Minnesotans in the Movies

Minnesotans in the Movies

Rolf J. Canton

NODIN PRESS

Acknowledgments

I would like to thank Pete Bateman and staff of the Larry Edmunds Book Shop, Inc. Hollywood, CA; Ron Boorst of Hollywood Posters, Hollywood, CA; the Hennepin County Southdale Library staff, the staff of the Special Collections Departments at the downtown Minneapolis and St. Paul Libraries (especially JoEllen Haugo), and Frau Claudia Trimborn of the Bonn Bibliothekcentral. I thank Robert, Bret, and Wade Sommer, Roy Blakey, and Randy Adamsyk and staff of the Minnesota Film Board office for the information, service, and materials they provided. A big thank you also to the Academy of Motion Picture Arts & Sciences.

I would also like to thank the Minnesota History Center and the many county historical societies throughout the state, especially Olmsted, St. Louis, Crow Wing, Stearns, Pipestone, Ottertail, Brown, Rice, Redwood, Douglas, McLeod, Beltrami, Carlton, and Freeborn Counties.

A special thank you goes to Tamin Haron for computer assistance, and to Tom McCoy, Elvin Jensen, David Ouse, Bob Peterson, and Dick Strand for their invaluable contributions. Without them this book would not exist.

A special thank you goes to Barbara Flanagan, whose columns for the *Minneapolis Star-Tribune* newspaper over several decades often mentioned notable Minnesotans who had achieved show business fame. Those columns were my inspiration for writing this book.

ISBN 13: 978-1-932472-41-7
ISBN 10: 1-932472-41-X
Library of Congress Control Number: 2006937002

Design and layout: John Toren

Nodin Press is a division of Micawber's, Inc.
530 North Third Street, Suite 120,
Minneapolis, MN 55401

*Dedicated to the
Oscar-Winning Actors and Actresses with
Minnesota connections:
Jessica Lange, Gig Young,
Judy Garland, and Gale Sondergaard*

*and also, especially,
to film archivist Bob DeFlores*

Bob DeFlores was born in San Francisco in 1935 and grew up in Los Angeles a few doors down from the Ozzie and Harriet Nelson family. He and David went to school together and were good friends.

Bob's parents were in show business and often performed with the Cansino Dance Company. Bob's father, now well into his 90s, still plays trumpet in a mariachi band in California.

As an adult Bob became a film archivist. He helped Bing Crosby, Loretta Young, Ginger Rogers, and Eleanor Powell assemble their film libraries. He once showed Bing a home movie of the first Crosby Pro-Am Golf Tournament, and Bing cried out, "There's my father in the background there. This is the only film I've got of him. Where did you find this?"

In the course of his research Bob has found several "lost films" including *Outside the Law* (1921) starring Lon Chaney, Sr; *Here Is My Heart* (1934) starring Bing Crosby; *Enoch Arden* (1911) directed by D. W. Griffith; and *Song O' My Heart* (1930) starring Irish tenor John McCormack. Bob sends these films to the American Film Institute or the Library of Congress for restoration.

Over the years Bob has organized many film events in the Twin Cities and trhoughout the country. In recent years he has been a frequent contributor to A&E Biographies. He has lived with his wife, Brenda, in the Minneapolis area since 1969.

Contents

Foreword

I love history—European, American, Minnesotan, all of it. But Minnesota's Hollywood history is special, particularly to a movie fan like me. I grew up with the movies and I continue to love them. In this collection of renowned Minnesotans and occasional Minnesotans—those who lived here awhile—just about everybody is covered.

I was amazed to see that the legendary movie cowboy William S. Hart spent his boyhood years in Minnesota, learning to ride a horse and to speak the Sioux Indian language.

A couple of visitors from Nebraska, Henry Fonda and Marlon Brando, are covered because Fonda attended the University of Minnesota and Brando attended and was kicked out of The Shattuck School in Faribault, Minnesota.

There are big names and small names and such super names as Richard Widmark and the Andrews Sisters. Reigning over them all, in my opinion, is Judy Garland, truly a superstar.

Tracking down all of the "names" must have been total devotion and it's clear that Rolf Canton is a major movie fan.

Horray for Hollywood—and its many Minnesota contributions!

– Barbara Flanagan
Star Tribune columnist

John Aasen

Born 1887,
Minneapolis, MN.
Died 1 August, 1938,
Mendocino, CA.

Ninety-nine actors out of a hundred seek employment in show business. John Aasen is one of the few who did not knock on Hollywood's door; instead Hollywood came to him.

Many comedians in the early film days had a sidekick—for example, Eric Campbell often served as Charlie Chaplin's oversized counterpart. When he was planning his movie *Why Worry* in 1922, Harold Lloyd decided he needed one too. His first choice was George Auger but George died before production began. Then Hal Roach told him of a Norwegian in Minnesota of such large proportions that only a specialist in Los Angeles, an acquaintance of Roach's, could make the man's shoes. They sent the fellow a telegram inviting him to come to Hollywood as quickly as possible for a movie job that would pay him handsomely. Though he had appeared in Barnum and Bailey shows as early as 1912, at the time Aasen was working as a carpenter in Minneapolis. He came to Hollywood, and the rest, as they say, is history.

Aasen was an extraordinary 8 feet 9 inches tall, according to his obituary in *Variety*, and he weighed about 550 pounds. It took eight yards of material to make him a suit. In **Why Worry,** one of the biggest box office attractions of 1923, Aasen plays a character named Colosso who is suffering from a toothache while stuck in jail during a revolution in Chile. Lloyd plays the part of a fellow-inmate, a rich hypochondriac named Harold von Palham. Von Palham cures

Colosso of his toothache and in return the giant assists von Palham in escaping. How do they do it? Easy. They just strap a cannon on Colosso's back, sling belts of bullets around his neck, and blast their way to freedom.

Aasen's mother, Kristi Danielsen, was born in 1868 in Numedal, Norway. While working in the town of Eggedal, she met a Swede named Nils Jannson Bokke. Both parents were unusually large people. Kristi emigrated to the United States alone in the spring of 1887, the year John was born.

Aasen made five films in all before retiring from movie making. He played a giant in *Two Flaming Youths* (1927); "Shorty" in *Legionaires in Paris* (1927); a bit part in *Should Married Men Go Home* (1928); and a circus giant in *Growing Pains* (1928). *Growing Pains* is an Our Gang Comedy/silent movie. But *Why Worry* remains his masterpiece.

When not making movies Aasen became a sideshow attraction for C. A. Wortham, a carnival owner-manager. Coming from Norwegian parentage, he certainly qualifies as a true Viking, at least in appearance, wouldn't you say? He died in Mendocino, California, at the relatively young age of fifty-one. Perhaps John's somewhat freakish body size was responsible for his early death. (Andre the Giant, who appeared in *The Princess Bride* (1987), died young, too, because of his unusually large proportions).

Walter Abel

Born 6 June, 1898,
Saint Paul, MN.
Died 26 March, 1987,
Essex, CT.

Walter grew up at 457 Ohio Street in St. Paul. His father was a barrel maker. Walter was active in the theater at Humboldt High School, and left home in 1916 to try his luck in New York City, where he quickly became part of the theatre crowd in Greenwich Village. He graduated from the American Academy of Dramatic Arts in 1918 and made his professional stage debut in 1919 in *Forbidden*.

Abel's first steady theater job was as stage manager to Minnie Maddern Fiske's stock company. He later joined the Provincetown Players and Eugene O'Neill personally cast him in *Desire under the Elms* and *Mourning Becomes Electra*. "No role, no review," said Walter very proudly, "has ever done for me what those two [plays] did. To please O'Neill was, to my generation of actors, the ultimate creative accomplishment."

In November of 1924 Walter happened to be playing in two Eugene O'Neill plays simultaneously. He appeared in the one-act play "Bound East for Cardiff" (under the collective title *S. S. Glencairn*) at the Provincetown Playhouse and in *Desire under the Elms* at the Greenwich Village Theatre. After finishing his role as Olson in "Bound East for Cardiff" in a Swedish accent, he would then run down the block to his New Englander role in *Desire under the Elms*. *New York Times* reviewer Brooks Atkinson praised him for being "deeply sincere" for his part of Olson the Swede, a part that Walter would be called upon to play often.

Abel's long film career began with a silent film in 1918, and ended 62 films later in 1984. At various times he was a contract player at both Paramount Pictures and RKO Studio. Among his many supporting roles are in *Fury* (1936); *The Witness Chair* (1936); to Errol Flynn in *Green Light* (1937); to Claudette Colbert in *Arise, My Love* (1940); to Charles Boyer in *Hold Back the Dawn* (1941); to Dorothy Lamour and Richard Denning in *Beyond the Blue Horizon* (1942); to Claudette Colbert in *So Proudly We Hail* (1943); and to Bette Davis and Claude Rains in *Mr. Skeffington* (1944). Walter played Shirley Temple's distraught father in *Kiss and Tell* (1945); he supported Danny Kaye in *The Kid from Brooklyn* (1946); and James Cagney in *13 Rue Madeleine* (1946). He also appeared in *Night People* (1954); *Raintree County* (1957); *Bernadine* (1957); and *Grace Quigley* (1984). Critics agree he was mis-cast in a prominent early role as D'Artagnan in the 1935 version of *The Three Musketeers*.

In *Arise, My Love* Walter uttered the lines, "I'm not happy. I'm not happy at all," which caught on like wildfire and became a catch phrase throughout America for a couple of years. Beginning with his role in *Skylark* (1941), we find him doing farcical characters brilliantly. A few other examples: the perpetually harassed studio chief in *Star Spangled Rhythm,* the comically long-suffering father to Shirley Temple in *Kiss and Tell.* He's equally hilarious in *Fired Wife, The Affairs of Susan,* and *Duffy's Tavern,* though perhaps his best-appreciated part today is as Broadway agent Danny Reed in the Christmas classic *Holiday Inn.*

Walter married Marietta Bitter in 1926. She was a harp player in the Carlos Salzedo Quintet, and also performed in the pit of many Broadway shows. Her father, noted sculptor Karl Bitter, had designed the fountain at Grand Army Plaza, and his work adorned the couple's brownstone on Manhattan's East Side. Marietta died in 1979. They had two sons—John, a Vietnam Marine veteran, and Michael, a film producer—and several grandchildren.

From film Walter moved into television, then back to the stage. In 1950 he appeared with Helen Hayes in both *The Wisteria Trees* (produced by Joshua Logan), and James M. Barrie's *What Every Woman Knows*. He later appeared with Katherine Cornell in Maxwell Anderson's *Wingless Victory* and with Judith Anderson in *Mourning Becomes Electra*. Mr. Abel's last Broadway appearance came in 1976 with the Shakespeare Festival at Lincoln Center's production of *Trelawney of the Wells*.

In the 1950s Walter served as vice president of the Screen Actors Guild under Ronald Reagan's presidency of that union. In the 1960s he served as president of the American National Theatre and Academy during a major expansion of that group.

In 1985 Walter went backstage after the Broadway show, *Aren't We All?* to meet his favorite screen partner, Claudette Colbert (three films together), but otherwise just lost track of his colleagues because he said, "Either they're dead or they believe I am." When you've been Shirley Temple's father, played D'Artagnan in *The Three Musketeers,* and been Bette Davis' suitor, you've had a full movie life.

Walter also loved boxing and winter sports. Maybe his Minnesota roots had something to do with that?

Kathryn Adams

Kathryn Elizabeth
"Betty"Hohn
Born 15 July, 1920,
New Ulm, MN.

While studying psychology at Hamline University in 1939, Kathryn tried out for a "Gateway to Hollywood Contest"—the *American Idol* of its day—and won the Midwestern District with her partner, Hugh Beaumont. Film Director Gregory La Cava liked her audition and immediately cast her as Katherine Borden in *5ᵗʰ Avenue Girl* (1939) starring Ginger Rogers.

Adams soon appeared in another RKO movie, *That's Right, You're Wrong,* featuring an all-star comic cast based around band leader Kay Kyser and singer Ginny Simms, along with Lucille Ball, Adolph Menjou, and Edward Everett Horton. Kathryn liked the offset activity as much as being in front of the camera during that shoot, because there was always a bridge game going among Edward Everett Horton, Franklin Pangborn, and Donald Woods. The film's producer, David Butler, became a good friend of Kathryn's, and when RKO did not pick up the option on her contract, he signed her to a two-year contract with Universal Studios, and almost immediately cast her in *If I Had My Way* (1940) starring Bing Crosby.

Kathryn met W. C. Fields when director Greg La Cava invited her to his beach house and asked her to bring her mother. While the others swam, Fields shared his life story with the very down-to-earth Mrs. Hohn, who, in the midst of her crocheting, was able to make Fields laugh quite easily. He liked her natural, non-pretentious manner—a trait which her daughter also possessed.

Kathryn's personal favorite among her films was *Love, Honor and Oh Baby!* (1940) with Donald Woods, followed by *Ski Patrol* (1940) in which she played opposite Philip Dorn, *Black Diamonds* (1940) co-starring St. Paulite Richard Arlen, and *Bachelor Daddy* (1941). Kathryn talked about Minnesota incessantly with Arlen during the filming of their movie. She especially liked to talk about her beloved roots at her parents' cabin at Lake Pokegama in Itasca County.

She appeared in *The Invisible Woman* (1941) with another all-star cast featuring John Barrymore in his last film. (Barrymore had to be physically propped up for each scene and giant cue cards were placed strategically behind the cameras to allow him to read his lines—his memory had long ago drowned in alcohol abuse, and he died the next year from alcoholism.) Other notable appearances were in Hitchcock's *Saboteur* (1942, as a young mother), *The Hunchback of Notre Dame* (1939), and *Spring Parade* (1940).

By the age of twenty-two Kathryn had already made twenty-three films. She and her former dancing partner Hugh Beaumont (who later gained fame as Ward Cleaver on the *Leave It to Beaver* TV series) were cast together in *Unfinished Business* for Universal Studios in 1941, and since it was well-known that they were in love, director Greg La Cava suggested they get married *during* the filming of the movie. It would have been a great promotional bit, perhaps, but the couple eventually decided the ritual of marriage was too sacred to be trivialized by Hollywood cameras, and they were married on Easter Sunday just after completing the film.

Married life appealed to Kathryn, and she soon lost interest in her film career. She appeared only once thereafter, in *Blond for a Day* (1946), which starred her husband as private detective Michael Shayne. This budget detective series proved to be a successful vehicle for Beaumont.

Adams and Beaumont were married for forty years. During that time Kathryn went back to school, completed her degree in psychology, and worked as a therapist for twenty years. The couple had three children, and enjoyed spending their summers at their log cabin lake home near Park Rapids, Itasca County. Beaumont died in 1982.

Though born in New Ulm, Minnesota, Kathryn's family moved to Warrenton, Missouri, then to Prospect Park in Minneapolis for two years of Kathryn's grade school life, before settling in Crookston, where her father, a Methodist minister, had been assigned to a congregation. On one Sunday in 1932 her father was too ill to deliver his sermon so thirteen-year-old Kathryn delivered it for him, and by all accounts she enunciated very well. The sermon was "And the Angels Sang."

Kathryn's mother was born in a sod house in Nebraska, the daughter of German weavers whose ancestors had immigrated to Russia during the reign of Catherine the Great.

As a high school junior Kathryn won the State Tuberculosis Essay Contest, which was broadcast over WCCO Radio in Minneapolis, and she also placed second in the dramatic division of the State Declamation Contest. But the next year her mother was invited to be a dormitory mother at Hamline University by the school president. She accepted and brought Kathryn with her. Kathryn tested into her freshman year of college without graduating from high school.

Kathryn, now remarried, lives in Mankato, Minnesota. She has written several childrens' stories, and is now at work on her autobiography.

Eddie Albert

(Edward Albert Heimberger)
Born 22 April, 1906,
Rock Island, IL.
Died 23 May, 2005.

Eddie Albert grew up in the Clinton and Franklin Avenue neighborhood of South Minneapolis. As a youth he attended St. Stephen's parochial school and was an altar boy at St. Stephens Church. He earned money delivering newspapers for ten years, and then took a job at a soda fountain which ran from six in the evening until one in the morning.

Eddie graduated in 1926 from Minneapolis Central High School, where he appeared in the plays *Dorothy* and *A Kiss for Cinderella*. This jingle accompanied his senior class picture: "Were all the world a stage, then every girl would plan—to be the leading lady, were he the leading man." During the summers Eddie would stay with his aunt and uncle in Fergus Falls, Minnesota, where he befriended future actor Frank Albertson.

Albert moved on to a three-year stint at the University of Minnesota. During those years he washed dishes and also worked as a movie house usher. One thing led to another, and before long he was an assistant manager at the Grand movie house, a manager of the Lyndale Theater a half block north of Lake Street (now an antique store), and manager for the Paramount Publix movie house. "They found out I could pull bum theaters out of the red," he later remarked. One of his duties as manager was to be Master of Ceremonies, and the magic show he developed was his first real stage experience. The public always liked it. The theater was "calling him" and after three years Eddie left the University behind to go into show business, becoming a "song, dance and patter man" with a trio for a Minneapolis radio station. When the radio announcer repeatedly referred to him as Hamburger instead of Heimberger, he decided to change his name to Eddie Albert. The trio eventually toured to Cincinnati, Chicago, and New York before breaking up. NBC was looking for a singing team at the time, and Albert auditioned as a duo with Grace Bradt. They won the spot and were heard every morning at eleven as Grace and Eddie—The Honey-mooners. After a stink playing summer stock theater Eddie appeared in his first Broadway play, *O Evening Star*.

One day writer Garson Kanin was a guest on Eddie's radio show. Kanin invited Eddie to appear in the Broadway production of *Brother Rat* in 1936 as Bing Edwards. He followed this with appearing in producer/director George Abbott's *Room Service*. Another promising young actor named Hume Cronyn joined Eddie in that cast. This great success led to Warner Brothers asking him to reprise his role of Bing Edwards in his 1938 movie debut of **Brother Rat**, which brought him together with President-to-be Ronald Reagan and Reagan's wife-to-be, Jane Wyman. After the filming of this debut, he rushed to New York to appear in the musical comedy version of Shakespeare's *Comedy of Errors*. His take on the West Coast scene at the time was that "in Hollywood stars are too busy trying to be a success to spend much time learning how to act."

Albert returned briefly to Broadway to appear in *The Boys from Syracuse*, another great success, but Hollywood called again and he quickly churned out three more films, **Four Wives, Angel from Texas**, and **Dispatch from Reuters**. By this time he was making a thousand dollars a week.

Yet Hollywood acting made Eddie restless, and he began to take long sailing trips into the Pacific in a boat that had been specially fitted for solo travel. After another picture for Warner Brothers, he went to Mexico to join the Escalante Brothers' Circus as a trapeze aerial artist. During his sailing trips he had noticed Japanese fishermen were making hydrographic surveys of the coast line, and while in Mexico he also noticed some strange goings on, all of which he later reported to Army intelligence. In July of 1942 he actually joined the Navy, and after a stint at Cornell Officer's Training School, he was assigned to the amphibious transport, *U.S.S. Sheridan*, and saw action in the South Pacific

During the first landings on the island of Tarawa Atoll in the Gilbert Islands, Albert commanded a salvage boat. It was a brutal assault, and American troops suffered heavy casualties. The beach was covered with dead and wounded, and many wounded Marines were still being picked off by sniper fire when Lieutenant Heimberger arrived to rescue them and bring them to safety. He made three trips, during which his vessel absorbed about a hundred bullets. Then, on his own initiative, Albert commandeered a second boat and made two more trips into the brunt of enemy fire. Tarawa was one of the bloodiest battles of Marine Corps history. Eddie was awarded a Bronze Star with a "V" for rescuing seventy marines in twenty-six missions, all of which were under enemy fire. (In 1944 an Oscar for Best Documentary of Short Subjects was awarded to the U. S. Marine Corps for *With the Marines at Tarawa*.)

In January of 1944 Albert was recalled to the States to make training films. He was finally discharged on December 7, 1945, whereupon he formed the Eddie Albert Productions, a film company dedicated to making educational films. He had to make five regular movies in order to amass the $200,000 start-up capital to finance the operation. By 1951 he had completed fourteen twenty-minute 16mm films. The best known is *Human Growth*, a sex-education movie aimed at eleven-year-olds, made in collaboration with the University of Oregon.

Yet Eddie's new-found passion for educational films hardly put a dent in his acting career. He continued to appear in commercial films, including *The Perfect Marriage; Time out of Mind; Smashup: The Story of a Woman; Hit Parade of 1947; You Gotta Stay Happy*, in which he co-starred with Jimmy Stewart; and *The Dude Goes West*. He returned to Broadway to be the leading man in *Miss Liberty*, which ran for 308 performances. In 1950 he was back in Hollywood, co-starring with Lucille Ball in Columbia Picture's *The Fuller Brush Girl*. He appeared with Betty Grable in *Meet Me after the Show*, and with Laurence Olivier and Jennifer Jones in *Carrie*. In *Roman Holiday* (1953) Eddie received an Oscar nomination for the Best Supporting Actor. That movie starred Gregory Peck and introduced Audrey Hepburn to the world.

Eddie Albert was outstanding as the Persian peddler, Ali Hakam, in *Oklahoma* (1955). He was great in support of Frank Sinatra in *The Joker Is Wild*; of Errol Flynn in *The Sun Also Rises* (1957); and of Flynn and, Trevor Howard in *The Roots of Heaven* (1958). He was in *Teahouse of the August Moon* (1956) with Marlon Brando. In 1959 he appeared with Gregory Peck, Deborah Kerr and Minneapolis' own Karin Booth in *Beloved Infidel*, a retelling of the difficulties experienced by novelist F. Scott Fitzgerald adjusting to Hollywood.

The list goes on. He was in *Captain Newman, MD* supported by Mike Farrell, a Saint Paulite of *M*A*S*H* fame. He received his second Oscar nomination as Cybill Shepherd's father in *The Heartbreak Kid*, a 1972 film made mostly in the Twin Cities. He appeared in *Foolin' Around* (1978) and in *Take This Job and Shove It* (1980), both Minnesota-made films.

Many younger folk may recognize Eddie Albert as Oliver Wendell Douglas in the hit TV series *Green Acres*, which ran from 1965 to 1968. This delightful farce was a spin-off of the even more popular show *Petticoat Junction*, which ran from 1963 to 1971. In *Green Acres*, a family of rich city-dwellers moves to the country to do some farming. They aren't very well equipped for the task, needless to say, and herein lies the humor. There is plenty of head-shaking and skull-scratching by the local townspeople, and the conflicts and confusion that arise between Albert and his sophisticated wife, played by Hungarian beauty Eva Gabor, adds to the fun.

Eddie married Mexican-born Margo on December 5th, 1945, at Saint Patrick's Cathedral in New York City. Margo died on July 17th, 1985. They appeared together in *I'll Cry Tomorrow* (1955). They had one child, Edward, born February 20, 1951. Eddie Senior enjoyed singing, he played the piano, violin and guitar, and collected first editions. He painted in oils and was an ardent physical culturist, which may explain why he lived to be ninety-nine. He was also an avid reader and especially loved the works of George Bernard Shaw.

In his later years Eddie became an avid environmentalist, and he was among the first celebrities to lend his considerable influence to the crusade to ban DDT. Because of his efforts in behalf of this and other environmental issues, his birthday, April 22, was chosen as the annual holiday Earth Day.

Frank Albertson

Born 2 Feb, 1909,
Fergus Falls, MN.
Died 29 Feb, 1964,
Santa Monica, CA.

Frank was raised in Fergus Falls until the age of thirteen, when his family moved to Puyallup, Washington. The family later moved to Hollywood, where Frank became an extra and a prop boy, and also a Hollywood High School basketball star. He appeared in several plays in high school and also met Virginia Shelley there. The two were married on March 7, 1931. (That marriage ended in divorce in 1935.)

Upon graduation from high school in 1927, Frank took work in the film laboratory at Paramount Studios. Later he became a prop boy there. About this time he was heard to say that he "Would rather act than eat." Frank had brown hair, blue eyes, a beaming smile and was considered good-looking. At nineteen he signed a contract with Fox Studios. They immediately featured him in *Prep and Pep* (1928) which was a great success for him. He is often seen as a cop, cab driver, or reporter, and he was considered a "light" leading man.

In 1930 he appeared in two Will Rogers films: *Happy Days* and *So This Is London*. At the time Will Rogers was the biggest money-earner in Hollywood as well as the nation's most popular humorist. He also scored a hit as Ranny Truesdale in *The Life of Vergie Winters* (1934). He was Katherine Hepburn's embarrassing brother Walter in *Alice Adams* (1935), and appeared with Gary Cooper in *The Plainsman* (1937); and with the Marx Brothers in *Room Service* (1938, as Leo Davis) In this film Frank brilliantly captures the ebullient spirit of a naïve young playwright as he and Groucho trade the phrase, "Hail, and Farewell," over and over again with great solemnity.

Perhaps Frank's most often-seen performance, however, is as Sam Wainwright, the hee-hawing pal of Jimmy Stewart in the Christmas classic *It's a Wonderful Life* (1946). Among notable later roles are with Spencer Tracy in *The Last Hurrah* (1958) and as the Mayor in the star-studded *Bye Bye Birdie* (1963). Perhaps his best movie was *Bachelor Mother* (1939) as Freddie Miller, the dim-witted boyfriend of Ginger Rogers, co-starring David Niven, Charles Coburn and E. E. Clive.

Frank's second wife was Grace Gillern. The couple had two children—Gretchen, born in 1942, and Juliet, born in 1946. Frank's mother was formerly Mary Healey, daughter of Fergus Falls pioneer Anthony Healey. Frank's father was also Frank Albertson, who was a nephew of Orris Albertson of Battle Lake, Minnesota. Frank had a cousin, Janet Pavlick, already under contract with Fox Studios when he arrived in Hollywood. Her stage name was Janet Dawn.

Frank did his share of early television. He appeared on *Perry Mason; Richard Diamond, Private Detective; Alfred Hitchcock Presents; The Untouchables; Mike Hammer; The Real McCoys; Zane Grey Theatre; The Andy Griffith Show; The Philco Television Playhouse; Maverick;* and many others. Frank appeared in 104 movies over a thirty-five year career. Not too shabby for anybody—much less a rural Gopher from Fergus Falls, Minnesota.

Lorand Andahazy

Born 15 April, 1914,
Lipto-Teple, Hungary
Died Feb. 19, 1986
Minneapolis, MN.

Lorand Andahazy arrived in Cleveland, Ohio, with his mother and two older siblings in 1922, when he was eight years old. Lorand's father had remained on the family estate in Hungary, but felt it was prudent, in the atmosphere of uncertain peace following WWI, to sent his wife and children to the relative safety of the United States.

As a child Lorand was compactly built, and he had the rugged good looks to match his well-muscled body. A serious young man with piercing blue eyes, he observed everything intensely and did not smile easily.

Lorand excelled in a number of sports as a youth, though equestrian events and gymnastics were his specialties. He was the Men's Gymnastics Champion three years running (1934-36) for the state of Ohio, which qualified him to go to the Olympic Games in Berlin in 1936. He competed that summer in Berlin on the same team as the black sprinter Jesse Owens and the heavyweight boxer Joe Louis, both of whom scored resounding victories over white opponents, to the exasperation of host (and Aryan supremacist) Adolf Hitler.

A year earlier Lorand had been introduced by his gymnastics coach to Serge Nadejdin, former director of the Imperial Dramatic Theatre of St. Petersburg. Mr. Nadejdin took Andahazy to a ballet performance of the Ballet Russe de Monte Carlo which happened to be touring the US at the time. Lorand had never seen a ballet before, and he was overwhelmed, not only by the ballet itself, but also by the women performing in it. He was enraptured with Anna Adrianova in particular—the first American dancer to be given a contract to dance for the Ballet Russe. (Her real name was Shirley B. Bridge).

When he had recovered from the effects of the dazzling performance, Lorand announced to his friends that, "with only three years of study, I will be a member of that company and marry that angelic woman." In fact, it took him only a single year to become a member of Colonel W. de Basil's Ballet Russe de Monte Carlo, heir to the group that had produced Nijinsky, the greatest dancer of the twentieth century. He was also off the mark with his second prediction. It took him six years before Anna Adrianova agreed to be his bride.

In 1939 the twenty-five-year old Andahazy was given the honor of appearing in one of Nijinsky's signature roles, the Golden Slave in *Scheherazade*, during a tour of Australia. Lorand felt chills throughout his body as he read the name "Nijinsky" inside the costume. Though he'd only been given one day's notice, Andahazy won plaudits from all critics. His background in gymnastics made it possible for him to execute leaps reminiscent of Nijinsky's legendary Grand Jetés, and when he passed near the curtain where Fokine, the creator of the choreography, was sitting, he overheard the Russian word for marvelous.

Fokine had great plans for Andahazy, but they were dashed when the United States declared war on Japan and its ally, Germany. A few months later, after finally realizing his dream of marrying Anna Adrianova, Lorand was drafted. He became a Unit Commander of Armored Reconnaissance of the Third Armored Spearhead Division of the 33rd Infantry Regiment. His unit was dropped by parachute behind enemy lines two months before D-Day, with instructions to make as much mayhem for the German Army as possible. He was one of the few men from his unit to survive the war. In the course of fourteen months of action, Andahazy won the Silver Star, the Bronze Star, the Purple Heart, five Battle Stars and the ETO (European Theater of Operations) Ribbon.

Back in New York after the war, Lorand paid a visit to his old bosses, Sol Hurok and Lucia Chase, directors of the American Ballet Theatre. Hurok, who had long been the main importer of ballets from the Soviet Union and Europe to the USA, offered his old star a contract that would bill him as "The Most Decorated Dancer in the World." But Lorand found that his wartime injuries—and especially a knee wound—made it almost impossible to continue dancing.

Andahazy now had a family to support—Lorand Jr. had been born in 1942—so he took the advice of his Army chaplain, the Rev. John Buchanan, and paid a visit to Minneapolis-St. Paul, where he had friends, and where Hungarian conductor Antal Dorati worked. During their brief stay Andahazy was offered a job teaching Military Science and Tactics at Breck School on Como Avenue at Highway 280 in St. Paul. He held that job for seven years, though he also had plenty of time to travel with his family. He even joined a touring company of the Broadway show *Carousel*.

In 1951 Andahazy took a few months off to visit Hollywood, and he managed to land a few roles while he was there. He was a costumed buccaneer in several parades, and he posed as an Indian for a sculptor: The finished statue stands to this day at the entrance to the Chicago Museum of Art. He also appeared in several pirate movies where he could appear shirtless such as *Lady In The Iron Mask* (1952). With some extra money in his pocket, Lorand returned home to start a ballet school with his talented wife in downtown St. Paul. After a couple of years they moved to 1680 Grand Avenue in the Macalester area of St. Paul. In 1955 they moved their office and residence to St. Louis Park. By this time Lorand had given up his "day job" and was working with his wife teaching full-time.

Anna Adrianova died of cancer in 1983 but Lorand and his son Marius continued the school and ballet company. Lorand suffered a stroke in the winter of 1986 but recovered enough to resume teaching. During an angiogram test at Veteran's Hospital he suffered a puncture to the aorta and died immediately. He was survived by his sons, Lorand, Jr., Zoltan, and Marius. Marius continues to run the school and also teaches at The University of Wisconsin–River Falls, and at parochial schools in St. Paul.

Loni Anderson

Born 5 August, 1945,
St. Paul, MN.

Loni's father was a pharmaceutical chemist turned executive with a great sense of humor and she adored him. He was thrilled that Loni became a comedienne. Her mother had been a model. During the mid-1950s, her grade school days, Loni lived in New Brighton at 2134 Belle Lane. During her junior and senior high school days she lived in Shoreview and attended Alexander Ramsey High School, now called Roseville High School. As a kid she did lots of swimming, fishing, and water skiing, which she still enjoys today. She has one sister, Andrea.

Loni was active in choir at Ramsey and was crowned the Valentine Queen her senior year. (She had won her first queen title at the age of fourteen). She easily won the Miss Roseville contest, and was Miss Runner Up to the Miss Minnesota title in 1964 won by Barbara Hasselberg of Bloomington. By a strange twist of fate,

Loni was attracted to Barbara's brother, Bruce, and after a two-week courtship, the couple went off to South Dakota to be married. Their daughter Deidra was born a year later. The romance faded almost as quickly as it had developed, unfortunately, and they were divorced in late 1965.

After the divorce Loni devoted herself to studying art, theater, and music at the University of Minnesota. She performed on the Minnesota Centennial Showboat in the summer of 1968 (she was a brunette then) alongside Linda Kelsey, who later appeared as Billie Newman on the *Lou Grant Show*. Upon graduating she taught art in high school and acted in different community theaters including the Edyth Bush Theatre in Highland Park, The Lakeshore Players in White Bear Lake, and St. Paul's Eastside Theatre.

She gave up teaching after being cast in the lead of a professional production of *Born Yesterday* at the Friar's Dinner Theatre. She followed that in November of 1971 with a fifty-three-week run in *Fiddler on the Roof* at the Chanhassen Dinner Theatre. Peter Michael Goetz of Guthrie Theater fame played the leading part of Tevye. She played Tevye's oldest daughter. Other shows followed at the Old Log Theatre of Excelsior and the Friar's Dinner Theatre, where she performed with Alan Sues in *Send Me No Flowers* in the winter of 1973. (The Friar's was re-named the Minnesota Music Hall in 1974 having been even earlier named Diamond Lil's in downtown Minneapolis at the corner of 4th Avenue South and 8th Street.)

During the production of *Play It Again, Sam*, Loni fell in love with Ross Bickell, who was playing the lead, and they soon were married. The couple later appeared together with Mr. & Mrs. Pat O'Brien in the comedy *Paris Is Out* at the Minnesota Music Hall. Loni wore a blond wig, exposed lots of cleavage, and used a Swedish accent, which gave old film star Pat O'Brien plenty of opportunity to do sight gags for lots of laughs. The O'Brien's encouraged them to go to Hollywood and give it a real try, so off they went. (Pat, by the way, was part of the original Irish Rat Pack of the 1930s, along with Jimmy Cagney, Frank McHugh, and Allen Jenkins. His most famous part is the title role in **Knute Rockne, All-American** (1940) the story of Notre Dame's famous football coach.

Ross eventually found work on *Fantasy Island* and had a variety of roles here and there. Then it was Loni's turn. She wore a push-up bra and a tight sweater to auditions and was soon engaged in a very successful run on the TV comedy series, *WKRP in Cincinnati*, which aired from 1978 to 1982. Loni asked the director if she could portray Jennifer as a bright, sensitive woman rather than as a dumb blonde and he said Yes. She credits Ross for all of her success because she would have stayed in Minnesota without his encouragement and would not have lasted long in Los Angeles without his companionship. Her greater success put a strain on their relationship, however, and they were divorced in 1981. They had no children together.

Loni's major films are *The Magnificent Magical Magnet of Santa Mesa* (1977, TV); the title role in *The Jayne Mansfield Story* (1980); *Sizzle* (1981, TV); *Stoker Ace* (1983); and *Blown Away* (1983). She returned to TV in the mid 1980s with *Partners in Crime* in 1984 and *Easy Street* in 1986-87. Back to movies again with *Sorry, Wrong Number* (1989, TV) and *All Dogs Go to Heaven* (1989, voice only). Later films are *White Hot: Mysterious Murder of Thelma Todd* (1991, TV); *Munchie* (1992); *Three Ninjas: High Noon at Mega Mountain* (1997); and *A Night at Roxbury* (1998).

Loni has always attracted attention. Even when she was a teen, she was asked to pose for magazines like *Playboy* and *Ebony*. She has always turned such offers down. When Burt Reynolds proposed marriage, however, she did not turn him down. Loni's mom, Maxine, was being psychic one day when she told Loni to come look at the TV screen. She said, "There, now, that's the kind of man you should marry." How right she was! That marriage lasted only from 1988 to 1993, however. The couple tried to get pregnant but ended up adopting a son, Quinton. She tells about the marriage in her book, *My Life in High Heels* (1995). Also in the book she tells of a serious flirtation with a young attorney named Wendell Anderson, who later became Governor of Minnesota. The trouble was that Loni was only sixteen when Wendell was so smitten with her. Her parents strongly objected to the relationship and their passion slowly simmered down.

Loni is a workaholic and that gets her by many of life's problems. She doesn't drink or smoke, eats lots of fish, chicken, and vegetables, and rarely eats red meat. She exercises every day. She prefers animated films and *Snow White and the Seven Dwarfs* (1937) is her very favorite. She is a former Lutheran Sunday School teacher; she admits to a shoe fetish and she adores her daughter, Deidra, and son, Quintin. Loni has wanted to be an actress since she was five years old. She has two granddaughters, McKenzie and Megan, a boyfriend named Geoff, and three Persian cats—Cloudsley, Raffles and Winkle.

Richard Dean Anderson

Born 23 January, 1950,
Minneapolis, MN.

Richard Dean Anderson is not only Angus MacGyver but a multi-talented showman. Besides being active as an actor these past twenty years, specializing in TV, he has been executive producer of four movies and composer of a song, "Eau d'Leo", that was used in "The Negotiator" episode (1988) of *MacGyver*.

Richard and his three brothers grew up in Roseville and attended Alexander Ramsey High School. Though he was born in Minneapolis his family moved to Dellwood Street near County Road C2. He attended Capitol View Junior High and graduated from Ramsey in 1968. He attended St Cloud State University and Ohio University but never graduated. Why? He was offered a part in a play in Los Angeles.

His main acting teacher was Peggy Fleury. His father, Stuart Anderson, was a jazz bassist, high school English teacher, and community theatre director; his mother was an artist. Stuart was born in Buhl, Minnesota, on the Iron Range. There are Iron Range ties lasting to this day for Ricky and his brothers.

Richard's acting career started in elementary school. In fact, he decided to become an actor when he was five years old. He was visiting a rehearsal of his father's when a cast member offered him a plate full of Twinkies. He thought that free Twinkies came with the play, which made acting seem like the best job in the world.

The other childhood career goal was playing hockey. Breaking both arms in a game brought that dream to rest, however, at age fifteen.

Another event tempered Richard's lust for wild adventure. He crashed two racing cars in two months. "Coming close to death humbles you," says Richard.

In another life-changing experience, he and two friends biked into Canada when he was 17. His two buddies dropped out but he continued through the Yukon into Alaska biking 7,000 miles in three months. He felt it was the single best memory of growing up and his perspective of the world changed during that trip.

He has served on the board of directors for Handgun Control, Inc. and makes the point that his MacGyver portrayal refuses to use guns but does not shy away from daredevil stunts. Each stunt is scientifically planned—authenticity is integral to the show. *MacGyver* ran for seven seasons, a very respectable run as TV shows go. Richard later appeared in several other short-run shows.

Richard is 6'2"; he has homes in Vancouver, British Columbia, and in Los Angeles. His favorite movie is *Lawrence of Arabia* (1962); guitarist Leo Kottke is his favorite musician. He has dated German Olympic skater Katharina Witt; he has a daughter, Wylie Quinn Annarose Anderson, born August 2, 1998. Her mother is Apryl Prose.

His movies are as follows: *Today's F. B. I.* (1981, TV); *Young Doctors in Love* (1982); *Odd Jobs* (1984); *Ordinary Heroes* (1986); *In the Eyes of a Stranger* (1992, TV); *Through the Eyes of a Killer* (1992, TV); *The Lost Treasure of Atlantis* (1994, TV); *Beyond Betrayal* (1994, TV); *MacGyver: Trail to Doomsday* (1994, TV); *Past the Bleachers* (1995, TV); *Pandora's Clock* (1996, TV); and *Firehouse* (1997).

The Andrews Sisters

LaVerne
Born 6 July 1911, Mpls, MN
Died 8 May 1967, Brentwood, CA

Maxene
Born 3 Jan. 1916, Mpls, MN
Died 21 Oct. 1995, Hyannis, MA

Patty
Born 16 Feb. 1918, Mound, MN.

Peter Andrews and his wife, Olga Sollie, were the proud parents of three girls: LaVerne Sophie, Maxene Angelyn, and Patricia Marie Andrews. Peter, a restaurateur, ran the Pure Food Café, a Greek café in Minneapolis. It was Greek because Peter was born in Greece and had come to America to find a better life. Olga Sollie was born in Norway and came to the USA to find greater opportunities. Here in the great melting pot of the American heartland, it was natural that a Greek Orthodox would marry a Norwegian Lutheran and raise a family. They married in 1910 and lived at 1600 Lyndale Avenue North in what was considered then to be an "old-fashioned house."

It was Olga who encouraged the girls to sing together so they would have a strong common interest. It would also keep the girls busy. Their father disapproved. All the same, starting in 1929 the girls sang on local radio stations, in kiddie revues, and in local talent contests. They greatly admired the Boswell Sisters, a group that sang on Bing Crosby's radio show, and they listened to them whenever they could. In 1931 the girls entered and won a talent contest sponsored by the Clausen School of Dance at the Orpheum Theatre in Minneapolis. At this time Laverne was 20, Maxene was 15, and little Patty was 13.

The trio was soon touring during the summer months with the Larry Rich Orchestra, and later with the Leon Belasco Orchestra, but the absolute highlight was singing with the Glenn Miller Orchestra. The girls also loved to visit their mother's brothers, Pete and Ed Sollie, who operated a grocery store in Mound, Minnesota, at the western end of Lake Minnetonka. (In fact, the family lived in Mound from 1920 to 1924.) The grocery store closed for good in 1964.

The trio earned enough to keep the family afloat through 1937, with their father driving them from stop to stop while Olga sewed their dresses and the girls practiced in the back seat.

In 1938, the Andrews Sisters broadcast every weekday night at 10 PM over WCCO on a program called *Just Entertainment* where they co-starred with Jack Fulton, a romantic radio tenor. Richard Post was the announcer. This show was aired coast-to-coast through CBS.

One of the many vaudeville stops they made in 1938 was with Ted Mack, famous for his *Amateur Hour* radio show. Dave Kapp happened to be listening that day and liked what he heard. He lined up a session with Decca Records through his brother, Jack, who ran the label. The sisters did a cut of "Nice Work If You Can Get It" on one side with "Bei Mir Bist du Schoen" on the flip side. The "hit" side didn't do so well but the flip side sold over a million copies.

For their efforts the girls earned the standard fee of fifty dollars. But after the success of this song, Decca agreed to give them a five-percent royalty on every record sold, which put them in the company of only one other recording star: Bing Crosby.

Their next hits were: "The Hut Sut Song," "Three Little Fishes," "Rum and Coca-Cola," "Apple Blossom Time," and "The Beer Barrel Polka."

Comedian Morey Amsterdam had found the song "Rum and Coca Cola" in Trinidad and brought it to the Andrews Sister's manager, Lou Levy—he was also married to Maxene. Their recording of it was the first calypso hit in the US, selling 7 million copies. In fact, there wasn't enough shellac at Decca to fill the orders so RCA and Columbia lent them the necessary amount.

The money that was now coming in was much appreciated because the Depression had wiped out their father's restaurant next to the Orpheum Theatre on Ninth and Hennepin Avenue. The family relocated to Southern California and both Peter and Olga died not long after.

The sisters' other hits included "Boogie Woogie Bugle Boy," "Don't Fence Me in," "Tico Tico," "Chattanooga Choo Choo," "Patience and Fortitude," "Pennsylvania Polka," "Oh Johnny, Oh Johnny, Oh," "Shoo Shoo Baby," "I Can Dream, Can't I," "All I Want for Christmas," and "Don't Sit under the Apple Tree." In all they made 900 recordings—19 of them gold records—and sold 100 million copies. During their remarkable career the sisters had more top-ten hits than either Elvis or the Beatles. Yet stange to say, none of them ever learned to read music.

The Andrews Sisters made quite a few films during their heyday, and they epitomize the war years as much as the music of Glenn Miller does. Many are genuine "morale boosters." Here is the list: *Argentine Nights* (1940); *Buck Privates* (1941); *In the Navy* (with Abbott & Costello, 1941); *Hold That Ghost* (starring Abbott and Costello again but also Joan Davis from St. Paul and Richard Carlson from Minneapolis, 1941); *What's Cookin'?* (1942); *Give Out, Sisters* (1942); *Private Buckaroo* (1942); *How's About It?* (1943); *Swingtime Johnny* (1943); *Always a Bridesmaid* (1943); *Follow the Boys* (1944); *Hollywood Canteen* (1944); *Moonlight and Cactus* (1944); *Her Lucky Night* (1945); *Make Mine Music* (1946); *Road to Rio* starring Bing Crosby and Bob Hope (1947); *Melody Time* (1948); and *Little Toot* (1954).

Once the sisters had all married they performed only sporadically as a group, though they appeared occasionally on TV variety shows well into the 1960s.

Patty never really left show business. Following a stormy marriage to film producer, Marty Melcher, she married Walter Weschler, a pianist-conductor. They had no children but have two dogs and live in Encino, CA. Patty appeared in *The Phynx* in 1970 and *The Gong Movie Show* in 1980. She and sister Maxene performed together in the smash Broadway show *Over Here* in 1974.

Richard Arlen

(Cornelius Richard
van Mattimore)
Born 1 September, 1899,
Charlottesville, VA.
Died 26 March, 1976,
North Hollywood, CA.

Richard Arlen spent his childhood and grade school days in White Bear Lake, a suburb of Saint Paul. He went to Cretin School until shortly after the United States declared war on Germany in March of 1917, when he dropped out to join the RCAF (Royal Canadian Air Force). He became a pilot but never saw combat. Upon returning from the war, he graduated (via his GED) from Saint Paul Central High School in 1918. At Cretin he was active in the "C" Club, lettering in football, hockey, and baseball; he pitched for the baseball team and was captain of the hockey team for two years. He was 5' 11" tall and very muscular as well as highly athletic.

After the War Arlen returned to Minnesota to enroll in the College of St. Thomas but dropped out to become a sports writer in Duluth. He also contributed sports articles to the *Pioneer Press* and the *St. Paul Dispatch* with M. T. "Empty" Caine, and worked as a swimming instructor at the St. Paul Athletic Club.

After a stint in the Texas oil fields, Arlen went to Hollywood in pursuit of adventure. His father, an attorney, disapproved of the idea but could not dissuade his son. How could he have guessed that twenty years later, Richard would be making six films a year for Universal Studios for $90,000 a year—and 4 months vacation!

But the early days were rough. Arlen lived on fourteen cents a day for over three weeks in Hollywood while seeking a job. His first job was as a motorcycle messenger at Paramount Studios. He broke his leg on the job one day and while in the hospital was spotted by a director who promised him a part when he got well.

The first important role Richard won was in the 1923 film, *Vengeance of the Deep*. He was on contract with Paramount by this time. He made dozens of silent movies but the 1926 films *Coast of Folly* and *Figures Don't Lie* are perhaps the most memorable.

Then came the big break. After five years on the Paramount payroll, Richard was cast in *Wings*, which won the first-ever Academy Award for Best Picture (1927). Richard played a tough, cynical fighter pilot, a characterization that became standard for him in later films. Gary Cooper, Clara Bow (the original "it" girl) and Buddy Rogers were also in the cast. A reviewer for the *New York Times* was struck by the film's "amazing air duels."

The film's director, William Wellman, personally chose Richard for the starring role. (A few years later Wellman discovered Jimmy Cagney and after featuring him in *Public Enemy* Cagney too became a superstar.) Arlen appeared in four more Wellman films in the next few years: *Beggars of Life* (1928), *Ladies of the Mob* (1928), *The Man I Love* (1929) and *Dangerous Paradise* (1930).

Following *Wings*, Arlen appeared in four more action movies, all of which we released in 1928: *The Four Feathers; Feel My Pulse; Beggars of Life*, and *Manhattan Cocktail*. The next year he made *Thunderbolt* and also appeared in *The Virginian*, starring Gary Cooper. *Only Saps Work* followed in 1930.

During that golden period of his career Arlen was earning about $200,000 a year, some of which he invested in a flying service. As a result of his aeronautical expertise Arlen became a civilian liaison air safety expert with the Army Air Corps in 1942.

Later notable films of his were: *Touchdown* (1931); *Alice in Wonderland* (1933) in which he played the Cheshire Cat among an all-star cast and *College Humor* (1933); *Come on Marines* (1934); *Call of the Yukon* (1938); *Mutiny in the Arctic* (1941); *Storm over Lisbon* (1944); *Kansas Raiders* (1951); *Warlock* (1959); and *Fort Utah* (1967), which was not only his last film, but also the 250th of his forty-year career.

James Arness

James King Aurness
Born 26 May, 1923,
Minneapolis, MN.

Jim and his brother, Peter Graves, grew up at 2324 Cromwell Drive in southwestern Minneapolis, near Penn Avenue South, West 54th Street, and Minnehaha Creek. In those days everything south of 54th Street was farmland. Jim attended Burroughs Grade School, Ramsey Junior High School, Washburn High School, and West High, where he graduated in 1941. At Washburn Jim was active in both sports and arts, participating in the operetta "Rose Marie" in which he played an Indian who did not speak. Yet the critics acknowledged even then that his presence was very noticeable.

Jim's parents, Rolf Aurness and Ruth Duesler, were both born and raised in Minneapolis. Rolf graduated from Minneapolis' original Central High School, which was downtown. Though neither of his parents were theater people, they were married in New York City at the Church of the Transfiguration, generally known as "The Little Church around the Corner," or "the actor's church." Ruth's father, Hess Graves Duesler, did have a strong love of theater and everything to do with it. Hess served as comptroller and treasurer of the Minneapolis Gas Light Co. Ruth recalled that her father would recite Shakespeare, Byron, Thomas Moore, and others to Jim and Peter, sometimes for hours.

While in school Jim's dream was to become a marine architect. He loved ships and the sea perhaps because his father's father had been a genuine Norwegian seaman from Alesund, Norway. That grandfather, however, changed his vocation dramatically when he decided to come to America. He settled in Minneapolis and studied medicine at the University of Minnesota. Instead of Seaman Aurness he became Dr. Peter Aurness, who was also a sculptor of note and inventor; he invented the duplex stethoscope.

Soon after graduation Jim entered Beloit College but the Second World War put an end to that. Jim joined the U. S. Army's 3rd Infantry Division and was part of the Anzio Beach landing on February 10th, 1943. He was wounded in the leg.

Big Jim is 6 foot 6 inches tall. He has natural blond hair and Viking-blue eyes. He tried working in real estate and advertising before going into movie making. His first film was *The Farmer's Daughter* (1947), which was appropriate because the Congressman in the film is supposed to be from Minnesota. Loretta Young won an Oscar for her portrayal of a young Swedish maid who re-educates the Congressman for whom she works.

His next notable film was the William Wellman film *Battleground* (1949), which won Oscars for screenplay and cinematography.

Jim's first starring role was as a giant carrot in the title role of Howard Hawk's *The Thing* (1952).

In 1952, with minor roles in a dozen movies under his belt, Jim appeared in *Big Jim McLain*. The movie starred John Wayne, though Arness was 2½ inches bigger. According to legend, during the filming Wayne was offered the part of Matt Dillon for the TV series, *Gunsmoke*. Wayne had absolutely no interest in being a TV cowboy, which he considered to be a major step down from his status as a bona fide film star. After sternly rejecting the offer, he is reported to have said, "Give it to my understudy," and stomped off. James Arness took the role of Marshal Matt Dillon and played it for twenty years on TV, adding another ten years in made-for-TV movies. Another Wayne remark was, "This guy is my protégé. All he has to do in my pictures is stand up straight."

Sometime during his long run of *Gunsmoke*, Jim shrewdly bought up the rights to the series, and the reruns brought him big returns. Jim was a natural blond, so his hair had to be died dark brown to fit the image of a lawman. Because he weighed 235 pounds at the time a special horse had to be selected to support him. Arness's measurements at that time were 48-36-39. He is the tallest man ever cast in a lead role.

Jim has made 38 movies and 5 TV series in all, among them *Them* (1954), a highly regarded science fiction movie; *The First Traveling Saleslady* (1956) starring Ginger Rogers; and the 1987 TV movie *The Alamo: Thirteen Days to Glory*. He also he starred in John Wayne's role in the remake of *Red River* in 1988 for TV.

Jim has had two marriages, the first to Virginia Chapman from 1948 to 1960 and the second to Janet Surtees from 1978 to the present. From his first marriage Jim had three children: Craig, Jenny Lee (now deceased) and Rolf. In 1981 he was inducted into the Hall of Great Western Performers of the National Cowboy and Western Heritage Museum in Oklahoma City.

Jim said, "I just wanted to see California. I wasn't thinking of acting." He has also said, "The greatest spiritual cleansing I can imagine is to dive into a big surf."

Lew Ayres

(Lewis Frederick Ayer III)
Born 28 December, 1908,
Minneapolis, MN.
Died 30 December, 1996,
Los Angeles, CA.

L ew Ayres was born in the West Lake Harriet area of South Minneapolis and went to the Lake Harriet School at 42nd and Sheridan Ave. So. from first through eighth grade. He grew up in the neighborhood around 44th and Upton Avenue South, which bordered on his old school grounds. The school has been razed and condominiums now stand on the grounds. His parents, who were musicians, divorced when Lew was four. He lived at 2721 W. 44th St. with his paternal grandmother, Anna Ayer, who taught piano at 43rd and Upton. It was she who introduced him to religious philosophy and metaphysics as she was a Theosophist. Lew also took piano lessons from her but he discovered that the banjo, guitar, and the saxophone were more suited to his taste and talents. In 1923 he moved to San Diego with his mother and stepfather.

A few years later, pursuing his musical interests, Lew dropped out of high school to join the Harry Halstead Band and a bit later the Ray West Band, which played at the famed Coconut Grove in the Ambassador Hotel in Los Angeles. Lew returned to school, and upon graduation he formed his own band in the summer in 1926.

Lew attended in the University of Arizona's School of Medicine only briefly the next fall before dropping out. His big break came at a tea dance when a movie executive caught sight of him dancing with Lily Damita (later to marry Errol Flynn and bear him a son). He signed Lew to a six-month contract with Pathé Studio, where he made his film debut in *The Sophomore* (1929). MGM executive Paul Bern saw the film and recommended Lew as a possible co-star for Greta Garbo in her upcoming film, *The Kiss*. Garbo herself chose Ayres from the candidates Bern had assembled. At the age of twenty-one Lew was on his way to being a star.

Lew's next role was as Paul Baumer in **All Quiet on the Western Front** (1930). He was sensational as the sensitive young German soldier who comes to realize the futility of war. This film, directed by Lewis Milestone, won Oscars for Best Picture and Best Director in

1930. It was the first anti-war film and Lew was deeply moved by both the book (by Erich Maria Remarque) and by being in the film itself. He became a pacifist.

Roles of such stature and meaning were few and far between, however, and for many years Ayres was content as a popular leading man who attracted lovely leading ladies. He starred opposite Constance Bennett in *Common Clay* (1930); *My Weakness* (1933) with Lillian Harvey; *She Learned about Sailors* (1934) with Alice Faye; *Cross Country Cruise* (1934) with Alice White; *Panic in the Air* (1936) with Joan Perry; *Young Dr. Kildare* (1938) with Laraine Day; *Calling Dr. Kildare* (1939) with Lana Turner; *Maisie Was a Lady* (1941) with Ann Sothern (from Minneapolis Central High School, class of 1926); and *The Unfaithful* (1947) with Ann Sheridan. In *These Glamor Girls* (1939) Lew co-starred with fellow Minnesotan, Richard Carlson, and Lana Turner.

Though Ayres did not have an aptitude for genuine medicine, he played the role of a doctor in sixteen films. Nine starred a character named Dr. Kildare.

Ayres' star went into eclipse during the Second World War, however, due to his highly-publicized (and to many former fans, unpatriotic) status as a conscientious objector. Few seemed to be aware that he served in the US Army Medical Corps in the Pacific Theater and earned three battle stars during the invasions of Luzon, Hollandia (Kotabaru), and Leyte.

Looking back across Ayres' sixty-year career, a few among his ninety-three films stand out. He appeared in *Holiday* (1938) starring Cary Grant and Katherine Hepburn, playing Hepburn's sweet-tempered, alcoholic brother. After the war he appeared in the hit film *Dark Mirror* (1946) and *Johnny Belinda* (1947) in which he plays a doctor who treats a deaf mute girl (considered to be Jane Wyman's best portrayal ever). Lew was nominated for Best Actor that year but lost to Sir Laurence Olivier in *Hamlet*. Wyman did win an Oscar, however.

Also of note were the films *State Fair* (1933) starring Will Rogers, *Don't Bet on Love* (1933) with Ginger Rogers (to whom Lew was married from 1934-40); *Advise and Consent* (1962), and *The Carpetbaggers* (1964).

Lew also produced, directed, wrote, and narrated two religious documentaries, *Altars of the East* (1956) and *Altars of the World (1976)*. These were critical successes and the second one earned Lew a Golden Globe.

B

Belle Bennett

*Born 22 April, 1890,
Milaca, MN
Died 4 November, 1932,
Hollywood, CA*

B elle was born into show business. Her father ran a tent show based in the Twin Cities in the 1890s. She spent a short time in the Sacred Heart Convent in Minneapolis, but most of her childhood and early teen years were devoted to being a tent-show trouper. Belle made her first film in 1913, but was also a member of several theatrical stock companies before turning to motion pictures full time in 1924.

Considered one of the outstanding leading ladies of the silent screen, Belle became famous for her "mother" roles, chief of which was the mother in *Stella Dallas* (1925). She beat out seventy-two other actresses for the role, and became "the perfect screen mother" to thousands when the film was released. Her son Billy was fatally injured while Belle was making the film, and at the funeral Belle flung herself across the deathbed and sobbed. A day after the funeral, however, she insisted on returning to the studio to complete scenes in which she sacrifices everything for her son, played by sixteen-year-old Douglas Fairbanks, Jr. Ronald Colman plays her husband. Stella eventually loses both husband and son in this four-handkerchief tearjerker. Had Academy Awards existed in 1925, Belle would probably have won Best Actress for the title role in *Stella Dallas*.

Belle was very generous to movie extras and gave several of them "breaks" in the trade. Perhaps this was because Belle herself had had a sadly scandalous childhood, marrying at thirteen and becoming a mother a year later. The baby died in infancy. She had a second child, William Jr, by a La Crosse, Wisconsin, man she divorced in 1924. At that point she began introducing Billy to everyone as her baby brother. (It's likely that the above listed year of birth is wrong by perhaps five years.) After losing her second son, she adopted a boy, Teddy, and went on to adopt twenty-nine children in all, supposedly all children of poor relatives from the Midwest. Belle's early marriage and early arrival at motherhood caused a minor furor in Minnesota and instigated a change in the state's marriage laws making early teen marriages illegal.

Bennett made fifty-five films in all. *The Way of All Flesh* (1928) brought her a nomination for Best Actress as the wife of a respectable man whose life deteriorates to the point that he is too ashamed to return home. The film was nominated for Best Picture of 1928, and Emil Jannings won Best Actor as the husband.

In 1928 director D. W. Griffith remade *The Battle of the Sexes*, which had been hugely successful for him in 1914, with Belle, Phyllis Haver, and Jean Hersholt. In *The Iron Mask* (1929) Belle co-stars with Douglas Fairbanks, Sr. and Marguerite de la Motte. Belle starred in *Courage* (1930) once again as the universal mother.

Bennett has a star on the Hollywood Walk of Fame.

Roman Bohnen

Born 24 Nov, 1894,
St. Paul, MN.
Died 24 Feb, 1949,
Hollywood, CA.

Roman appeared as a character-actor in thirty-nine films, all but three of which were made during the 1940s. He played Candy in *Of Mice and Men* (1939) starring Burgess Meredith and Lon Chaney, Jr. He appeared in *The Hard Way* (1942, *The Edge of Darkness* (1942), *The Song of Bernadette* (1943) starring Jennifer Jones (Roman played her father), and *The Hairy Ape* (1944) starring William Bendix.

He was one of many character actors who starred as a group in *The Mask of Dimitrios* (1944). The film lacked bona fide stars and was probably all the better for it. The ensemble cast included Peter Lorre, Sydney Greenstreet, Florence Bates, Eduardo Cianelli, and Zachary Scott. In *Mission to Moscow* (1943) the cast is similarly loaded with foreign-looking character actors with Walter Huston in the middle.

Roman plays the part of Krestinsky. Also in 1944 he played Dad Pettyjohn in another classic, *None But the Lonely Heart* which starred Cary Grant and Ethel Barrymore, (who won an Academy Award for Best Supporting Actress).

Every film Roman made in 1944 was a classic and *The Hitler Gang* was no exception. He played Captain Ernst Rohm, the leader of Hitler's "brown shirts." In 1945 he appeared in *A Bell for Adano*, based on a hugely popular book, and a year later he was Able Seaman Macklin in *Two Years before the Mast* (1946). He was Mr. O'Neil in *The Strange Love of Martha Ivers* (1946) starring Barbara Stanwyck and Kirk Douglas. He played Warden A. J. Barnes very effectively in *Brute Force* (1947).

Bohnen played doctors, lawyers, military officers, priests, coal stokers, dock loaders, and maybe best of all, he played fathers. He was Dana Andrews' father, Pat Derry, in his most acclaimed film, *The Best Years of Our Lives* (1946), which won Oscars for Best Picture, Best Director (William Wyler), Best Actor (Fredric March), and Best Supporting Actor for Harold Russell, a genuine handless veteran with no acting training. In a poignant performance, Roman is reunited with his son who has just returned from the war.

Marlon Brando

Marlon Brando, Jr.
Born 3 April 1924,
Omaha, NE.

Yes, Marlon Brando has a Minnesota connection. He attended Shattuck School in Faribault as his father had before him, and that qualifies him as an adopted Minnesotan.

Marlon was third of three children of Marlon Sr. and Dorothy Brando. His oldest sister, Jocelyn, became an actress. The middle child, Frances, became an artist. Both Marlon and his sisters took after their mother's looks. His nickname was Bud and he grew up in a financially comfortable household. Marlon, Sr. was of French extraction and his name was originally spelled Brandeau. Dorothy was called Dodie and she was very artistic. She wrote, painted, sculpted, and acted; she was liberal and emotional and attracted to advanced ideas, while her husband was a conservative businessman, unfeeling except for occasional outbursts. Bud was closer to his mother than to his father.

Dodie, a blonde who wore her hair in bangs, was a longtime participant in the Omaha Community Playhouse, which was an important stop off for Henry Fonda and Dorothy McGuire early in their careers. Wally Cox went to elementary school with Brando (later they were roommates in New York), but the two did more fighting than studying. Bud was a daydreamer who was usually shy but sometimes craved to be the center of attention, which he rarely got from his father. He was never a good student.

Being a rebel made for difficult times throughout school. In his junior year Brando was expelled for smoking in the gym. It was decided that Bud needed more discipline so he was packed off to Shattuck Military School in the fall of 1940. Marlon looked grown up and handsome in his cadet uniform but his nature was still to be a prankster.

He called it "The Military Asylum." Of all the things he hated at Shattuck, which included everything, he hated most the chapel bell, which chimed every fifteen minutes. Late one night Marlon snuck out of the dormitory and climbed the bell tower. He seized his most hated enemy—the clapper—wrested it from the bell and buried it. He was not caught. The next morning, however, bugles blared in lieu of the chimes. That was equally unpleasant.

At Shattuck Brando spent much of his time in the infirmary. He had learned how to raise the mercury of a thermometer by rubbing it on his bed sheets whenever the nurse wasn't looking. Next, he created a bomb of two-inch firecrackers and placed them just under the door of a teacher he disliked. He used a trail of hair tonic for a fuse, but rather than burning dryly and cleanly, it scorched the wooden floor and left a track back to Bud's room. Marlon was expelled again, and before long he was back at his parents' home in Libertyville, Illinois, telling people he was going into the ministry. His parents began to see, in this fantasy statement, that Bud was fated to be an actor. He had not quite completed two years at Shattuck, leaving in the spring of 1942 (before graduation).

It's worth noting that while at Shattuck Marlon's interest in sports declined though his interest in theater increased. He took part in two school plays, as a sword carrier in one and a watchman in the other. The Dean of the English Department, Duke Wagner, was also the Director of Theater. He praised Marlon and Marlon adored him in return. Wagner introduced Brando to Shakespeare.

In 1943 Marlon went to New York to explore the possibility of working in the theater. He became a pupil of Stella Adler, who discovered the immense talent behind his pranks. He loved to experiment with false whiskers, foreign accents, nose putty, and dialects. He was taught that ham acting was wrong, that inner truth was the goal, and that drama was a social force, a serious teaching of life. He also studied dance, fencing, and yoga. Shelley Winters and others noticed that Marlon was a brooder. He suffered from melancholic fits and would withdraw from people for days and days. Then childish exhilaration took over and he would rejoin the human race and attend parties and do favors for people.

By the fall of 1944 Brando got the part of Nels in *I Remember Mama*. It was a long-running success, and Brando met all the members of the Group Theatre; Clifford Odets, the playwright; Elia Kazan, the director; Luther Adler and John Garfield, both actors; and others like Karl Malden. His reputation was growing.

In 1947 Brando became an overnight sensation as Stanley Kowalski in Tennessee William's play, *A Streetcar Named Desire*. Jessica Tandy played Blanche, Kim Hunter played Stella, and Karl Malden played Mitch. Williams won a Pulitzer Prize for writing the play, and it also won the New York Drama Critics Award. Brando was 5' 10" but looked strong and slightly husky. He had been lifting weights, which added to the animal energy underlying his portrayal of Stanley.

The rest is history. Brando went to Hollywood where he appeared in the long-awaited filming of *A Streetcar Named Desire* (1951). Other films followed including *The Wild One* (1954), and an Oscar-winning performance as Terry Mulloy in *On the Waterfront* (1954).

The remainder of Brando's career had more than its share of ups and downs, perhaps, with *Mutiny on the Bounty* (1962), *Last Tango in Paris* (1972), *The Missouri Breaks* (1976), and *Apocalypse Now* (1979) among his better efforts. Brando won a second Oscar for his compelling performance as Don Vito Corleone in *The Godfather* (1972).

Thanks, Marlon, for your stopover in Faribault, Minnesota.

A couple of Brando quotes: "An actor is at most a poet and at least an entertainer." "The only thing an actor owes his public is not to bore them."

Virginia Bruce

(Helen Virginia Briggs)
Born 29 September, 1909,
Minneapolis, MN.
Died 24 February, 1982,
Woodland Hills, CA.

Virginia's first address in the world was 2617 Harriet Avenue South but Earll Briggs moved the family the next year around the corner to 1402 W. 26th Street in Minneapolis. The family also lived at 2566 Lake of the Isles Blvd for a while before moving to Fargo, North Dakota, in 1912.

Virginia was often teased about her allegedly rural roots and was even called a "hick." She resented it because it wasn't true. In any case, by the early 1930s she had become the epitome of the glamorous Hollywood chorus girl, with her sophisticated swagger, her large, taunting, sparkling-blue eyes, and a smile that blended youthful enthusiasm with a sense of worldly experience. She was 5' 4" yet seemed petite (one newspaper source cites her as 5' 6"). She loved swimming, tennis, riding, and fishing, yet more than fishing she loved fishing stories. Virginia became a big fan of prizefighting and boxing. She never dieted because she didn't need to, but ate whatever she wanted and always kept her figure and her milky white complexion.

Ginny Briggs attended Agassiz Grammar School and Fargo Central High School. The Briggs family lived in a squarish brick house on the corner of Fifth Avenue and Fourteenth Street. Ginny often played in her front yard with her friends, and she once tended nine kittens in the basement of her family's home through a severe North Dakota winter. Even as a child she was pretty and well mannered, yet there was always that pensive and soulful expression.

The Briggs were financially comfortable and Virginia's mother was a championship golfer at the Fargo Country Club. She won the state championship three times. Mrs. Briggs also was active in Fargo Fine Arts Club. Ginny became quite proficient at the piano and entertained with dance music for both family events and young people's parties. In the summer the Briggs family went to Detroit Lakes for long vacations. In winter there was ice skating in the park rink, basketball games in the school gym, and sleigh rides over the countryside. Ginny had one brother, Stanley, a few years younger than she.

By 1928, Earll, an insurance broker, had lost all his money due to massive crop failures throughout the Dakotas, so the family moved to Los Angeles. Ginny was to start at UCLA and Stanley to start high school in L. A. However, director William Beaudine and his publicity man, Harry Wurtzel, spotted her one day when she was touring a movie studio and were immediately impressed by her looks. Beaudine signed her onto a personal contract for $25 a week.

The next year she made six pictures with Paramount Studios. Her debut came in *Fugitives*, which newcomer Jean Harlow also had a bit part in. Her third movie, *Love Parade*, starred Maurice Chevalier and Jeanette MacDonald and was directed by the legendary Ernst Lubitsch. Virginia had one line.

The next year she performed in eleven movies, and began to develop a reputation as a prankster on the set.

A friend named Jack Harkrider, a designer for the Ziegfeld shows, helped her get a job as a showgirl on Broadway in *Smiles* starring Fred and Adele Astaire. Flo Ziegfeld declared Virginia to be "The World's Most Beautiful Natural Blond." Ann Sothern and Madeleine Carroll completed the trio labelled as "the three most beautiful blondes in the world." After *Smiles* she appeared in *America's Sweetheart*, which lasted six months.

In 1931 Virginia returned to Hollywood, took a screen test for Metro-Goldwyn-Mayer (MGM) with newcomer Robert Young, and signed a contract. She was featured in *The Miracle Man* (1932) with Boris Karloff one year after his shockingly successful role in *Frankenstein* (1931). After a few more bit parts she was paired with John Gilbert for the film *Downstairs* (1932). The two fell madly in love, and after a whirlwind courtship they married at the conclusion of the filming. Irving Thalberg, the head of production at MGM, was the best man while his wife, Norma Shearer, was a bridesmaid.

In 1933 Virginia gave birth to Susan Ann. In accordance to her North Dakota values she retired upon becoming pregnant. By the following year thee marriage had gone sour, Gilbert and Bruce divorced, and Virginia returned to filmmaking. When Gilbert died two years later, it was discovered that he had bequeathed his entire estate to Virginia and Susan Ann, worth a quarter million dollars. A plot to kidnap Susan Ann was thwarted not long afterword, but the kidnappers were never caught.

Starting with the title role with *Jane Eyre* (1934), Virginia acted in fourteen movies in sixteen months. That's one way to recover from grief. The mid-and late-1930s were also her heyday in filmland when she enjoyed high recognition, popularity and respect. She starred as

Jenny Lind, the Swedish Nightingale, in *The Mighty Barnum* (1934) co-starring Wallace Beery. She starred with Lawrence Tibbett in *Metropolitan* (1935), a fictional account of the beginning of the Metropolitan Opera Company. She starred with Robert Taylor in the popular *Times Square Lady* (1936). She shared star billing in *The Great Ziegfeld* (1936) with William Powell, Myrna Loy, Ray Bolger, Fanny Brice, Frank Morgan, and Luise Rainer. Virginia sang the show-stopping finale, "A Pretty Girl Is Like a Melody," as chorus girls dance. The film won several Oscars, and Virginia became ensconced in the public imagination as the classic Ziegfeld Girl.

Virginia's other notable films include *Between Two Women* (1937), *Yellow Jack* (1938), *The First Hundred Years* (1938), *There's That Woman Again* (1939), with Melvyn Douglas, and *Wife, Doctor and Nurse* (1937) with Loretta Young. Virginia said that Loretta was the only person she did not like to work with.

In 1937 Virginia married film director J. Walter Ruben, and she had a son, Christopher, in 1941. Although they had known each other for nine years, a romance suddenly blossomed during Ruben's directing *Bad Man of Brimstone* (1937). Their marriage was successful but Ruben died suddenly in 1942.

Virginia's final marriage was with Ali Ipar from 1946 to 1964.

Virginia Bruce' appeared in seventy-nine movies in all over thirty-two years. Her last role was as Kim Novak's mother in *Strangers When We Meet* (1960) which also starred Kirk Douglas.

As an adult she liked to travel to New York, London, and Paris. Two of her best Hollywood friends were Mrs. Gary Cooper and Mrs. Donald Ogden Stewart. She collected first edition books. Her favorite films? *The Big Parade, The Merry Widow* and *The Constant Nymph*. She never tired of reading *School for Scandal* by Richard Brinsley Sheridan. Other favorite authors included Nathaniel Hawthorn, Eugene O'Neill, and William Faulkner. She loved bridge and golf, driving her roadster and tending the garden at her home in Pacific Palisades, California.

Phillip H. Bruns

Born 2 May, 1931
Pipestone, MN.

From farm kid to Fulbright Scholar, with Yale University in between, then on to Broadway, Jackie Gleason, George Shumway, and Morty Seinfeld—Phil Bruns has done a few things during his show business career.

Phil was born on a farm seven miles south of Pipestone, Minnesota. He was the last of three surviving children born to H. P. and Marge Bruns. Phil is a German-Irish American. His older sisters are Mildred Bruns and Dorothy Boese. His parents married in Doon, Iowa, on December 5, 1917. Their honeymoon to Pipestone took seven days, a long time even for the horse-and-buggy standards of that day, but as Phil says, "It was a case of fast hearts and slow horses."

His fondest memories of growing up are riding into Pipestone on balmy summer nights in a 1932 Ford. They would pick up a block of ice from the Reynolds Ice Company, then get ice cream bars for the whole family. Then they would race home before all the ice melted completely. At the age of six Phil was given his first B. B. gun and he immediately took target practice at gophers, rabbits, and a cow that had kicked him. He remembers his mother burning corn during the Depression as there was no market to sell it at a fair price. Whenever he slammed the screen door, his mother paddled his bottom. He loved fishing for bullheads at Lake Shetek. He loved picking wild asparagus along the roadside while walking the three miles to school. What he didn't eat, he sold to Reiff's Country Store for 25 cents—just enough for a movie ticket, a box of popcorn, and a triple-dipped ice cream cone. Ah, the memories.

Phil did well enough in high school football (class of '49), to earn a football scholarship to Augustana College in South Dakota. The scholarship did not entail cash, but provided Phil with a steady job—deputy sheriff in Augustana. He graduated with degrees in speech and physical education, and lettered in football, baseball, golf and track. He did so well in theater that he was accepted into graduate school at the Yale University Drama School, New Haven, Connecticut. Wow! Quite a distance from Pipestone!

At Yale Phil taught a few classes while completing a Master of Fine Arts degree (1956) and during that time he developed a strong interest in mime and comedy. His graduation recital was a one-man mime show. He was awarded a Fulbright Scholarship soon afterward, and spent the next fifteen months in England at the University of Bristol and the Old Vic Theatre and school. His Fulbright stipend was larger than the salary of most of the cast members, and he felt it his duty to be a willing host. It wasn't long before his house had become a center for cast parties. Among the regular guests was Peter O'Toole, who has remained a life-long pal. English writer and critic Kenneth Tynan praised Phil highly for his performance in *Home of the Brave* in the National University Drama Festival in London.

Through Peter O'Toole Phil met Albert Finney, who, like O'Toole, was a fair-haired boy from whom much was expected in the theater world. In fact, Finney was offered the lead role in **Lawrence of Arabia** but he happily turned it down and suggested O'Toole. The part made O'Toole's name a household word, but Finney's day was coming. He was given the lead role in **Tom Jones** and his position in the British world of film and theater was secured.

Phil had attracted a lot attention during his stay in England, and when his Fulbright was over he was invited to stay on. He was anxious to make his name on the American stage, however, and he returned to New York. He almost immediately scored a triumph in *Mr. Simian* (1963), which earned him an Obie award for Best Actor of the season. Among his thirty off-Broadway productions and ten Broadway productions, Phil was nominated three times for an Obie. Speaking of awards, Phil Bruns was voted "The Outstanding Young Man in America" in 1960. In 1976 he won the Augustana Alumni Achievement Award.

Phil's introduction to TV was on *Jackie Gleason and his American Scene Magazine*, which ran from 1962-1966. He joined Frankie Fontaine and the Gleason regulars (as replacements for the departing Art Carney) for thirty-nine shows per season for three years (1963-1966). Gleason had liked his audition because Phil made him laugh. It was not easy to make Gleason laugh.

Gleason made it clear to his people that no one, on any account, was to laugh at his own bit on stage. Gleason offered the challenge to Phil that if Phil could make him laugh (make him "break," in stage lingo), then Jackie would double Phil's salary. Well, three times that first season Phil's checks were doubled, and not for just that show but for the rest of the season.

Returning to the stage with Hollywood's Players Ring Gallery, Phil became part of the "MacBird" show, which satirized President Lyndon Johnson and family. Phil played LBJ, complete with rumpled ten-gallon hat, spectacles, and elevator-lift cowboy boots. The audience loved him, and the *Los Angeles Times* said of his portrayal, "Philip Bruns is all drawling, ignorant, power-hungry, nose-twitching, hypocritical politicians rolled into one." The IRS audited Phil from 1967 to 1993.

Perhaps Phil's most memorable TV role was as George Shumway on the *Mary Hartman, Mary Hartman* show, which ran from 1974-1976. Louise Lasser played Mary Hartman, Phil played her father. People still stop him on the street and call him George. He continued as George Shumway on *Forever Fernwood* in 1977-78.

Phil played another father, Morty Seinfeld, in the first episode of *Seinfeld* in 1990, and had major guest-appearances on other shows too numerous to mention.

Phil's first movie was **All Woman** (1958). He was in **A Thousand Clowns** (1965), **Jenny** (1969), and **Midnight Cowboy** (1969). He was in the original **Out-of-Towners** (1970); **Harry and Tonto** (1974); **The Great Waldo Pepper** (1975), and **Nickelodeon** (1976). For his stunts in **Nickelodeon**, Phil became an honorary member of the movie stuntmen.

Other films include **Corvette Summer** (1978), **The Stunt Man** (1980), **My Favorite Year** (1982) both starring Phil's old friend Peter O'Toole, and **Flashdance** (1983). He turned down the role of the referee in **Rocky** because he would have had no lines. Oh, well....

Phil Bruns married Jill Owens on June 28th, 1969, in New York. They divorced after some years and Phil has now been married to Laurie Franks for many years.

Phil owned a farm in Pennsylvania for many years. He just can't shake free of the beauty of pheasants suddenly bursting into flight out of a cornfield.

Phil was recently elected to membership in the Academy of Motion Picture Arts and Sciences. He is among very elite company as there are only 1,300 members out of 96,000 members of the Screen Actors Guild. Robert Redford wrote the crucial recommendation, it seems, as he had fond memories of their working together in **The Great Waldo Pepper**.

Forty years ago Phil said, "I'd just like to be known as a hell of an actor." To judge from his many excellent theater notices, plum TV roles, and varied film appearances, he has gotten his wish.

C

Richard Carlson

Born 29 April 1912,
Albert Lea, MN.
Died 24 November 1977
Encino, CA.

This man led three lives in the first television series of spies and counterspies. Yes, Richard Carlson, who graduated from Minneapolis' Washburn High School in 1929, played Herbert A. Philbrick in the 1950s TV series, *I Led Three Lives*.

Richard was the youngest of four children born to Mr. & Mrs. Henry C. Carlson. He had two sisters, Margaret Mabel and Ruth Elenor, and one bother, Henry Clay Carlson, Jr.. The family lived at 525 Park Avenue in Albert Lea, where Henry Carlson was an attorney with the law firm of H. H. Dunn. Mrs. Carlson was the former Mabel Du Toit and it was said that Richard inherited his good looks from her. Mabel's brother was a co-founder of Honeywell, Inc. Mabel was of French descent while Henry was Danish.

The family moved to Minneapolis in 1918 when Richard was six. His father became a partner in Fowler, Carlson, Furber and Johnson, which had offices in the New York Life Building in downtown Minneapolis. The family lived at 5103 Garfield Avenue South. Richard attended Margaret Fuller Elementary School, Ramsey Junior High, and Washburn, where he was class president in his senior year. The Wahian Yearbook states that Richard was "illustrious and most amorous and most imperious." Among a long list of extracurricular activities, he had the lead in two class plays: "*The Marriage of Nanette*" and "*Sweethearts.*" He also wrote, directed and appeared in "*The Masquerade,*" quite a coup for a high school lad.

Richard attended the University of Minnesota, graduating summa cum laude and Phi Beta Kappa in 1933, and he won scholarship prizes of $2,500. While he was a student, he appeared in plays at Scott Hall such as Shakespeare's *Henry IV, Part I*, in which he played Prince Hal. He later completed his master's degree in English Literature, also at Minnesota, but from that point on he followed the lure of the theater.

While working as an English instructor Richard wrote three plays, several sketches, and a novel. With scholarship prize money he formed a repertory company which toured the country performing his plays. It was an artistic success but a financial failure. He sought work at the Pasadena Playhouse in California to no avail, then headed for New York, where he made his debut in 1937 in *Now You've Done It*. Later that year he appeared with Ethel Barrymore in *The Ghost of Yankee Doodle*.

While playing in *Whiteoaks* with Ethel Barrymore, Richard talked with Sidney Howard regarding a script he'd written, *Western Waters*. Howard was duly impressed and called David O. Selznick—the crown prince of Hollywood at the time. Selznick mailed a contract immediately and Carlson signed in three capacities, as a playwright/author, actor, and director.

The next year Carlson made his film debut in a comedy-drama called *The Young in Heart*. Carlson was deemed to have good legs and good knees, which he used to good effect in the role of Duncan Macrae who wore a kilt.

Richard published articles during the 1930s in *Collier's, Woman's Home Companion, Ladies Home Journal, Good Housekeeping* and other national magazines. He sold a play about life on the Mississippi River during steamboat days to Broadway producer Harry Moses who produced it in the fall of 1938. Unfortunately, it was a "turkey" and folded early. His early dream of writing "the great American play" never materialized, but he bragged that he had a few flops to his credit. Writing had to give way to acting full time.

Carlson's career took off in 1939 when he co-starred with Lana Turner and Lew Ayres in *These Glamorous Girls* then co-starred with Ann Sheridan in *Winter Carnival* (1939). The next year he starred with Anna Neagle in the remake of *No No Nanette* (1940). Two comedies followed: *The Ghost Breakers* (1940) where Richard lent support to Bob Hope and Paulette Goddard; and *Hold That Ghost* (1941) starring Abbott and Costello. Richard also made his most important film in 1941, the post-Civil War drama *The Little Foxes,* starring Bette Davis, Herbert Marshall, Teresa Wright and Richard as David Hewitt. The film received nine Oscar nominations. It was written by Lillian Hellman and directed by William Wyler.

Carlson also appeared in **Back Street** that year in support of Susan Hayward. The film was written by Minnesota's Eleanore Griffin, who had recently won an original screenplay Oscar for **Boys Town** (1938).

Richard signed a contract with MGM in 1942. He appeared in **White Cargo** (1942) in support of Hedy Lamarr (as Tondelayo) and Walter Pidgeon. That same year he starred in **Fly by Night** (1942) which largely imitates Alfred Hitchcock's **The Thirty-Nine Steps** (1935).

In 1943 Richard played Owen Vail in support of Judy Garland in **Presenting Lily Mars**. This was a great venue for Judy to sing along with Tommy Dorsey and his band and Bob Crosby and his band.

Perhaps his next significant film was **King Solomon's Mines** (1950) starring Stewart Granger and Deborah Kerr, and also including Minnesota-born Lowell Gilmore. The cast flew from Cairo to the Ugandan headwaters of the Nile River, then across Lake Naivasha to Nairobi, Kenya, traveling fourteen-thousand miles in all through eastern and central Africa during the location shooting. They saw plenty of hippos, giraffes, baboons, zebras and several kinds of antelope. Compton Bennett, the director, saw a lion kill a gazelle one evening. The stars and cameramen were nearly trampled while filming an exotic native dance. In his notes Richard compared Nairobi to Paris.

Richard appeared in sixty-three films in all during a career spanning thirty-one years. He also directed eight pictures and made seventeen TV appearances. Yet he is perhaps best known for two things. Among science fiction fans he is a genuine cult hero because he acted in three ground-breaking 3-D movies: **It Came from Outer Space** (1953), **Creature from the Black Lagoon** (1954) and **The Maze** (1953). In these flicks he was able to project intelligence, boldness, tension, and earnestness that were perfectly suited to the unusual subject matter.

It is as Herbert A. Philbrick that most Americans remember Richard Carlson. *I Led Three Lives* was based on the best-selling book by the real Herb Philbrick, who really was a counterspy in the FBI. The series started in 1953 and lasted until 1956. Richard's Herb Philbrick was a Boston advertising executive by day and a member of the American Communist Party by night and a spy for the FBI in between times. Virginia Stefan played his wife, Ann.

When Richard died in 1977 at age sixty-five, he left a widow, Mona, and two sons, Christopher and Henry.

It is perhaps of interest that Richard Carlson, Arlene Dahl, Oscar-winning film director George Roy Hill, newscaster Dave Moore, Oklahoma Sooners national champion football coach Charles "Bud" Wilkinson, and national champion golfer Patty Berg, all lived within three blocks of the Bryant Drug at 50th & Bryant Avenue South in Minneapolis.

George Chesebro

Born 29 July 1888,
Minneapolis, MN.
Died 28 May 1959,
Los Angeles, CA.

G eorge has the Minnesota record for appearing in 355 movies during his long career. He was a featured player and occasional leading man in silent action movies but because of his natural scowl he became a villain in sound movies. Almost all of his movies were "B" budget westerns, and he became adept at playing robbers, cattle rustlers, and drygulchers—any role that called for a bit of crudeness and crassness.

George was born and reared in Minneapolis, yet horseback riding was his favorite sport. He was known as one of the best riders in all of movieland! His father, George E. Chesebro, was a switchman for the Northern Pacific Railroad. The family lived at 421 Bryant Ave N.

George joined a Minnesota stock company in 1907 while still a teen, and he played in vaudeville, too. Yes, folks, he also had a day job as a clerk at the N.E. Furniture Co. After leaving home he lived for a while at 116 S. 12th St. in Minneapolis. He toured the Orient from 1911 to 1913 in a musical spectacular, and by the time he arrived in Los Angeles in 1915 he was a seasoned veteran.

Following a stint in the armed forces during World War I, George became a leading man in the early days of movies, though his status slipped during the 1920s and he became a "heavy"—one of those ever-familiar faces whose names seldom appear in the credits.

Yet Chesebro was featured in several silent serials, including *The Lost City* (1920), *The Diamond Queen* (1921) and *The Hope Diamond Mystery* (1921). Early in his career he worked for Triangle Studios, and often found work in the 1930s and 40s with PRC, Monogram, Superior, and Reliable Studios. It seems all directors of oaters wanted

George Chesebro to take a pot shot at the hero or just poke at the good guy's jaw. Other noted films that George appeared in were *The Mexicali Kid* (1938, as Joe); *The Adventures of Wild Bill Hickok* (1938, as Metaxa); *Daredevils of the Red Circle* (1939, as Sheffield); *Mandrake the Magician* (1939, as Baker, a thug), *S. O. S. Coast Guard* (1937, as Chief Thug L. H. Degado, 1942); *Trial of the Silver Spurs* (1941); and *The Adventures of Frank and Jesse James* (1948).

As George aged he often landed roles as a gang boss. His best screen part was as the brains of a gang of robbers in *Cheyenne Takes Over* (1947) starring Lash LaRue.

Among the stars George worked with over the course of his career were Gene Autry in *Tumbling Tumbleweeds* (1935), Ken Maynard in *Lightning Strikes West* (1940), Tex Ritter in *Starlight over Texas* (1938), Tim McCoy in *Frontier Crusader* (1940), Hopalong Cassidy in *The Hills of Old Wyoming* (1937), Buster Crabbe in *Gangsters Den* (1945), Wild Bill Elliott in *Sun Valley Cyclone* (1946), Hoot Gibson in *Lucky Terror* (1936), Dick Foran in *Prairie Thunder* (1937), Bob Steele in *Billy the Kid's Fighting Pals* (1941), Clayton Moore in *Ghost of Zorro* (1949), and with Charles Starrett in *Lawless Empire* (1946).

A bit of trivia: George was one of three Minnesotan cowboy actors with large filmographies. Terry Frost and William Fawcett are the other two. In *Black Hills* (1947) all three appeared together.

George's last name has been listed as Cheeseboro, Cheesebro, Chesboro, Chesborough, Chesbro, Cheseboro and Chesebro. He died at age seventy in Hermosa Beach, California.

Rachael Leigh Cook

Born 4 October, 1979
Minneapolis, MN.

By the age of twenty-one Rachael Leigh Cook had already spent over half of her life in show business. She started modeling at age ten. Specifically, she was a print model on Milk Bone boxes and on Target ads nationwide. Her most effective ad was an anti-drug ad in which she smashed an egg with a frying pan. Then she faces the camera and says, "This is your brain on heroin." She goes on to trash the whole kitchen saying, "This is your family, friends, career, etc." It was considered a very effective anti-drug ad.

After five years of modeling (she is 5′ 2″), her agency sent her to an audition for a short film called *26 Summer Street* (1996). She got the part and has been hooked on acting ever since. Later that year she traveled to Los Angeles with her mother and at her first audition she landed a major role in *The Baby-Sitters Club* (1995). She plays Mary Anne Spier, the blossoming entrepreneur who organizes her girlfriends into a baby-sitter agency of sorts. From there Rachael was whisked into *Tom and Huck* (1995) in which she plays Becky Thatcher, Tom's love interest. In those days she was still commuting between Hollywood and classes at Minneapolis South High, though she also attended the Laurel Springs School, a school for young actors who are unable to live a regular agenda due to movie commitments.

In the modern Pygmalion film *She's All That* (1999) co-starring Freddie Prinze, Jr., Rachael did a wonderful transformation from an ugly duckling to a ravishing beauty, and won several teen awards as a result. A year later she appeared as a troubled teen in Sylvester Stallone's *Get Carter*. She had long since become a hot item in Hollywood, and in 2001 she appeared in no less than four features, most notably as the girl-band lead singer in *Josie and the Pussycats*. She also played a frontier gal, Caroline Dukes, in the Civil War-era western, *Texas Rangers*. More recent films have included the teen thriller *Tangled, Sally, Palms,* and *The Big Empty* (2003).

Perhaps Rachael came to her career through growing up with a father (Tom) who did stand-up comedy on the side as he pursued his day job of being a school social worker. Her younger brother, Ben, also wants to be an actor. Her fast-track career includes twenty-two films in only six years. She has appeared on a half dozen TV shows, including *Dawson's Creek, The Outer Limits* and *WOAK Live*. She was also featured with Freddie Prinze, Jr. in the music video, *"Kiss Me,"* by Six Pence None the Richer.

Rachael is left-handed and is a vegetarian. She says, "I'm not small, I'm space-efficient." Also, "If this whole acting thing doesn't work out, I'll just get a talk show."

D

Arlene Dahl

Born 11 August, 1924
Minneapolis, MN.

This very successful health and beauty columnist, consultant and businesswoman is one of Minneapolis Washburn High School's most illustrious graduates (1943). President of Arlene Dahl Enterprises, Arlene has written some fourteen books on secrets of health and beauty. She began her post high school life as a model for Harry Conover, was the Rheingold Beer Girl in 1946, and went on to appear in more than thirty films.

Known for her lush red hair, Arlene is of Norwegian extraction and has been dubbed "the living Dahl." Everyone who works for her, coincidentally, has red hair, too. Arlene visited Minneapolis in 1987 to play a celebrity hostess to Norway's King Olav at the downtown Marriot Center on 7th Street between Hennepin Avenue and Nicollet Mall. It was her first trip back since 1983 when she attended her fortieth class reunion.

Arlene was born at Fairview Hospital and was an only child. In her early years she lived at Fremont Avenue North. At five she began to study dance at Dorothy Lundstrom's School of Dance, Charm and Fashion at nearby Ascension School. That same year her grandmother put her on the picnic table at a family gathering and told her to sing "Polly Put the Kettle On"—her first public performance.

At ten Arlene and friends started a Hollywood Revue group that performed at such places as the Mabeth Hurd Paige Club and the Monday Welfare Club, where underprivileged children could enjoy Christmas entertainment. She also performed at the Minneapolis College of Music where she sang "Alice Blue Gown," "Mechanical Doll," and "Fairy Queen."

Her parents, Rudolph and Idelle (Swan) Dahl, moved to 4636 Lyndale Avenue South. In this neighborhood Arlene attended Margaret Fuller Elementary School, Ramsey Junior High, and Washburn Senior High. While in seventh grade at Ramsey she appeared in productions of *Tom Sawyer* (as Becky Thatcher) and *Dear Octopus*, sponsored by the Council of Parent-Teachers Association and the Better Drama League, which later sponsored Arlene (as the heroine) on national radio for children's adventure serials. She knew from seventh grade that she wanted to be an actress.

Arlene's mother sewed all of her costumes, and the two were constant companions until Idele had a stroke and died. Arlene was eighteen at the time.

As a student at Washburn, Arlene was in the National Honor Society, the U.C. Club, French Club, Glee Club, dramatics, the Social Entertainment Committee and was a drum majorette. She was voted by her class as the "most likely to succeed." She wrote a term paper on legendary actress Katherine Cornell for graduation.

Throughout her school days she studied singing at the Minneapolis College of Music at 11th Street and La Salle Avenue. She also studied dramatics at the University of Minnesota during summer vacations. She studied painting, drawing, and design at the Minneapolis Art Institute's School (now the Minneapolis College of Art & Design), and after graduation she took a job with Dayton's Department Store as an interior window display artist.

At age nineteen Arlene did some modeling of bathing suits and sports togs for the Sportsman Show at the old Minneapolis Auditorium. When the show moved to Chicago, she moved there with it. After two years of modeling there, she left for New York and a life on the stage.

Arlene made her first appearance on Broadway in *Mr. Strauss Goes to Boston* in 1945 lasting all of 12 performances. It was said that Mr. Strauss should have stayed in Boston rather than coming to New York. After the show closed Arlene took to modeling for $30 an hour with the Harry Conover Agency.

At twenty-two she signed a contract with Warner Brothers Studios. Her debut film was in a bit part in **Life with Father** (1947) starring William Powell, Irene Dunne, and Elizabeth Taylor. Glory arrived with **My Wild Irish Rose** (1947, as Rose Donovan) in which she co-starred with Dennis Morgan.

The next year Dahl signed with MGM, where she made her most memorable films. (Why the short stay with Warners? It seems that Jack L. Warner went to Europe having forgotten to renew Arlene's option. Louis Mayer had seen *My Wild Irish Rose* and wanted Arlene at MGM so he signed her away from Warners before anyone was wise to it.) Her first film there was *The Bride Goes Wild* (1948) starring June Allyson, Van Johnson, and Hume Cronyn. That was followed by *A Southern Yankee* (1948) in which she co-starred with Red Skelton in a marvelous, heart-warming comedy.

Next came *Reign of Terror* (1949) in which she co-starred with Robert Cummings; *Scene of the Crime* (1949); *Border Incident* (1949, with Ricardo Montalban); and *Ambush* (1949) in which she co-starred with Robert Taylor. She co-starred with Red Skelton again plus Fred Astaire and Vera-Ellen in *Three Little Words* (1950), a musical comedy biography of songwriters Bert Kalmar and Harry Ruby. Arlene's singing "I Love You So Much" made a great impression. (Debbie Reynolds also made a terrific impression in this film, her debut).

Arlene co-starred again with Red Skelton in *Watch the Birdie* (1950); with Barry Sullivan in *No Questions Asked* (1951); with John Payne in *Caribbean* (1952); with Ray Milland in *Jamaica Run* (1953); with Alan Ladd in *Desert Legion* (1953); and with Fernando Lamas in *Sangaree* (1953).

Meeting Fernando Lamas was quite significant for Arlene. Two years earlier she had divorced Lex Barker, husband number one, after less than a year of marriage. She was ready to become involved with a steamy Latin lover. Dahl and Lamas were married for six years and had one son, Lorenzo, born in 1958—he is a TV star and heart throb.

Arlene co-starred again with Lamas in *Diamond Queen* (1953); with Bob Hope, Rosemary Clooney, and Tony Martin in *Here Come the Girls* (1954); and in *Woman's World* (1954) with another star-studded cast. At about this time Arlene also found time to star on Broadway as Roxanne opposite Jose Ferrer in *Cyrano de Bergerac*.

Arlene was so elegant and beautiful that her appearance often seemed to overshadow her talent, and she was not always paired well with leading men. Late in her career she often played hard-edged women—for example, the klepto-nympho ex-con in *Slightly Scarlet* (1956), the frigid title character in *Wicked As They Come* (1957), and the arsonist in *She Played with Fire* (1958 also titled in England as *Fortune Is a Woman*).

The best of her later pictures is definitely *Journey to the Center of the Earth* (1959) co-starring James Mason and Pat Boone. Arlene tumbles with the best of them when the volcano erupts, and even when smeared with dirt she is drop-dead gorgeous.

Arlene Dahl's Hollywood life wasn't the most important thing for her. She valued theater work more highly, and considered fashion, beauty, and health more important still. She parlayed this love into a second career in 1950, when *Chicago Tribune* founder Robert McCormick offered her a position writing about beauty and style. Her first interview was with Ava Gardner, who had once occupied the dressing room across the hall from hers at MGM. In another early interview Greer Garson told her that she washed her hair in champagne. Arlene's column was off and running, three times a week for the next twenty-one years.

At various times Arlene has designed sleepwear for A. N. Saab & Co., served as beauty director of Sears, Roebuck & Co., and worked with advertising agencies. In 1969 she was named Woman of the Year in Communications by the New York Advertising Club! She has also found the time to write several best-selling books, including *Always Ask a Man* (1965), *Beautyscopes* (1968), and *Secrets of Hair Care and Secrets of Skin Care* (1970).

Dahl's later husbands include the Texas oil millionaire Chris Holmes and wine connoisseur Alexis Lichine.

Movie columnist Louella Parsons once singled out Arlene and Elizabeth Taylor as the only two natural beauties in Hollywood who could step in front of a camera without a spot of makeup.

Arlene has been asked many times what she thinks of Women's Liberation and she quotes Coco Chanel, "Equality? Why step down?"

Irene Dare

(Irene Davidson)
Born 14 February, 1931
Saint Paul, MN.

Irene Dare, called the Shirley Temple of the Silver Skates, was discovered when a talent scout saw newsreel footage of her skating for the 1937 St. Paul Children's Hospital Ice Follies. The scout was dazzled by the performance and immediately contacted Hollywood producer Sol Lesser, urging him to sign Irene to a movie contract. He told Lesser that she was a miniature Sonja Henie, the Norwegian skater who had won five Olympic gold medals in the 1930s.

At the time Irene lived with her parents, Harry B. and Violet P. Davidson, at 1628 Juno Avenue, near Randolph and Snelling Avenues in Saint Paul. The family could not agree about Irene's future. Mr. Davidson, a photo-engraver for the *Saint Paul Daily News*, reflecting on the uncertainties of the Depression-era times in which they lived, wanted his daughter to have a college education and live a practical life. Irene's mother, on the other hand, pushed for glamour and a life in show business. Eventually Mrs. Davidson won the debate, after scouring the directories for all fields of entertainment and convincing her husband that no child skating star was currently active who might undercut their daughter's career.

Prior to taking skating lessons in 1935, Irene had taken acrobatic dance lessons. This enabled her to do the stunt skating that she became known for in her movies. She mastered "the Charlotte" during his first year of lessons. This manoevre entails gliding at full speed forward or backward on one skate while the arms, body and one leg resemble a gliding plane. She mastered the splits on skates at age six. Her skating teacher was Orrin Markhus, the best skating teacher in Minnesota at the time.

Irene attended the Mattocks Elementary School during those years but she preferred skating to school. In fact, her natural ambition was so strong that her parents never had to coax her into practicing. She quickly learned the fan, the cartwheel, and a stunt that had her doing a headstand on ice. She had no fear of falling because her acrobatic training had prepared her to recover from spills on the ice. (Besides, it wasn't such a long way down.)

By age five Irene had performed in sixteen ice carnivals in and around St. Paul and then the big break came. The Club New Yorker in New York City made her an offer through Evelyn Chandler, considered by St. Paulites as the best professional woman skater in the world. The first night of her scheduled week of performances was personally cancelled by Mayor Fiorello LaGuardia. He said that she could not be present at a place where liquor was served. This controversial publicity put Irene in the front-page headlines, and inspired Fox Newsreel to make a special short film about her career.

After the New York tour Violet Davidson took Irene out to Hollywood and lived on an allowance Harry sent them each week. At age seven Irene began a six-year film contract with producer Sol Lesser, who had developed such stars as Jackie Coogan, Jackie Cooper, Baby Peggy, and Bobby Breen. Irene would start at $125 per week rising to $1,200 a week in the sixth year.

Her first film was *Breaking the Ice*. In the cast were boy-soprano Bobby Breen, Charles Ruggles, Dolores Costello (wife of John Barrymore), St. Paul's Dorothy Peterson, Margaret Hamilton (the Wicked Witch of the West) and comedian Billy Gilbert. The following year Irene appeared in *Everything's on Ice* (1939) starring Edgar "Slow Burn" Kennedy (a graduate of the Mack Sennett Keystone Cops movies and comedies of the Hal Roach Studios), Roscoe Karns, and young Bobby Watson. Mary Hart, formerly a leading lady of the Arthur Casey Players in St. Paul, also shared the bill.

At one point in the latter film Irene dances on skates with a dummy like Charlie McCarthy with a Palm Beach nightclub as the swanky background for her maneuvers. The scene is reminiscent of Ginger Rogers and Fred Astaire dancing.

In preparation for the filming of *Everything's on Ice* Irene followed a rigorous schedule. She was up at 6; at the rink at 9 where she skated until 11. She ate, then took ballet lessons from 12:30 until 1:30. At 2 she returned to the rink and practiced her skating until 4. From 4:30 to 5:30 she studied dramatics and she went to bed at 7:30. This may seem tough on a young girl of eight but she considered it playing, not working. She did this six days a week. She also considered making $125 a week better than being in grammar school—in today's dollars that would be $2,500 a week.

In 1939 Harry Davidson filed guardianship papers with the California Superior Court to be appointed Irene's legal guardian under the "Jackie Coogan" law, whereby a portion of a minor's salary must be placed in trust for the child. The family of six was by now permanently relocated in the Los Angeles area, and Mr. Davidson himself was working as a photo engraver again.

Irene's final movie, *Silver Skates* (1942) is loosely based on the Dutch classic *Hans Brinker or the Silver Skates*. It featured singer Kenny Baker, Patricia Morison, and the skating comics, Frick and Frack.

Joan Davis

(Madonna Josephine Davis)
Born 29 June 1907,
Saint Paul, MN
Died 22 May 1961,
Palm Springs, CA

One of the great queens of slap-stick comedy in movies and TV, and twice voted Radio Queen of Comedy, Joan Davis was the only child of LeRoy and Nina Davis, who lived at 161 Aurora Avenue in St. Paul. They moved to 275 Bates Avenue in 1915 and to 558 St. Peter in 1920, also in St. Paul. Joan's father was a train switchman and later a dispatcher.

At three Joan—or Jo as she was called then—began singing, danc-ing, and reciting at various local functions. A vaudeville scout spotted her and persuaded LeRoy and Nina to let Jo go on tour with the Pan-tages Theatre Circuit. Her "Toy Comedienne" act was fourteen min-utes long. A tutor accompanied her whenever she was on the road but she managed to attend school a few months each year. Her grades did not suffer at all because she graduated from St. Paul's Mechanic Arts High School in 1925 as valedictorian (or the academic equivalent: she took many of her courses through correspondence.) After graduation she worked at a Five and Dime store where she especially liked selling goldfish, asking customers if they wanted them gift-wrapped.

For the next several years Jo toured the vaudeville circuit, amuse-ment parks, summer camps, and Elks lodges. Then, in March of 1931, her manager hired a "straight man" for her. Si (Serenus) Wills became her husband after five months of performances and also the father of her child, Beverly, born in 1933. Within three years they (as Wills and Davis) played the Palace Theatre in New York, the goal of all vaudevil-lians. But life on the vaudeville stage was dimming so she and Si went to Hollywood in 1934.

Joan (as she was now called) made a short comedy for Mack Sennett, a hillbilly story called *Way Up Thar,* for Educational Films (where Shirley Temple had started in 1932). RKO was impressed and gave her a featured part in the comedy *Bunker Bean* (1935). Two years later Twentieth Century Fox signed her to a four-year contract under which she made twenty-five pictures. Some of the more notable are *The Holy Terror* (1937) starring Jane Withers, (who was Shirley

Temple's only real competitor); *On the Avenue* (1937); and *Time Out for Romance* (1937). The best of the lot was probably *Thin Ice* (1937) starring Sonja Henie, the Norwegian Olympic gold medal skater, and Tyrone Power.

The next year she moved up to star billing in *Hold that Co-Ed* (1938) with John Barrymore. In this improbable tale, Joan plays a girl who dresses as a boy to win a football game and thereby helps Barrymore win re-election as governor. Kyle Crichton wrote at the time of the film's release, "Miss Davis makes flying tackles.... She takes off in an array of limbs and arms resembling nothing other than an octopus taking a flying test, she ends by falling on her caboose with a crash that not only shakes the stadium but shakes the inherent faith of man in the frailty of woman." Director George Marshall sent her to UCLA's Izzy Cantor for training in kicking the football and very quickly she could kick the pigskin right between the goal posts.

In *Just Around the Corner* (1938) Joan appears in support of Shirley Temple, Bill Robinson, and Bert Lahr. *Tail Spin* (1938) was a star vehicle for Joan, Constance Bennett, Alice Faye, and Jane Wyman, all of whom play civilian pilots. This film is full of romance, tears, smiles, and great flying scenes.

Joan and Warren William (From Aitkin, Minnesota) played in support of Tyrone Power and Linda Darnell in *Daytime Wife* (1939). *Manhattan Heartbeat* (1940) stars Joan with Robert Sterling. (Harold Buchman from Hibbing, Minnesota, co-wrote the screenplay.) *Sun Valley Serenade* (1941) starred Sonja Henie, Glenn Miller and his Orchestra, Milton Berle, and Dorothy Dandridge. As you can see, the casts in all these movies are deep with talent.

Another gem for Joan was *Hold that Ghost* (1941) starring Joan with Abbott and Costello, the Andrews Sisters, and Richard Carlson, Ted Lewis and his Orchestra, and Mischa Auer. Not only does Joan shine as the leading lady, among strangers in a haunted house, but the film has long been considered the finest work by Abbott and Costello.

Joan Starred with Eddie Foy, Jr. in *Yokel Boy* (1942) and in *Around the World* (1943) with Kay Kyser and his Orchestra, Ish Kabibble, Mischa Auer (the bartender in *Casablanca,* 1943) and the band's lead singer, Ginny Simms.

Another high water mark was *Show Business* (1944) starring Joan with Eddie Cantor, George Murphy, and Constance Moore. The film focuses on the lives of four old friends in vaudeville and it recaptures the true spirit of vaudeville as well as any film made on the subject.

Joan's final great movie was *George White's Scandals* (1945) where she co-starred with Jack Haley, who had played the Tin Man in the *Wizard of Oz*. Her daughter, Beverly Wills, plays Joan at age twelve. After making *Harem Girl* in 1952—her fiftieth film in seventeen years—Joan said goodbye to the movie industry. But by this time she was enmeshed in a TV serial, *I Married Joan*, a domestic sit-com which ran from 1952-56. Joan starred as Joan Stevens (the ever perplexing), with Jim Backus as her husband Judge Bradley Stevens, and her daughter, Beverly Wills, playing Joan's sister. Ninety-eight half-hour episodes were filmed.

Joan was 5'5" tall, had reddish-brown hair and green eyes, and weighed 120 lbs. She was one of the best-dressed women in Hollywood though none of that mattered when she entered the world of radio in 1941. Rudy Vallee invited her to be a guest on *Village Store* and by 1942 she became a regular stock member of the show. When Vallee went into the U S Coast Guard, she took over the show and brought it to new heights. By the end of 1943 she was voted America's top radio comedienne. She won again in 1944 as well as being voted to the *Motion Picture Daily's Fame Poll*. By 1945 she became the third most popular radio person after Bob Hope and the team of Fibber McGee and Molly.

Joan's nuances, vocal modulations, and inflections could only be matched by Eve Arden, and Joan's physical pratfalls, facial gestures, and double takes could only be matched by Lucille Ball. But Joan could do it all whereas the others couldn't. She enjoyed swimming, horseback riding, tennis, and golfing, and she loved going to boxing matches. Her gag-file was large enough to fill twelve volumes.

Joan Davis died of a heart ailment in Palm Springs at the tender age of 48. Her services were held at St. Paul's Catholic Church of Los Angeles. Her TV co star, Jim Backus offered this tribute, "She was the greatest female comedy talent we've ever had."

Dora Dean

(Dora Dean Johnson)
Born in 1872,
Covington, KY.
Died 13 Dec, 1949,
Minneapolis, MN.

Dora Dean's beauty was legendary, and her acrobatic soft shoe dance sent men's heads spinning. The most important of her early conquests was tap dancer Charles E. Johnson, who fell in love with her at first sight and eventually married her in 1893. The two danced together professionally as Johnson and Dean—he in top hat, tails, and kid gloves, and she in elegant evening gowns—and are famous even today as the vaudeville team that introduced the cakewalk dance to show business. They introduced the step in 1895 in Madison Square Garden, and were among the pre-eminent dance teams prior to World War I.

The black entertainer Bert Williams (of the Williams and Walker team), was also smitten with Dean and was moved the write this song: "Oh, have you ever seen Miss Dora Dean, She is the sweetest gal you ever seen. Someday I'm going to make this Gal my Queen. On next Sunday morning, I'm going to marry Miss Dora Dean." The lyrics are not remarkable perhaps, but Williams and Walker sang this song every night during their own popular act, which went a long way toward elevating Dean and Johnson to the limelight.

Dora was born Dora Babbige, and was the sister of Clarence Babbige, who eventually became the first black judge in Kentucky. Her mother was a former slave. She worked as a nursemaid in Cincinnati, Ohio, before going on the stage, prompting her name change. In 1889 she joined the chorus of Sam T. Jack's Creole Show. Because of her lovely figure Jack hired her to be a "statue girl." It was while touring with this show that she met Minnesotan Charles Johnson, who was also in the company.

Johnson was the son of Eliza Diggs Johnson, a former slave from Missouri. She told her son of the cakewalks on the plantation. When her husband died, the family moved to Minneapolis and Johnson became locally famous as a dancer, while also working as a shoe shine boy at the Nicollet Hotel barber shop for three dollars a week plus tips.

He eventually joined the Creole Show where he earned seven dollars a week plus room and board. His style was considered eccentric but audiences grew to like it and he soon became the star of the show. The Sam T. Jack Creole Show was different from other minstrel shows because he replaced the traditional row of male performers with a semi-circle of well-dressed, beautiful women, along with a female interlocutor. Only two men appeared in the line-up, and they told the jokes and played tambourines and bones. It was a radical break with the male minstrel tradition.

The writer and composer Bob Cole developed a sketch for Johnson and Dean to perform in the show, and it was so successful that on May 20, 1895, they left the Sam T. Jack Creole Show to headline themselves in Madison Square Garden. It was on this occasion that they introduced the cakewalk to the audiences of the Big Apple and the world.

The team of Johnson and Dean was a class act, and Dora was the first dancer of any race to wear expensive evening gowns during a performance. She had several gowns in the $300-$500 range (quite a sum in those days) and she often did three costume changes a night. Johnson was the first to wear evening dress. On the technical side he introduced steel plates, or taps, for his dancing shoes.

The remarkable duo also introduced the flicker spotlight, which they dubbed a kinetoscope, into their act. It emitted regular flashes of light to reflect the white accents on their costumes as they danced to an otherwise black background. (We call this a strobe light effect today.) Dora pioneered the use of tights to discreetly display her special charms. One pair showed a light flesh color between the knee and hip that was seen as she extended a leg through a slit skirt. When she did an English theme she wore all white tights. She always wore dazzling diamond earrings. They dropped the traditional "black-face, minstrel makeup" entirely and influenced other acts to do so—for example (Rufus) Greenlee and (Teddy) Drayton.

Johnson and Dean were the first black act to receive top billing at Tony Pastor's Theatre in New York. They were the first to bring a jazz band to Europe on tour in 1913. They set many vaudeville records such as playing one hundred fifty consecutive nights at Koster and Bials in New York. They played three months every summer for three years at Hammerstein's Roof Garden; two months every year for five years at Wintergarten in Berlin; three months every summer for five years at Os-Budavara in Budapest, Hungary; six months over Richards Circuit, Australia; two months every year at the Palace Theatre, London, England; and fifteen years as a featured act over the Keith-

Proctor and Orpheum Circuits especially the Union Square Theatre in New York City.

While on a German tour in 1902 the painter Ernest Hellman painted Dora posing in a cakewalking attitude, and paid their wages for the two weeks it took him to do it. The finished work was displayed in the Paris Exposition that year. Over the years it became Johnson's most prized possession. She was thirty at the time.

During the huge success they enjoyed up until the outbreak of World War I, Dora's body grew a little wider each year, and jokes and jingles began to circulate. "Miss Dora Dean, no longer lean…" yet she and Johnson retained their remarkable charisma. Neither sang very well, and they talked their way through the songs. Nor was either of them a great dancer technically. But as a team they worked well and the public always loved them.

When attendance dropped during the war, Johnson and Dean split up to perform independently, but with less success. Dora headed a "Pick Act"—a woman surrounded by black children—pickaninnies, who were to sing and dance. She was the first black woman to do a Pick Act. It had previously always been a white woman surrounded by black children. They appeared in Minneapolis in July of 1914 and the *Minneapolis Journal* reorted that Dora Dean and Her Fancy Phantoms was a great success. It noted that she and Johnson had been booked for thirty-five weeks on the Lowe's Circuit but, she, as a separate act, would still do well on the smaller circuits. Dora also cast, trained, and directed other Pick Acts for European tours.

The two revived their act in 1934 after a twenty-year hiatus, and they appeared once again in nightclubs and in vaudeville houses such as Connie's Inn in New York. Johnson suffered a leg injury in a Minneapolis nightclub in 1942. In his later years he talked about doing a dance act with Dora's portrait on stage. Dora stopped dancing about 1939 and died ten years later after a lengthy illness. Charles died in Minneapolis in 1953.

Dora made only six films in all, though little is known about them other than the titles. Here they are: *Time Lock No. 776* (1915), *Silver Threads Among the Gold* (1915), *Eyes Right!* (1926), *Bouncing Babies* (1929), and *Dancing Sweeties* (1930). In 1930 she also appeared in *Georgia Rose* (1930) starring Clarence Brooks and Evelyn Preer.

Looking back at their legacy, Johnson and Dean were major stars on the white circuits. They increased the range of opportunities in show business for black performers and especially black women. On the basis of her renown Dora's image was displayed on cigarette cards as the Sweet Caporal Girl. And the couple amassed quite a bit of wealth during their heyday. They purchased all the houses on one side of one Minneapolis city block, but with all the expense of Dora's years of poor health, they had to sell them one after another to pay medical bills. Charles had only two houses left when Dora died.

In 1946 WCCO's John Reed King asked radio audiences every Saturday morning, "Who is Dora Dean?" As far away as New York this question was heard for weeks and large prizes were offered for the correct answer. No one knew the answer! How soon we forget.... And she was still alive at this time! After reading this book, you readers will know the answers to this and many similar such questions.

Marguerite de La Motte

Born 22 June 1903 (possibly 1892) Duluth, MN. Died 10 March, 1950, San Francisco, CA.

Marguerite made sixty movies between 1918 and 1942 though all but the last four were silent films. She was born to Joseph Van Buren De La Motte and Nellie Claribelle Pinney, who were from Wisconsin and Indiana respectively. Though her date of birth is unclear, and the 1910 and 1920 censuses support the 1903 birth date, dates for 1902 and 1892 have also been assigned to her, and in show business the earliest birth date is nearly always the true date.

Marguerite may have attended Endion Elementary School in Duluth, but the family moved to Los Angeles in 1914, and before long she was studying ballet with the famous ballerina, Anna Pavlova. She became a dance star of the "prologue" to the motion pictures at Sid Grauman's Theatre. In those days all theaters had live entertainment "warm-ups" before the movie began.

In 1918 Marguerite was discovered by the man who became the first "King of Hollywood"—Douglas Fairbanks, Sr. She was Fairbanks' leading lady in three of his most prestigious films: *The Mark of Zorro* (1920, as Lolita Pulido), *The Three Musketeers* (1921, as Constance Bonacieux), and *The Iron Mask* (1929, as Constance again). Her debut film, *Arizona* (1918), was written and directed by Fairbanks, and she also appeared in his last silent comedy *The Nut* (1921). In this movie Fairbanks makes use of trick photography to suggest that the two are climbing through the heating pipes of a house to reach the furnace. In another scene, set in a wax museum, Doug pretends to be a dummy and does a wax cop routine—all very entertaining.

Marguerite later appeared in four Cecil B. De Mille movies: *The Girl Who Wouldn't Work* (1925), *The People vs. Nancy Preston* (1925), *Red Dice* (1926), and *Montmartre Rose* (1929), her last silent film. Though *The Iron Mask* was part-talkie, her first talkie cast her as the heroine, Ruth Cameron, in the western drama *Shadow Ranch* (1930). She has small parts in three other talkie films.

Marguerite married twice, first to John Bowers, a matinee idol of the stage and later a silent film star. Their marriage ended in divorce. During the Second World War, she was an inspector in a Southern California war plant. Later she moved to San Francisco and worked for the Red Cross.

Marguerite has a star on the Hollywood Walk of Fame.

William Demarest

Born 27 February, 1892,
St. Paul, MN.
Died 28 December, 1983
Palm Springs, CA.

Yes, Uncle Charley from TV's *My Three Sons* is a Saint Paulite. Bill's family moved from their home at 468 Rice Street to New Jersey in 1906, however, when he was a teenager. By that time he was an experienced vaudeville performer, and out East he continued to work in vaudeville with two older brothers, Rubin (born 1886) and George. The brothers also performed in carnival shows and burlesque houses. As new mediums appeared, Demarest mastered them, eventually appearing in over 150 movies spanning more than 50 years. There was radio too, of course, and later television. Bill was also a professional boxer and a serious student of the cello. He retired from show business in 1978 after seventy-five years in the trade.

It was in Saint Paul, however, that Bill got his first taste of show business. Arthur Bonnycastle White, the manager of the Variety Theatre, gave Bill and his brothers their start in vaudeville, and by the time he was thirteen Bill was certain that he wanted a life on the stage.

Forty years later, in 1945, on a swing through St. Paul, Bill looked up his old boss and other friends and favorite old haunts. Much later, in 1972, at his eightieth birthday party at a Palm Springs country club, Demarest warmly reminisced about growing up in St. Paul. He said his professional discipline was first grounded in routines learned and performed in St. Paul.

During a tour of cello concertizing Bill's schedule brought him to the Windsor Theatre in St. Paul (now the site of the Saint Paul Hotel.) He expected the usual Midwestern blah reaction to his program of Bach and Beethoven, so he planned a surprise for them. As he plucked a string five pigeons and two chickens burst out of his cello. "The audience woke up with howls, whistles and foot-stomping. They pretty near tore the roof off. That St. Paul audience didn't know it at the time, but that episode changed my act and my career. From that time on, I've played everything for laughs."

Bill played on the nation's stages for twenty years before going to Hollywood. He played the Palace Theatre on Broadway in 1917, which was the highest goal of all vaudevillians. During a five-year hiatus from movies between 1929 and 1934, Bill appeared in the Broadway productions of the Earl Carroll musicals *Sketch Book* (1929) and *Vanities* (1931) co-starring with Lillian Roth and Jack Durant.

His movie debut came in 1926 in *When the Wife's Away*. A year later Bill became a part of movie history by appearing in *The Jazz Singer*, the first sound movie.

Among Demarest's best movies are *Sullivan's Travels* (1941), *Hail the Conquering Hero* (1944), and *The Miracle of Morgan's Creek* (1944). All three were written and directed by Preston Sturges for Paramount Studios, and they are as funny now (and also as meaningful and problematic) as on the day they were released.

Demarest was nominated for a Best Supporting Actor Oscar in 1946 for his performance as Steve Martin in *The Jolson Story*. *The First Legion* (1951) is also ranked among his best films.

A couple of Bill's cult movies are *A Girl in Every Port* (1928) and *It's a Mad, Mad, Mad, Mad World* (1963) which sports a veritable Who's Who of comic performers in the cast. His other notable performances for director Preston Sturges are *Christmas in July* (1940); *The Great McGinty* (1940); and *The Lady Eve* (1941). Bill was in Frank Capra's notable populist film *Mr. Smith Goes to Washington* (1939) which starred Jimmy Stewart. (Incidentally, this film's screenwriter was Sidney Buchman, born in Duluth, Minnesota. Sidney won an Oscar nomination for writing the script. He won the full Oscar two years later for penning *Here Comes Mr. Jordan* (1941).)

Demarest appeared in several other notable films, including *Easy Living* (1937, as Wallace Whistling), a romantic, "crazy" comedy with a touch of farce starring Jean Arthur, Ray Milland ,and Edward Arnold. He was in *Big City* (1937, as Beecher) starring Luise Rainer and Spencer Tracy. Bill was in support of Shirley Temple in *Rebecca of Sunnybrook Farm* (1938, as Uncle Henry Kipper) also starring Randolph Scott, Gloria Stuart (of *Titanic* 1997), Jack Haley, and Bill Robinson. In *The Great Man Votes* (1939, as Charles Dale) Bill shines with star John Barrymore, Donald MacBride, and child star Virginia Weidler. The film focuses on a drunken professor who casts the deciding vote in a local election. Bill also played support to Jean Arthur and Charles Coburn in *The Devil and Miss Jones* (1941, first detective), a sociologically uplifting comedy.

Bill appeared in one film with his brother Rube: *The Gracie Allen Murder Case* (1939). Though he did three TV series, his portrayal of crotchety Uncle Charley O'Casey in *My Three Sons* (1965-1972) has endeared him to millions. The popular CBS show starred Fred Mac-Murray as a West Coast aerodynamics engineer trying to raise three boys. Bill came into the series to replace William Frawley who left the series because of health problems in the beginning of 1965. This sitcom was the second longest in TV history after *Ozzie and Harriet*.

Demarest played cunning but kind characters, crotchety, cynical, gruff but golden-hearted characters. His vaudeville background had given him so much experience that he was labelled an "old pro" by his colleagues in movies. Bill has a star on the Hollywood Walk of Fame. For a while in the 1930s he was an agent.

One day he bought some chocolates from a pretty girl named Terry Ray at C. C. Brown's, a candy store at 7007 Hollywood Boulevard, across the street from the Hollywood Roosevelt Hotel. He told her she was pretty enough to be in movies, and he took her to Paramount for a screen test. She passed with flying colors and went on to a twenty-year film career as Ellen Drew.

Bill married twice, first to Estelle Collette, then to Lucille Thayer, who survived him. Having lived in Hollywood from 1936 to 1968, he moved with Lucille to Palm Springs where they lived from 1968 to his death in 1983. Bill created the William Demarest Foundation charity in the 1970s and the William Demarest Golf Tournament. He lived to be nearly 92 years old.

Carol Dempster

Born 9 December 1901?
New York City, NY.
Died 1 February, 1991
La Jolla, CA.

Carol Dempster was D. W. Griffith's last great discovery in Hollywood. Before going into movies she
studied dancing with Ruth St. Denis,
who later formed the Denis-Shawn Dancers with Ted Shawn. Like
Marguerite De La Motte she danced in the live prologues which almost
invariably preceded the movies. She had dark hair and a rather narrow
face with close-set eyes. Cameraman Karl Brown thought she was hard
to photograph but D. W. Griffith was smitten with her, and the two
were romantically involved for years. Many people thought Carol was
inept at acting and were frustrated that Griffith spent so much time
trying to develop her "talent."

Besides "discovering" Carol and the Gish sisters (Lillian and
Dorothy), Griffith also had a touch of responsibility for discovering
Rudolph Valentino, who used to "hang out" at the Alexandria Hotel
bar. In 1918, when he was not well-known, Valentino used to go to
the Alexandria every afternoon around five o'clock to be noticed,
mooch drinks, and eat free sandwiches. Griffith noticed him there
and offered him a chance to dance with Carol in a prologue to his
movie *The Greatest Thing in Life* (1918). Valentino happened to be an
accomplished dancer and the duo created some magic on the dance
floor.

In 1919 Carol plunged into movies, making five that year. She
played in support of Lillian Gish in *A Romance of Happy Valley* and
True Heart Susie, and she also had prominent parts in *Scarlet Days*,
The Girl Who Stayed Home, and *The Hope Chest*.

After some disappointing reviews from three Griffith films, *Love
Flower* (1920), *Dream Street* (1921) and *One Exciting Night* (1922),
Carol struck some gold playing the leading lady in the Goldwyn pro-
duction of *Sherlock Holmes* (1922) which also starred the heart throb
of Broadway, John Barrymore. The outstanding cast also included
Roland Young (the original Topper) as Dr. Watson, and William
Powell (Philo Vance and Nick Charles). This was the first important,
American-made Holmes movie. It was based on a stage play by Wil-
liam Gillette, who played Holmes for thirty years. With Sam Gold-

wyn's stamp the film became a "prestige film," and many scenes were shot on location in London. The film was lost for decades but was rediscovered in the 1970s.

Carol was disappointed by the lukewarm reviews for the Griffith epic, *America* (1924), which critics felt was something of a rehash of *Birth of a Nation* (1915). (Recent appraisals have been more favorable.) She won praise, however, for *Isn't Life Wonderful* (1924), in which she and Neil Hamilton played poor, struggling Polish refugees in post-war Berlin. A *New York Times* critic said, "Miss Dempster is excellent in her exacting role. She looks delicate, wistful and natural without any exaggerated makeup." More great reviews came for *Sally of the Sawdust* (1925, as Sally) a Griffith production starring W. C. Fields. It was hailed as a "great comedy with wonderful acting." Based on their success together Fields was teamed up again with Carol in *That Royle Girl* (1925). Her final film, and perhaps her best, was *The Sorrows of Satan* (1926).

Carol left her film career on a high note and never looked back. In 1929 she married a wealthy financier, Edwin Larsen. They had no children but they traveled widely and had two homes, one in Palm Springs and the other in La Jolla. It was noted by visitors to the Larsen house that Carol, even in her 70s and gray-haired, was quite vital and attractive. Her movie career lasted just seven years but she left a legacy to be proud of—fifteen films; the adoration of the film world's first genius, D. W. Griffith; the experience of working with Lillian Gish, the Barrymore brothers, and W. C. Fields; followed by a long life of financial security, leisure, and travel.

As to her Duluth roots, don't be deceived by the New York birth date. Her father, John W. Dempster, worked for the Inman Tugboat Line, first as a watchman, then as a dispatcher, and later as a purchasing agent. Carol was born while her father was on a business trip with his wife, Cassie. At the time of Carol's birth John was a deputy sheriff and they lived at 1904 60th Avenue East. Later they lived at 412 4th Avenue East.

Richard Dix

(Ernest Carlton Brimmer)
Born 18 July 1893
Saint Paul, MN.
Died 20 September 1949
Hollywood, CA.

Yes, The Whistler is from Saint Paul. Richard Dix was a major leading man at RKO Studios from 1929 through 1943 and made a total of 100 movies over a thirty-year career. He grew up at 1208 Raymond Avenue in St. Paul. His six-foot frame and 180 pounds made football and baseball easy sports for him in school. Richard also displayed obvious acting talent in the dramatics club and acted in school plays. However, his father, Arthur C. Brimmer, was a surgeon who encouraged practical endeavors for his son, so Richard entered a pre-med program at the University of Minnesota, but dropped because the sight of blood made him sick. He then took a banking job, followed by a clerical job at an architectural firm. All the while he continued to study dramatics at night.

The stage bug bit Richard at the age of seventeen when he appeared in a St. Paul stock company as a spear carrier. The legendary actor-producer E. H. Sothern saw the performance and was quite impressed by the thunderous applause Richard got for his bit part, unaware that Richard had brought every friend he had to the theatre as shills. Sothern offered him $18 a week to play small parts in his company while they were in St. Paul. Richard landed another role when the James Neill and Edythe Chapman Company came to town and needed a college-aged football player for their production of *The Widow's Son*.

After playing in stock companies in Dallas and Pittsburgh Richard finally made it to Broadway. By that time he was no longer Ernest Brimmer. He was Richard Dix. He spent a year in New York in various stock companies. When his father saw him in *The Song of Songs* on Broadway, he withdrew all opposition to Richard's stage ambitions. For a couple of months in 1918 he was unemployed so he enlisted in the army, but the Armistice was signed soon afterward and he was promptly discharged.

In early 1919 Richard's brother Archie, who had provided him with both money and encouragement, died suddenly. Richard returned home, but it was not long before his father, too, had died, leaving Richard responsible for the welfare of his mother and sister. He spent two years acting in local acting companies before heading west to seek fame and fortune in theater and movies.

Dix quickly became a leading man with the Morosco Stock Company in Los Angeles, replacing the popular Edmund Lowe. As a stage star he befriended David Butler and Douglas MacLean, who played supporting parts in his plays. They encouraged him to take a screen test, and the test brought him to the attention of producer Joseph M. Schenk who signed him to play the lead in *Not Guilty* (1921) for the First National Studio. (For the record, his actual film debut was as a butler in *One of Many*(1917)). Schenk persuaded Dix to switch to Goldwyn Studios where he starred in *Dangerous Curves Ahead* (1921), *Racing Hearts* (1923), and *Souls for Sale* (1923).

In 1923 Richard signed a long-term contract with Paramount Pictures, and the studio made use of his rugged good looks in a string of westerns. Key movies during that period were *The Christian* (1923), *Quicksands* (1923), *The Ten Commandments* produced by Cecil B. DeMille (1923), *Call of the Canyon* (1923), *The Lucky Devil* (1925), *The Vanishing American* (1925), *Womanhandled* (1926), *Nothing But the Truth* (1929), and *Seven Keys to Baldpate* (1929), an all-talking movie based on the best-selling book and mystery thriller. In *Warming Up* (1928) Dix displayed his great athletic ability in the role of a baseball pitcher. It was Paramount Studio's first feature with synchronized sound effects.

In 1929 Richard switched to RKO studios and in 1931 he really struck gold in making *Cimarron*, which was voted Best Picture of 1931. It was the high point of his career. He played Yancey Cravat, an Oklahoma homesteader. Irene Dunne was his co-star. Both were nominated for Academy Awards. The director, Wesley Ruggles, received a nomination for Best Director, and Howard Estabrook won the Academy Award for Best Screenplay.

Throughout his career Dix was known for his self-effacing, forthright manner. He was sincere, hardworking, and a "regular fellow." He was very athletic and did most of his own stunts. He suffered a broken rib and had two teeth punched out in *Knockout Reilly* (1927) in the course of shooting a scene with Jack Renault, a professional boxer. During this filming he also suffered an appendicitis attack.

Dix was handy with a whip; he loved hunting, boxing, golf, fishing, and tennis. He loved to dress in old clothes but he also liked soft collars and bow ties. He had thick, dark brown hair and brown eyes. He loved to socialize with the cooks in the kitchen at a party.

He told Louella that the reason he wasn't married at age 37 in 1931 was that he wanted a woman who had Norma Shearer's nose, Bebe Daniel's eyes, Irene Dunne's voice, Ann Harding's hair and a personality like—Louella Parsons. In 1931 he married a non-actress, Winifred Coe, of San Francisco, and they had one daughter, Martha Mary Ellen Brimmer. They divorced in 1933.

The next year Richard married his secretary, Virginia Webster. They remained together until his death in 1949. They had twins: Richard, Jr. and Robert, and they also adopted a daughter, Sara Susan.

Richard Dix was one of the few silent movie actors who had little trouble making the shift into talkies—his deep voice matched his commanding presence perfectly. He directed a few films, and in his later westerns he succeeded in elevating the genre. These include *Man of Conquest* (1939), *Cherokee Strip* (1940), *The Roundup* (1941), *Badlands of Dakota* (1941), *Tombstone, the Town Too Tough to Die* (1942), *American Empire* (1942), *Buckskin Frontier* (1943), and *The Kansan* (1943).

His last movies starred him at Columbia Studios in a half dozen of *The Whistler* series (1944-1947). But his health had began to decline. He decreased his drinking and refrained from heavy action scenes, but in October of 1948 he had a serious heart attack.

A year later, after several more attacks, Dix died at the age of 56. He had just sold a 148-acre ranch in the Santa Monica Mountains near Topangas where he had raised turkeys and dogs for more than twenty years. On that ranch was a fifteen-room house with every convenience except a telephone.

Warren Douglas

(Warren Douglas Wandberg)
Born 29 July, 1911,
Minneapolis, MN.
Died 11 November, 1997,
Jackson, CA.

Warren acted in forty-four movies and wrote sixteen over a span of thirty-five years, including a long stretch at Warner Brothers in the 1940s. He seemed to have outgrown his acting by 1957, though he continued screenwriting until 1967. He was also a dialogue director in four movies. His final film as an actor was *The Red Pony* (TV, 1973). He was also a lyricist and a novelist. As a child Warren often went to the movies with his mother. He fell in love with Charlie Chaplin and could imitate the Chaplin walk perfectly. Warren graduated from South High School in 1929. He worked in the University of Minnesota theater while a student there in the 1930s. He also performed at the Moorish Room of the old West Hotel at 5th and South Hennepin Avenue. He traveled to the East Coast for summer stock productions, eventually made it to Broadway, and was discovered by a Warner Brothers talent scout who signed him to a contract in 1938.

Douglas's first film role was a bit part in *First Offenders* (1939). The next year he appeared in a more important film, *Northwest Passage* (1940) starring Spencer Tracy, Robert Young, and Ruth Hussey. He was in four action thrillers in 1943: *Northern Pursuit* starring Errol Flynn, directed by Raoul Walsh; *Mission to Moscow* starring Walter Huston, directed by Michael Curtiz; *Destination Tokyo* starring Cary Grant and John Garfield; and *Air Force* starring John Garfield and Gig Young.

Warren was featured in *Pride of the Marines* (1945) starring John Garfield and Eleanor Parker. Another 1945 hit movie was *God Is My Co-Pilot* which starred Dennis Morgan and Raymond Massey. As the decade advanced he appeared in *The Man I Love* (1946), *High Conquest* (1947), *The Babe Ruth Story* (1948), and *Task Force* (1949) starring Gary Cooper and Walter Brennan. *Homicide* (1949) was Warren's thirtieth movie of the 1940s—a pretty busy decade. He also appeared in a host of World War II training films and short subjects including an Oscar winner entitled *I Won't Play*.

As middle age approached, however, the parts grew smaller and also harder to come by, and Douglas turned his attention to screenwriting. In the end Warren penned the scripts for sixteen films, and in five of them he wrote a part for himself. These were: *Yellow Fin* (1951); *Torpedo Alley* (1953); *Fangs of the Arctic* (1953); *Cry Vengeance,* and *Dragoon Wells Massacre* (1957). After appearing in *The Deep Six* (1957) and *The Helen Morgan Story* (1957), Warren stopped acting altogether and focused his attention on his writing. Perhaps the best of his scripts is *Jack Slade* (1953), although *The Night of the Grizzly* (1966) also has its devotees.

E

Kimberly Elise

(Kimberly Trammel)
Born 1967,
Minneapolis, MN.

I always knew I wanted to be an actress," Kim told an *Essence* Magazine interviewer in January of 2001. "No one in my family acted but ever since I was little, it's all I ever wanted to do." She grew up in Minneapolis—until her family moved to Wayzata, a wealthy, western suburb of Minneapolis, and the Marvin and Erma Trammel Family became one of the first Black families in the neighborhood. Kim is the third of their four children. She thought long and hard about her goal to be a professional actress—but how would she actually make it happen?

Well, she wrote to "Mr. Fixit" in the *Minneapolis Star* newspaper and he gave her a list of things to do, including getting photos taken to present herself and hiring an agent to secure auditions. When she graduated from high school, Kim followed the advice exactly and landed a few commercial roles that paid her way through four years at the University of Minnesota. She graduated in 1990 with a bachelor's degree in speech-communications.

The Trammels lived at 1519 Washburn Avenue North in Minneapolis in the early 1970s and Kimberly attended Hall Elementary School at 1605 Aldrich Avenue North. They next lived at 1615 Queen Avenue North before moving to Wayzata in 1980.

It may seem odd that Kim, who always wanted to be an actress, never appeared in a play in college. She was a speech major trying first to conquer her fear of public speaking. She also avoided acting classes in school. "[Acting classes] work for some people but I always wanted my work to be free-spirited, organic and natural... The real heart of acting is honest reacting." Her first major role in the Twin Cities was at the Walker Art Center. The play was *Enlightenments*, and she was cast as Diva Sanchez, a mentally-retarded tough girl from the Bronx ... with cerebral palsy ... who is an albino ... who raps. Wow!

After college graduation, Kimberly visited her father's employment agency, an executive search firm. She met Maurice Oldham there and was impressed. "He was so striking and so well-mannered," she said. They met again at a party a couple of weeks later and the two became inseparable. After three months of courtship they married, and within a year they had their first child, Ajableu.

Kim did her best to juggle motherhood, family life, and her career goals. She acted in a few local plays, and was also able to direct a short film in her loft, *The Joy of Mama's Recall*, which was screened at the Walker during the 1992-93 season. This short film brought Kim an invitation to attend the American Film Institute in Los Angeles, and the entire family packed up in 1994 and moved to L.A.

At AFI Elise made a film entitled *The Race*, which was shown in the Walker's "Women in the Director's Chair" Festival. The family struggled to make ends meet, but in 1996 Kim was chosen to co-star in *Set It Off* (1996), along with Queen Latifah, Jada Pinkett Smith, and Vivica A. Fox. The next year she won the Cable Ace Award for Best Supporting Actress in the TV movie *Ditch Digger's Daughter*.

Her performance in Oprah Winfrey's *Beloved*, (1998) brought her to an entirely new level of recognition. The film focuses on the generation of African Americans who came of age just after Emancipation. Ms. Winfrey later described Kim's performance as an extension of that spirit. "Kimberly is an extraordinary human being because of her willingness always to show her grace. You see that grace in her work, in the attention she pays to it, how she makes everyone who works with her better." She plays Denver in the film, the daughter of Winfrey and Danny Glover, and she later remarked, "[While] doing that film, I never thought about anything. I just trusted and allowed Denver to flow. It was a possession."

Her next role was equally challenging. She starred in *The Loretta Claiborne Story* (2000, TV) about a championship athlete with severe mental limitations. The same year she appeared in *Bait*, followed by a prominent role in *John Q* (2001) starring Denzel Washington. Most recently she appeared in *Mr. Bojangles*, a TV biography of Bill Robinson, the famous tap dancer.

Kimberly has come to understand her career as an actress in both historical and spiritual terms: "It's about our ancestry. It's about spirits that are still broken and hurt. And what I know now is that my responsibility, part of the reason that the Creator gave me this assignment, is to help fulfill what wasn't fulfilled before."

During her years in Hollywood, Kim has found that in the entertainment industry sexism is a bigger problem than racism, "Maybe it's an industry thing, but you really have to fight for your respect as a woman in this town." Asked about race relations in Minnesota, Kim said, "I don't find Minnesota to be a hugely racist place, not at all. You find many interracial couples and my family is full of interracial children. That shows how accepting people in Minnesota are of different cultures."

Muriel Evans

Born 20 July 1910,
Minneapolis, MN.
Died 26 October 2000,
Los Angeles, CA.

Known for her "prairie flower" roles, this innocent-eyed blond beauty was a popular leading lady in "B" westerns during the thirties and forties, appearing in forty-two movies in fourteen years.

Muriel was of Norwegian heritage, her parents being recent immigrants, but her father died when she was two months old, and her mother took her to California, where Mrs Evanson landed a job at First National Studios. All the wardrobe department and movie sets became Muriel's special playground. One actress gave her a French porcelain doll and Charlie Chaplin gave her a Chinese tea set.

Muriel started her career under contract to MGM, co-starring with Buck Jones in *Boss Rider of Gun Creek* (1936), *Law for Tombstone* (1937) and five other films. She co-starred with William Boyd, who became known as Hopalong (Hoppy) Cassidy, in *Call of the Prairie* (1936) and two others. She co-starred with John Wayne in *The New Frontier* (1935) and in *King of the Pecos* (1936) as well as several films with Tom Mix. She worked with the best.

Not all of her films were westerns, however. She appeared with (and dated) Gary Cooper in *Mr. Deeds Goes to Washington* (1936) and with Laurel and Hardy (no dates) in *Pack Up Your Troubles* (1931). She was in *Manhattan Melodrama* (1934) starring Clark Gable, William Powell, and Myrna Loy in their first pairing together before the *Thin Man* series got going. (Legend has it that this was the film that gangster John Dillinger was watching just before he was cornered and shot by FBI agents.)

She also appeared in *Broadway to Hollywood* (1933) a film about a vaudeville family making it in the movies. She made an appearance in a Tarzan movie entitled *Nature in the Wrong* (1933) starring Johnny Weissmuller. Another notable performance was in *Queen Christina* (1933) starring Greta Garbo.

Greta Garbo called her after hearing that Muriel was Scandinavian and could speak Norwegian. They met for lunch at the MGM commissary during the shooting of *Queen Christina* and soon became close friends. Muriel was as impressed with all the famous faces at the commissary as anybody else. Its publicity department coined the phrase, "More stars than there are in heaven," and it seemed quite true.

Muriel had such dazzling beauty that she caught the attention of handsome men, rich men, playboys, and charmers such as Clark Gable, Gary Cooper, and Prince Louis Ferdinand. This lead to her first marriage, at eighteen, to wealthy industrialist Michael Cudahy. It was short-lived. After leaving Cudahy and his opulent lifestyle behind in Paris, Muriel entered the Hollywood dating game. She dated Clark Gable during *Manhattan Melodrama* and watched all the women buzzing around him. She once asked him, "Hey, Gorgeous, what is it like being God's gift to women?" Gable answered, "Wanna see?" She blushed a little and nodded. Gable pulled a plug of candy from his blazer pocket and bit into it. He chewed a little and then pulled out his false teeth, which had become stuck to the candy. After a moment of shock, she joined him in uproarious laughter. Asked Gable, "So, my darling, what do you think of me now?" Muriel recalled later, "He had a great sense of humor. He was one of my favorite leading men. We were in love for a while."

After her marriage to stockbroker Marshall Worchester in 1936 Muriel pulled out of the movies. The couple settled in Washington, D.C. where she had four radio shows of her own and was also later the star of the TV show *Hollywood Reporter*. In 1936 a *Los Angeles Times* entertainment reporter evaluated Muriel Evans as "minus the sham and hypocrisy, the false glitter, glamour and tinsel of make-believe… (with) sterling qualities, a versatile flair for comedy and dramatic acting, a lovable nature, loyalty for her friends." He went on to predict that she would achieve the pinnacle of filmdom.

After her busy years in front of the camera Muriel retired to Tarzana, California, and did volunteer work at the Motion Picture Country Home. She remained a beautiful blond for many years and attended Hollywood parties into her eighties. She also regularly attended reunions at the "Way Out West" Tent of *Sons of the Desert* (of Laurel and Hardy) and described working with them in *Pack Up Your Troubles*.

Before she died Muriel recorded her story of Hollywood life for the documentary *I Used to be in Pictures*. In that film she said, "I lived in one of the most jubilant times in Hollywood. Today actors are actors, period, not stars. We had to shine on and off the camera. We were not merely actors—we were gods."

Yet, when summing up her career, Muriel was largely a god of the Western, and she properly earned her "Golden Boot Award" which is presented only to the top stars of that genre.

William Fawcett

(William Fawcett Thompson)
Born 8 September, 1894,
Rochester, MN.
Died 25 January, 1974,
Sherman Oaks, CA.

William Fawcett was a Professor of English, Speech and Drama at Michigan State University (1936-1942) before throwing it over to see if he was really the viable actor he was training others to be. It worked. Fawcett acted in over one hundred movies, and went on to play a prominent role in the long-running 1950s TV series *"Fury"* (1955-1960) as the hired hand Pete.

Bill's father, William E. Thompson, hailed from Australia, while his mother, Zilpah (Lijah/Ti-ah/Zilfoah), was from Wales via Australia. Mr. Thompson listed his profession as minister (Methodist) on the 1895 census and he would continue to serve in that capacity until America entered World War II, at which time he retired to Rochester, Minnesota. He was still living there in 1956 at the age of 87. Young Bill probably inherited those long-lived genes.

Bill followed in the cowboy boot steps of William S. Hart, the first real cowboy star in Hollywood, by learning how to ride horses around the countryside of Olmsted County, where Hart had galloped a generation earlier.

Young William went to elementary school in High Forest village and prep school at Rochester Academy. He received his baccalaureate degree from St. Paul's Hamline College in 1917, and not long afterward he organized a road company of actors with which he toured the Upper Midwest for the next ten years.

With the onset of the Great Depression Bill returned to school, enrolling at the University of Nebraska at Lincoln. He graduated in August of 1932 with an masters degree in English. Four years later he added a Ph.D. to his resume and took a post in the English Department at Michigan State University.

While at MSU Bill directed the first production at the George T. Fairchild Theatre. The play was *High Tor* by Maxwell Anderson. In fact, Fawcett is credited with revitalizing the drama school as MSU, but he was also active in the Civic Players Guild, and he served as President of the Michigan Association of Little Theatres for a while. And yet, as he approached fifty, Bill Fawcett decided to leave the prestige and security behind and return to the challenges and vagaries of an acting career.

Though he had already appeared in two movies, Fawcett's *bona fide* movie career began in 1946 at the age of fifty-two. He was thin, wiry, and sunken-cheeked, and for the next twenty-five years he often played ornery, cantankerous old coots whose loyalty ran deep. His real specialty was mangling the English language, which he did a lot as the character Pete in *Fury*. As a former English professor, it must have given him a degree of secret pleasure.

"Doc T," as he was known in Tinseltown, decided to use his middle name as his last name because "there were too many Thompsons on the Hollywood scene when I arrived here after leaving Michigan State." Though ornery coots were his forte, Fawcett's professorial demeanor led to significant roles as Judge Smith in *Stars Over Texas* (1946), as Judge Town in *Tumbleweed Trail* (1946), and as Professor Hammil in the 1949 serial, *Batman and Robin.* He did seven movies in 1947 and seven more in 1948. The happy grind was on. He was Andre, the beachcomber in *The Sea Hound* (1947), a newshawker in *Superman* (1948, a serial), and Merlin in *The Adventures of Sir Galahad* (1949).

Bill acted in support of Gary Cooper in *Springfield Rifle* (1952) but perhaps the highlight of his career was playing Andy Griffith's Pa in *No Time for Sergeants* (1958). Another notable film Fawcett appeared in was *King Rat* (1965) starring George Segal. His final film was *Blackbeard's Ghost* (1967, starring Peter Ustinov, Dean Jones, and Suzanne Pleshette).

He made over a hundred fifty TV guest appearances on various series such as *Annie Oakley, The Adventures of Rin Tin Tin, Circus Boy, Wagon Train, Maverick, Gunsmoke, Mr. Lucky, Perry Mason, The Wild, Wild West,* and early episodes of *The Lone Ranger.*

Bill attributed much of the typecasting to his excellence in horsemanship. He didn't think he stepped down in the world to play inebriated, unschooled cowboys. He had fun. He was always busy and making much more money than he would have made teaching, and perhaps he found it more stimulating, too. He worked til he was 75 years old.

Ed Flanders

Born 29 December, 1934,
Minneapolis, MN.
Died 22 February, 1995,
Denny, CA.

Ed was considered a "character-lead" and he is known for having played the role of Harry Truman in three different productions. He was on stage at the Guthrie Theatre in its inaugural season (1963), and he was widely praised for his TV performances in both character and leading roles.

Ed's father was a machinist from Winnipeg who worked in an auto supply company. His mother was born in Indianola, Iowa. He had sparkling blue eyes and dark, curly hair. The family lived at 3500 Queen Avenue N., and Ed attended Patrick Henry High School, graduating in 1952. In the Pat Yearbook Ed was described as "a lover" whose biggest thrill was "girls." His silly ambition? "To act on the stage." He played Professor Willard in *Our Town,* the senior class play.

After high school Ed went to the West Coast and made his professional debut at San Diego's Globe Theatre in *Mr. Roberts.* He later appeared in the American Conservatory Theatre in San Francisco, the

Milwaukee Repertory, and the Manitoba Theatre Center before arriving at age twenty-eight at the Guthrie Theater with his actress wife, Ellen Geer, (daughter of character actor Will Geer.) Among several parts he played at the Guthrie was the role of Fluellen in Shakespeare's *Henry V*, which showed off his skill with dialects. His ancestors were mostly Irish but he also has Welsh and Flemish roots, so perhaps it's not surprising that he easily did Irish, Welsh, English, Scottish, and other accents. He and Ellen had a son, Ian, in 1964.

Flanders' Broadway debut was in Harold Pinter's *The Birthday Party*, and he won both Tony and Emmy Awards for his portrayal of Phil Hogan in *Moon for the Misbegotten*, but the emotional high point of his career was playing Reverend Daniel Berrigan in *The Trial of the Catonsville 9*. Ed said, "It was the whole experience…Dan and I are greatly similar in many ways. We're both Irish and are both devout muggers. It wasn't a difficult role for me, but it was appearing with all those super-loving people in a play about the Vietnam War that greatly needed saying. It was the big time for me in the theater."

Following his 1974 appearance in *Moon for the Misbegotten* Colleen Dewhurst described Flanders as "a very inner actor. Working with him is like working with yourself and not having to worry what the other person is going to do."

For recreation Ed went to sea or for a walk in the woods or went fishing. He kept a 30-foot trimaran in Oxenward Harbor near Santa Barbara. He always felt he kept some of Minnesota in him but he loved California. He liked New York but less than L. A. and he liked an occasional Heineken beer. He and Ellen divorced in 1968.

His first film was *The Grasshopper* (1970) followed by *The Trial of the Catonsville 9* (1972) in which he reprised his stage role of Rev. Daniel Berrigan. He played President Harry S. Truman (for the third time) in *MacArthur the Rebel General* (1977) starring Gregory Peck as MacArthur. (The other two were TV movies.) *The Ninth Configuration* (1980), *True Confessions* (1981), *The Pursuit of D. B. Cooper* (1981), and *Exorcist III* (1990) round out his non-TV movies. Ed made three dozen movies in all over a twenty-five year span, and a dozen notable TV appearances between 1967 and 1972. It was a fully career.

Ed was probably best known to the nation as the kind-hearted Dr. Westphall on *St. Elsewhere*, the 1980s NBC series for which he won an Emmy in 1983. Sadly, Ed's second marriage fizzled out in 1994, leaving him very depressed, and he took his own life with a shotgun.

Henry Fonda

Born 16 May, 1905,
Grand Island, NE.
Died 12 August, 1982,
Los Angeles, CA.

Henry Fonda, famous for his portrayals of Mister Roberts, Clarence Darrow, Frank James, Tom Joad, Professor Norman Thayer, Jr., Abe Lincoln, and many other characters, attended the University of Minnesota for two years between 1923 and 1925. He came to the U from Omaha, Nebraska, to study journalism. At first his hobby was painting theater scenery, but during his two-year stay at the U of M Henry changed his mind—he wanted to become an actor.

Henry and his two younger sisters, Harriet and Jayne, grew up in Dundee, a suburb of Omaha. At age eleven he won a short story contest sponsored by *Dundee News*. His father William owned or operated a printing plant. He attended Dundee Grade School and graduated from Omaha Central High School in 1923. He was a Boy Scout and later Eagle Scout and he played lots of baseball. His name comes from a titled Italian or Spanish family from which a distant ancestor fled from political persecution to the Netherlands and eventually to America. Their family gave its name to Fonda, New York. Henry was 6' 1", with dark hair, blue eyes, a lanky body, an honest face, and a Midwestern drawl.

Henry chose to attend the University of Minnesota because that was the home office of Northwestern Bell Telephone. Since he already worked at the Omaha branch he could land a job in the home office to pay his expenses while in school. Arriving at the University of Minnesota in September of 1923, Hank lived at the Dinkytown YMCA for a while. He and his roommate, Glen Doty, slept on cots. They had a dresser, a chair and an unpainted desk for furniture. He often ate at the Bridge Cafe on 15th and 4th Street SE. One frequent lunch partner was Don Oathout, who went to engineering school, and eventually became a board member at AT&T. Don and Hank would often double or triple date. On one occasion Hank's date announced to the group that her hands were cold (they were in an open touring car). Instead of taking the hint to hold her hands in his, Fonda said, "Sit on 'em. That'll warm 'em up."

Though Henry did not join a fraternity, he did accept the invitational "rush" tour for prospective pledges and was invited to their parties and sorority parties. On one occasion, at a Phi Mu Sorority House party, Fonda was dancing with Mildred Sommer. According to her he confessed that he couldn't decide whether to pursue acting or scenery painting as a career. He really liked painting but felt pressure to act because some people thought he had the talent for it. Mildred persuaded him, she felt, to try the acting.

To pay expenses his freshman track coach lined up a job for him at the Unity Settlement House at 1716 N. 3rd in Minneapolis where Hank taught physical education. He coached softball, touch football, basketball, and track. His classes started at eight in the morning and he worked from three in the afternoon to eleven at night, which didn't leave him much time for his steady girl.

Henry eventually flunked out of the U. He was so tired at finals time that he used his blue book for doodling and never answered a single question. He returned to Omaha and in 1925 made his first stage appearance, in Philip Barry's *You and I* at the Omaha Playhouse. In one of those odd cinema coincidences, it was Marlon Brando's mother (Brando himself was one year old at the time) who cajoled Fonda to be in the play.

Henry made his first professional stage appearance two years later at the Variety House in Des Moines, Iowa, where he had been hired by Minnesota's George Billings to be his assistant. Billings, famous for his portrayals of Abraham Lincoln, liked the sketch that Fonda did of his Lincoln act. Fonda later went back to the Omaha Playhouse where he was made assistant director at a salary of one hundred dollars a month.

Lured by the lights of Broadway, Fonda moved to New York in the summer of 1928, but the theatres had shut down for summer so he promptly left for Massachusetts, where he became assistant director of the Cape Cod Playhouse at Dennis, Massachusetts. His salary was ten dollars a week plus board. Later that summer he formed a summer stock theater company of his own at Falmouth along with some students. Among them were future director Joshua Logan, a gangly young actor named Jimmy Stewart, and Margaret Sullavan, whom he married in 1931. (They were divorced two years later.) Stewart and Sullavan later starred together in Ernst Lubistch's delightful comedy *The Shop Around the Corner*.

Fonda's later career has been the subject of many articles, books, and encyclopedia entries. He had bit parts in Broadway productions for several years before his impersonation of Max Gordon in *New Faces* caught the attention of Leland Hayward in 1934. Hayward became his agent, and renegotiated his contract with Hollywood producer Walter Wanger from a hundred to a thousand dollars a week.

Later that summer, playing in summer stock at Mount Kisco in 1934, Hank appeared in *The Swan* as a tutor. Actress June Walker saw him and thought he would be perfect for the farm boy lead in *The Farmer Takes a Wife*, his first important Broadway role, which ran over one hundred performances in thirteen weeks before closing with rave reviews. His portrayal of Dan Harrow was typical of later Fonda roles—"a manly, modest performance" in a style of "captivating simplicity" said Brooks Atkinson of the *New York Times*. Wanger then loaned him to Fox so that Fonda could appear in the screen version.

While Henry was in Hollywood making the film Jimmy Stewart once again became his roommate. One night they double-dated—Jimmy escorted Ginger Rogers and Henry with Lucille Ball. They danced at the Coconut Grove and ended up at dawn in Barney's Beanerie. Stewart commented that the women's makeup looked a little heavy in the morning light, and Fonda tactlessly agreed, quickly cooling the evening's ardor. Hank later quipped that if he had behaved himself he might have had a studio named Henrylu instead of Desilu.

Once Fonda had become an established star the films followed one after another with regularity. He was in westerns, comedies, and even rather dire noir films like Fritz Lang's *You Only Live Once* (1937). That year Fonda also made *Wings of the Morning*, which brought the great Irish tenor John McCormack to the screen. It was Britain's first Technicolor film, and it caught grand views of race horses galloping on the rolling green hills in this little romantic gem.

While making *Wings of the Morning* in England in 1936, Fonda fell in love with Frances Seymour Brokaw. They were married on September 16th. She is the mother of Jayne and Peter. It was the second marriage for both. Frances committed suicide in 1950. She also had a daughter, Pamela.

Bette Davis co-starred twice with Fonda, once in *That Certain Woman* (1937), and the following year in *Jezebel* (1938), which earned five Academy Award nominations and won an Oscar for Davis.

Among Fonda's period roles of the era was a fine Frank James in *Jesse James* (1939) starring Tyrone Power, and the title role in *Young Mr. Lincoln* (1939), brilliantly directed by John Ford. He was the faithful assistant of the inventor of the telephone in *The Story of Alexander Graham Bell* (1939) starring Don Ameche, and he starred with Claudette Colbert in the entertaining *Drums along the Mohawk* (1939) also directed by John Ford.

Henry's most famous performance, however, was as Tom Joad in John Ford's *The Grapes of Wrath* (1940). This film earned six Academy Award nominations, though Fonda was not among them. Based on John Steinbeck's best-selling novel, the film depicts the lives of Dust Bowl Okies who leave their farms to make an epic journey west to become orange pickers in far-off California. Fonda and the other members of the cast capture the human suffering and also the undying spirit perfectly, so that social commentary and film art are inextricably fused with one another. Incidentally, Henry and John Steinbeck became good friends for the next forty years.

Fonda's most notable films of the 1940s include the comedy *The Lady Eve* (1941) with Barbara Stanwyck; an unconventional and somewhat grueling western about lynching, *The Ox-Bow Incident* (1943),

Following a three-year stint in the Navy during World War II, Fonda made another western, *My Darling Clementine* (1946), which was a great success at the box office. The *New York Times* said that Fonda's portrayal of Marshall Wyatt Earp was "as real as the dirt on which he walks."

Fonda now decided to return to the stage where he felt his work would be more relevant. He did three plays on Broadway over seven years: *Mister Roberts, The Caine Mutiny Court Martial,* and *Two for the See-Saw.* In 1948 he won the Antoinette Perry Award, the Barter Award, the Academy of Arts and Letters Awards, and the 1948 Tony for the Most Outstanding Portrayal of the season for his work in Mr. Roberts. When the play was made into a movie seven years later he was naturally chosen for the part. John Ford was chosen to direct, and he wanted to add a few of his signature hi-jinks to the story. Fonda resisted the idea. Things eventually came to a head on the set, and Ford jumped out of his directing chair and punched Fonda in the chin, sending him reeling. Though Ford later apologized, their sixteen-year professional association had been permanently ruptured. Mervyn Le Roy was hired to finish the film, and Ford and Fonda never worked together again.

Other films from Fonda's later career include *War and Peace* and Alfred Hitchcock's *The Wrong Man.* Fonda finally won an Oscar in 1981 for his work in *On Golden Pond* (1981), a film which also allowed him to appear on the scene with his daughter Jane for the first time. Three years earlier Henry had won the Life Achievement Award from the American Film Institute.

James Garner had the good fortune to be a juryman for one year during the run of *The Caine Mutiny Court Martial.* Because Garner had no dialogue he could focus on the acting by Fonda going on every night right in front of him. "Fonda had such stage presence it was unbelievable," he said. "He would come on and every eye in the audience would go to him and not leave him. He had charisma and technique. He knew how to draw an audience to him."

Susanna Foster

(Suzanne DeLee Flanders Larson)
Born 6 December, 1924, Chicago, IL.

A phonograph record bought Susanna Foster a ticket to California and a contract with Metro-Goldwyn-Mayer Studios in Hollywood. This golden-haired songbird was brought up at 1811 First Avenue South in Minneapolis. When Suzanne was eleven, Carl Johnson, violinist and leader of the Palace Theatre, recorded her at the microphone and sent the record to MGM Studios. Deanna Durbin had just left MGM to join Universal Studios and MGM needed another pretty, singing child. So, at the age of twelve, Suzanne Larson, with only amateur talent shows behind her, was embarking upon a career in musical film. Or so she thought. So did her parents, Mr & Mrs. L.L. Larson and her sister.

When Susanna arrived she was excited to see the faces of famous actresses and actors such as Jean Harlow, Virginia Bruce, Spencer Tracy, Eleanor Powell, Lionel Barrymore, Allan Jones, and Jimmy Stewart in the studio commissary. She studied singing and acting at the studio school alongside Judy Garland, Freddie Bartholomew, and Mickey Rooney. The school had three teachers and seven students. At the age of seventeen she was still in the "child star" category by the studios. She could sing the A above high C and later said that there were only two notes on the keyboard she couldn't reach. MGM's vocal teacher, who Suzanne later stated had never had any musical training, nearly ruined her voice, however. An MGM executive, Nicholas Nafack, told her that though she was not a singer, she might be able to act a little. (One is reminded of the assessment of Fred Astaire: "Can't act, can't sing, can dance a little.") But three years passed and Susanna was never used in a film. When her option with MGM expired in 1939, Susanna signed with Paramount Studios.

Foster's debut movie at Paramount was *The Great Victor Herbert* (1939). She was cast as an extra but the director Le Roy Prinz was so impressed with her audition that he gave her a much bigger part. William Randolph Hearst liked her singing so much that he had her flown to his mansion at San Simeon for a private recital.

Her next three films at Paramount were *Glamour Boy* (1941) starring Jackie Cooper; *The Hard-Boiled Canary* (1941); and *Star Spangled Rhythm* (1942). Paramount offered to renew her contract but without a raise, so she walked off the studio lot then and there.

The next year Universal studio cast her as Christine Dubois in *The Phantom of the Opera* (1943) starring Nelson Eddy and Claude Rains. This part was first offered to Deanna Durbin who rejected it.

Susanna was only nineteen at the time, and she looked forward to a bright career in films, but her roles became less plum with the passage of time. Her other films with Universal included *Top Man* (1943); *Follow the Boys* (1944) with an all-star cast including the Andrews Sisters, W. C. Fields, and George Raft; and a starring role in *This Is the Life* (1944).

By the time she made *That Night with You* (1945) Susanna was completely unhappy with her film career. She went to Europe to study voice for three years at Universal's expense, but upon her return in 1948 she rejected the lead in *The Countess of Monte Cristo* (the part went to Sonja Henie), and Susanna became *persona non grata* in Hollywood. Her career was over.

Foster went on to sing operettas with her husband, the tenor Wilbur Evans, for several years. They had two sons, Philip and Michael, but were divorced in 1956. Putting show business aside, she held down a variety of jobs to support herself and the boys, including switchboard operator, swimming instructor, and receptionist/typist. She also had a stint as an office clerk in the dividend department at the Wall Street office of Merrill, Lynch, Pierce, Fenner & Smith.

Susanna has always been a maverick. She would rather buy a horse than go nightclubbing, dancing, and "tearing around." She puts her perfume on her nose so she can smell it rather than on her neck for others to smell. She has said that Turhan Bey was the real love of her life. She did reestablish contact with him when he was doing commercial photography in Vienna, Austria, in the 1970s.

Her last film effort was *Detour* (1992, as Evie), a remake of a movie by the same title made fifty years earlier. So far, her career is closed out with a video called "*The Opera Ghost: A Phantom Unmasked.*" (2000, also containing archival footage). She played herself. She weighed having a career in the opera but didn't really pursue that because the politics in opera, she said, is even worse than in movies. She admits to not having the intense ambition and drive to succeed in show business. Her story asks the question: can a talented person succeed on a high moral level without the overriding ambition that is expected in show business and, probably, most professions?

Jane Frazee

(Mary Jane Frehse)
Born 18 July, 1916,
Duluth, MN.
Died 6 September, 1985,
Newport Beach, CA.

Jane Frazee's parents wanted her to be a lawyer when she grew up. Instead, she became the singing star of "B" budget musicals and westerns, just as Judy Garland became a star of the "A" budget musicals. Her father, Walter, a valuation engineer for the Duluth, Winnipeg and Pacific Railroad, didn't live long enough to see his daughter succeed in show business. Her mother, Olga, did, though, and she was as proud of Jane's success as a hoofer and singer as all of Duluth was.

Jane and her sister, Ruth, were just kids when they formed a sister-act known as "The Frehse Sisters." The family lived at 3506 West Third Street, but when Walter died in 1926 they moved to 4319 West Sixth Street. Olga moved them again two years later to 116 North Seventh Avenue East. Ruth and Jane probably attended Merritt Elementary School and Washington Junior High.

Jane was eight and Ruth ten in 1924, when the sisters started with singing and dancing at businessmen's luncheons and PTA meetings for $10 a performance. At one point the pair toured for an eight-month stretch, budgeting a dollar a day for food. The sisters should have attended Duluth Central high but there is no record of it.

By 1934 their mother, Mrs. Olga Frehse, became their manager and went with them on the vaudeville circuit. They ended up in New York City, and eventually graduated to the Lyceum Theatre, their first grade-A professional appearance. They reached their peak on the NBC radio network with the Larry Clinton Orchestra, broadcasting

Monday evenings at 8:30 p.m. and airing in Duluth on WEBC. The sponsor for the show was Sensation Cigarettes which cost 10 cents a pack. For a stretch they were also featured nightly at Ben Marsden's Riviera Club, a leading Gotham night club (NYC).

Mrs. Frazee observed, "You discover that it's a great deal tougher booking dates for an act in New York than it is getting dates in Duluth. You have to get tough in dealing with the agents and you have to keep right after them to see that there are regular bookings." This quip appeared in the *Duluth News Tribune,* July 27, 1939. Olga Frazee added, "Getting the spot with the Larry Clinton program was a wonderful break for the girls because now they can place their music before millions each week."

The sisters appeared in the Lowe's theaters around the country. They also appeared at the Chez Paree in Chicago; at the Coconut Grove in Hollywood; the Clover Club on Sunset Strip in Hollywood where they appeared on the bill with Joe E. Lewis. (The Clover Club was an illegal gambling operation which paid top money). While performing in Hollywood with Clinton's Orchestra, they naturally took screen tests, and that was the end of the Frazee duo. Ruth failed her screen test, but married MGM producer-writer Norman Krasna. Jane passed the test and stayed single—for a while.

Jane turned down a stock contract with MGM in favor of co-starring in a Republic Studio feature with Johnny Downs named *Melody Ranch.* (It was never made.) Then she signed with Universal Pictures and made a series of low budget musicals for $250 a week. *Moonlight and Melody* (1940) was her first feature film. (She and Ruth had appeared together as The Frazee Sisters in three short films for Warner Bros in the 1930s). The next year Jane did eight movies, including *Buck Privates* with Abbott and Costello.

Her freckle-faced charm and superb singing brightened musicals done at Universal, Republic, Columbia and, finally, Monogram pictures in the 1940s and early 50s. While filming *Hellzapoppin* in 1941, which also featured Minnesota comics Olsen and Johnson, she met actor-director, Glenn Tryon, the first of her four husbands. Tryon, eighteen years older than Jane, had first appeared in movies in 1929. He went on from acting to become a writer, producer, and director. They had a son, Timothy Glenn Tryon, and they divorced in 1947. Tryon, primarily a western star, died in 1970.

Among the best of Jane's forty-some films are *Sing Another Chorus* (1941), *San Antonio Rose* (1941), *When Johnny Comes Marching Home* (1942), *Get Hep to Love* (1942), *Moonlight in Havana* (1942), *Swing in the Saddle* (1944), *Kansas City Kitty* (1944), *Practically*

Yours (1944), *Swing and Sway* (1944), *Beautiful But Broke* (1944), *Swingin' on a Rainbow* (1945), *Ten Cents a Dance* (1946) *Calendar Girl* (1947) *The Gay Ranchero* (1948) and *Rhythm Inn* (1951). *Practically Yours* was her only A-budget picture. She became known during the War years as "The Queen of B Musicals." All her films made money for the studios and many can be seen even today on late night TV.

Jane knew the end of her career was coming when she was switched from musicals to Roy Rogers westerns. She met with Matty Fox, then head of Universal Studios, for a salary discussion. He told her that her image and salary dictated that she continue working in cheapie films. Fox dismissed as irrelevant the comments critics were making that Jane was ready for bigger and better film material by saying, "We're running a business here." Jane was dissuaded by the studio from taking drama lessons because, "then you'll start acting and you won't be any good to us."

Her most memorable film, perhaps, was *Rosie the Riveter* (1944) in which she plays that perky industrial worker who became a wartime icon. Her co-star in this frolic is Frank Albertson, who hailed from Fergus Falls. In support of them was Carl "Alfalfa" Switzer, a principal player in The Little Rascals series of short films from the Hal Roach Studios.

A look at the film titles alone suggests the light content of many of Frazee's films. But to play the leading lady in forty-two movies ain't bad, whatever their budget happens to be.

Jane was 5' 4" and weighed 110 pounds in her heyday. She lived by the motto: early to bed, early to rise. She was a fine diver and did some swimsuit modeling. (Her sister, Ruth, owned the pool that Jane frequently swan in.)

In 1951 Jane became a part-time real estate agent in the Newport Beach area while continuing to do movies on the side. Spinning off the Monogram feature, *Rhythm Inn* (1951) she played comic George O'Hanlon's wife, Alice McDoakes, in eight of "Joe McDoakes" short films between 1954 and 1956. In 1952-53 she appeared regularly in the TV series, *Beulah*.

Jane had a half dozen notable TV appearances such as *The Lone Ranger* (1950); *The Gene Autry Show* (1952) and *Superman* (1953) where she met Minneapolis native, Noel Neill, playing Lois Lane. After 1956 she effectively retired and in 1960 Jane became a very successful full-time real estate agent in Newport Beach. Sometimes prospective home buyers would ask her, "Didn't you used to sing in the movies? Aren't you that Doris Day?"

Later in life Jane offered an answer to the question of why she had never progressed beyond B-pictures. "I wasn't bad looking but I was never a beautiful girl and in those days you had to look great." She added, "I had a drive to do better things than I was doing but not that great inner drive that very successful people have."

Though not among the truly glamorous or gorgeous, there was something about Jane that made her very likeable. Her hair stayed blond and she stayed attractive. She died at 67 of complications of a stroke.

Terry Frost

Born 26 October, 1906, Montevideo, MN. Died 1 March, 1993, Los Angeles, CA.

One of the better henchmen of "B" Westerns, Terry Frost appeared in over a hundred cowboy movies and in two hundred TV episodes during his long show business career. His specialty was losing a big gunfight to a cowboy star like Johnny Mack Brown.

Terry was born to Frank Joseph Frost and Minnie Drusella Williams in Montevideo, Minnesota, but the family moved to Bemidji when Terry was six. His father became co-proprietor of the Bemidji Hotel at 208 3rd Street, where the Frost family also lived. In 1924 Frank either died or deserted the family. The reason there is some confusion is that Minnie listed herself that year as a widow living with Terry at 817 America Avenue, but Frank is listed as dying in St. Paul in 1942. In any case, Minnie worked as a dressmaker, and later a presser, to support the family.

After high school Terry left Bemidji to find work on the vaudeville circuit, and he appeared in some thirty-five stage shows before going to Hollywood in the later 1930s. Once there, he freelanced among several studios including Republic, Monogram, RKO, Columbia, and Universal Studios. Because of a clubfoot Terry was rated 4-F by the Los Angeles draft board during World War II so he stayed in Hollywood and continued to make movies, but he also owned and operated a coffee shop called Terry-Gene's on Wilshire Blvd.

Westerns and action pictures were Frost's specialty. Among the best are *Rustlers' Hideout* (1945), *Outlaws of Texas* (1950) ,and *West of El Dorado* (1949). Terry usually wore a black hat, and was shot by the guy in the white hat before the end of the film. He often appeared in Gene Autry films including *Silver Canyon* (1951), *Valley of Fire* (1951), *Barbed Wire* (1952) and *Winning of the West* (1953). Other features are *Louisa* (1950), *The Far Country* (1954), *Calamity Jane* (1953), *The Spoilers* (1955), *Ten Wanted Men* (1955), *Top Secret Affair* (1956), *The FBI Story* (1958), *The Left Handed Gun* (1958), and *Ada* (1961).

As his movie-making slowed down in the late 1950s, Terry plunged into TV work, including a regular part in the series, *Highway Patrol* (1955-1959) starring Broderick Crawford.

Once his acting career was over, Terry became Executive Director of Drama at Patricia Stevens Colleges of Los Angeles and Pasadena. He spent his later years traveling all over the globe and writing magazine articles, books, and plays. He also enjoyed attending Western Film Fests. Terry was survived by his wife, Marion Callahan Frost, their daughter, four grandchildren and a great-grandson.

G

Verne Gagne

*Born 10 May 1923,
Robbinsdale, MN.*

Verne made just one movie but it's a doozie, *The Wrestler* (1974) also starring Ed Asner as Mike's fight arranger and Billy Robinson, a champion wrestler from England. Verne shows off his terrific athletic ability—including his signature drop kick and sleeper hold—in this mostly Minnnesota-made movie by producer W. R. Frank, Jr.

The film was well made, considering the limited budget. Verne supplied half the capital and Bill Frank covered the other half—$250,000 apiece. The film played in movie houses all around the country and did well in gross receipts, but when everyone took his respective share out, the net receipts were zero. It was so discouraging that any talk of a sequel was drop-kicked out of the question.

Verne's home on Lake Minnetonka was used for the family scenes, a warehouse in Chicago was converted into the wrestling arena for the fight scenes, and St. Paul provided the exterior shots. Ed Gump wrote the screenplay and appeared in the barroom scene, which was filmed at Mayslack's Restaurant and Bar in Northeast Minneapolis. Jim Westman directed; Gil Hubbs did the cinematography while Neal Chastain was film editor. The movie's running time is 95 minutes.

Several bona fide professional wrestlers appear in various roles including Hardboiled Haggarty, Dusty Rhodes, The Crusher, Dick Murdoch, Lord James Blears, Superstar Billy Graham, and Bob McNamara (of Gopher football fame in the 1950s). Sam Menacher is the mob leader and he is typecast with his surly, menacing looks and husky voice. Columnist Jim Klobuchar is also in the movie as a nay-saying critic.

Gagne, a three-sport man at the U, won two NCAA wrestling championships while at the University of Minnesota, and was a member of the 1948 US Olympic Wrestling team. He was drafted into the National Football League but declined all offers in favor of a pro-wrestling career. He liked football well enough but he just simply loved wrestling. (Besides, the money was better.)

During the 1950s Verne won a number of pro championships. When the American Wrestling Association (AWA) was formed in 1960, he won the first title and nine others. When he retired as champion of that association in 1981 at age 58 he had held the championship off-and-on for a total of thirteen years and ten months. Verne was inducted into the WCW Hall of Fame on May 23, 1993.

Verne's wife, Mary, died in 2002. He has three children: a son, Greg, who also wrestled until he hurt his back, and two daughters, Donna and Cathy. Verne's career spanned the eras of "real" wrestling to "fake" wrestling to "entertainment" wrestling. Verne himself was always considered a scientific wrestler—a good guy who never had to be unduly vicious or theatrical. He let his wrestling do the talking for him.

Judy Garland

(Frances Ethel Gumm)
Born 10 June, 1922,
Grand Rapids, MN.
Died 22 June, 1969,
London, England

Without a doubt Judy Garland is the greatest contribution to Hollywood history of all artists of Minnesota birth. "Baby" Frances Gumm was in show business as a toddler as part of the Gumm Sisters, an act which played the vaudeville circuit in the later 1920s to the mid 30s. She spent her first four years of life in Grand Rapids, Minnesota, before moving to California in 1927. Upon arriving in California her mother became one of the biggest stage mothers of all times, a fact which Judy hated. We audience members, however, still reap the benefits of Mrs. Gumm's brass and gumption.

Judy's parents were Frank Avent Gumm and Ethel Marion (Milne) Gumm. Her oldest sister was Mary Jane, who went by the name of Suzy and the middle sister was Virginia, who was called Jimmy. Until she took the name of Judy, she was called Baby Gumm instead of Frances. She was born with scoliosis, a lateral curvature of the spine.

Wayne Martin interviewed Judy in 1960. The following are excerpts from his article, "Judy Garland on Life in Grand Rapids, Minnesota."

About Minnesota: "It's a swell state, Minnesota. I'm proud it's my home, and I know a few hundred thousand of us who feel the same way. We've got to pull together, we Minnesotans, for just one more duration, that's all. Here's love and good luck.

"I do remember it was terribly happy, terribly happy, and possibly the only kind of normal, carefree time in my life, and that was for only three years. At the very beginning, I can go back to that time, you know, and I remember my mother and father. My father owned the (New Grand), a little theatre in Grand Rapids. We had a lovely house and he was very successful. That had happened since he had married my mother, and when they found they were gong to have a family, they settled down in Grand Rapids, and we bought a theatre. My mother used to play the piano at the theatre, and sometimes my dad would hire someone else to play the piano for silent movies. We lived in a white house with a garden, and I remember I went back there when I was about sixteen for the first time, and as I recalled it was so big, and you know how it happens when you go back years later, and you find out it wasn't big at all. Otherwise, it was very attractive. It's a beautiful town, beautiful town. Grand Rapids is right in the middle of the iron ranges of Minnesota, surrounded by lakes.

"I remember the snow. I remember also my grandfather and my grandmother lived in Duluth. We used to take train rides, the three kids and my mother, and go visit my grandmother and grandfather. Grandmother would meet us at the train with taffy to be pulled— we'd have a taffy pull. My grandmother used to let me drink tea at her house—it was always green tea. Her name was Fitzpatrick, my mother's mother. Her maiden name was Milne, but her name was Fitzpatrick, Eva.

"There was a lake, a Lake Pokegama ... We use to go there in the summertime. I can remember vaguely my father and mother taking me and the two girls to swim in Lake Pokegama. I remember one time I couldn't swim, and my oldest sister, I think it was, Mary Jane (Suzy), or Jimmy, carried me out into the water, stumbled, and dropped me, and there was a great fuss because I was scared, and I got wet, and the whole family gathered around.

"My two oldest sisters used to steal cherries. There was one man who grew cherries someplace in the summertime. They'd take their wagon, you know, they had a wagon, and they'd go and steal cherries. Anyway, they'd steal the cherries, and one night they got stuck with me. They had to take care of me, so they took me with them, and I guess I was awfully little, because I couldn't walk too well, you know. I was just barely sort of walking, and they got all the cherries in the wagon, and the fellow came out and yelled at them, so they just slammed me in the wagon on top the cherries and ran off. I looked like a cherry pie when I got home.

"But then sometimes in the winter, when my dad would be at the theatre, and my mother would be playing the piano, we would go out into the snow. I remember there was always a great big can of Thompson's Malted Milk, I think was the name of it, and it was just stuff you mixed in a malt, chocolate malt. My older sister took care of those two younger sisters, and we'd go out in the snow, and we'd make angels. We'd lie down and we'd do like this, with your arms, like a bird, and you'd get up and it looked like an angel. Then we'd all go in the house and have hot milk and that Thompson's cocoa, and I just adored that.

"Everything I can remember about Grand Rapids has charm and gaiety, you know, and I remember when I—the first time I can remember singing when anyone took any notice was, my father was playing the piano, and I had a little girlfriend I don't remember her name but she was so small, she couldn't have been more than about two, and he taught us to sing, 'My Country, T'is of Thee,' and he had an upright piano at home, and he played it, and he conned my mother and sisters into listening to this little girl; and I was terribly proud because they said she was good, you know. Baby. Baby Gumm.

"I really remember a white dress that my mother made for me too, uh—and that was the first dress I appeared on stage in, in my father's theater. There's a picture of it. You've seen that picture of a little white sort of net dress. I can remember her making that dress. Really.

"But evidently they told me later the first trouble started when I was going to be born, and they didn't want to have another baby. My mother didn't want to have another baby because I was five years after the other two, and there was a great deal of dissension about that, because my father wanted her to have a baby; but she didn't want to have a baby, so there was a lot of tension. But after I was born—(I think they were planning on a boy, at least they had a letter written, only it was another girl)—and then it got, things got all right again. Because what I recall was lovely.

"The only thing I recall that was very painful when I was little in Grand Rapids was terrible ear trouble. I lived my life with earache, and I'd have to go to the doctor. In those days they lanced your ear, and they [didn't] give you anything for it, and they just carried you down [to] sit in the house and lanced your ears, and you screamed bloody murder, you know. Then, I used to sit at home with great socks full of salt. You know, they'd take socks and fill the socks with salt and heat them, an old remedy. They'd tie two socks over your ears. You'd look like a cocker spaniel. And I did have a little trouble with hearing when I was a kid, because of so much ear trouble.

"That's about the only unpleasantness I can remember. Everything else was lovely.

"Then I remember snow fights, snowball fights in the back of my grandmother's house, and I know my older sister was just wonderful to me, because they let me come out into the fight. They'd build forts, and they'd have one gang on one side and one behind the other fort. And they'd throw snowballs. You'd look up, and if anybody got popped with a snowball it counted against you, I guess. And they never let me in them.

"But finally my older sister said one day, 'Well, you can come.' So I got into the snow with them, and I was so thrilled! You know, to be with older kids, and all. And I looked up once, and a kid named Bernard something-or-other threw a snowball with a rock in it, and it conked me. Well, my sister took out after him and just beat the dickens out of him, you know? And threw tin cans at him, and took me in her arms, and babied me—it was one of those—Now those are the kinds of things I remember.

"Anyway, for such a mixed-up life later, it started out beautifully.

"Then at one point, I don't remember just how, exactly—my sisters would remember this, I imagine—there was a show at my dad's theater, and I was two. And it was Christmas time. And I had this white dress that my mother made for me for something, and I was sitting on my grandmother's lap in the audience, and my two sisters were on the stage. They were 'old pros' by then. They'd been appearing in the theater, for years. And my grandmother pushed me off her lap and said, 'Go on, get up on the stage.'

"So I went to my mother, who was in the pit, and asked her if I could sing, and she said, 'Not tonight, but next week.' Evidently they had these once a week.

"Anyway…part of it, we went home, and she made this white dress. And they taught me 'Jingle Bells' to sing on the stage.

"So I remember going on the stage with the show. And then I sang "Jingle Bells," you know. And our group was run in a circle. And everybody started to say it was good, I liked it, and I just stayed there, and stayed, and I sang one chorus after another, and my mother was howling with laughter, but she kept playing, and my father was in the wings saying, 'Come on! (you know, get off), and I couldn't hear my father. I guess I fell in love with the lights and the music, and the whole thing. Anyway they couldn't get me off. I must have sung about nine choruses of "Jingle Bells." My father finally came out and got me over his shoulder as I wanted to go on still singing "Jingle Bells" into the wings, trying to get the last…and I was a big hit. So then it became 'The Gumm Sisters.'

The following paragraphs are from a Joey Adams interview. His article, "The Real Me" appeared in *McCall's* Magazine in April, 1957.

"I loved my father. He was a wonderful man with a fierce temper, a great sense of humor and an untrained but beautiful tenor voice. He ran away from home when he was ten and joined a minstrel show. He met my mother, Ethel Milne, when he was singing in a Wisconsin theatre where she was the pianist. They toured vaudeville together as 'Jack and Virginia Lee, Sweet Southern Singers.'

"My father had a special kind of love for me, the youngest of his three daughters. At night before he went to the theatre, I used to crawl up onto his lap in a white flannelette night suit while he sang 'Danny Boy' and 'Nobody Know de Trouble I've Seen' for me. It was a bedtime ritual in our house for Daddy to get me ready to sleep, and it was one I loved.

"My first two Christmases I slept in a dressing room while the rest of the family was on stage performing, but by my third year I was old enough to be jealous of my sisters, and I wanted to get into the act, too. My mother told me to sit quietly in a box during the performance, but she should have known better. The minute my sisters went on, I marched right out onto the stage. Whatever they were singing I've forgotten, but I paid no attention anyhow and launched into 'Jingle Bells,' the only song in my repertoire. I sang five straight choruses before Daddy carried me off the stage. From then on I was part of the act.

"Later we split up, Dad and Mother in their act and we three girls in ours. We always followed each other, so that when Dad and Mother were on stage we would sit in the audience and applaud and when we went on they would do the same for us. This is how I learned that it takes only one friend to start the applause rolling.

"One thing that always brought a lump to my throat and tears to my eyes was Dad's introduction of Mother as 'a tiny, pretty lady with pretty, tiny hands.' I don't know what it was about that introduction, but even as I write these words I have tears in my eyes.

"In 1927 Dad bought a theatre in Lancaster, California, on the edge of the Mojave Desert. The entire family made one-night stands along the road west. Those are days I'll never forget. Because I was the smallest I stood between Sue and Jimmy, and when I thought things were too dull I would tickle or pinch them. Sometimes we'd laugh so hard that we had to run off stage before we were finished. Though we worked a lot we were poor in those days, and I can remember when it was my turn to cook trying to make dinner for the family out of two eggs and a moldy loaf of bread. I would just scramble the eggs to make them go further and we'd do without the bread."

Lancaster was seventy miles north of Los Angeles. Ethel took her girls to auditions all the time but nothing came of it so they signed with the Meglin School for Kiddies, a talent agency specializing in child acts. Between 1929 and 1931 Meglin put the girls in four short subjects: *The Big Revue* (1929), *The Wedding of Jack and Jill* (1930), *A Holiday in Storyland* (1930) and *Bubbles* (1930).

They were booked to play the Chicago World's Fair in 1934, and found that they had been billed on the marquee as the 'Glum Sisters' rather than the 'Gumm sisters.' The master of ceremonies, George Jessel, remarked that it made no difference. "They both rhyme with crumb and bum," he said. "Why don't you change it?"

Jessel suggested they call themselves the Garland Sisters, after a friend of his, Robert Garland, who was drama critic of the *New York World-Telegram*. "We had never heard of Mr. Garland and we didn't know what the *World-Telegram* was." Judy later recalled. "But drama critics were important people, so we adopted the name."

Judy herself took the name 'Judy' from the Hoagy Carmichael song that was popular at the time.

The years in Lancaster weren't happy ones for Judy. The countryside was barren and harsh and so were the people. After almost a decade in Landcaster the family moved to Los Angeles.

Judy's signing her firm contract with MGM on October 15, 1935, with a weekly salary of $150—the basis of the family's income. As a young employee of MGM, thirteen-year old Judy attended the Little Red School House for special tutoring in acting, singing, etc. Her classmates in 1935 were Mickey Rooney, Deanna Durbin, Frankie

Darro, and Baby Peggy (Montgomery). Later, in 1936, Suzanne Larson (Susanna Foster) joined them.

Garland's dad died of spinal meningitis not long afterward. At that point MGM took over her life. "When Mother wanted to discipline me," she later recalled, "all she had to say was, 'I'll tell Mr. Mayer.'"

"Life at MGM wasn't exactly secure," Garland observed. "Deanna and I both were slated to be fired, and we knew it. Her option was up first, and as soon as it expired, Universal Pictures hired her. Then MGM discovered what a mistake they'd made letting Deanna go. So they decided to keep me on an exclusive contract, even though I wanted to go, too."

Under the MGM regime Garland was forced to diet to retain her appeal. Unsure of how to showcase the plump starlet, the studio put her first in a short subject with Deanna Durbin, *Every Sunday* (1936). Next they loaned her to Twentieth Century-Fox to co-star in *Pigskin Parade* (1936), her first feature, thinking that if Judy and/or the movie failed, the blame could be placed on the rival studio. She wore pigtails and cover-alls and sang "Balboa," a snappy swing song that went over really well. Judy's star was rising.

Her next significant film was the *Broadway Melody of 1938*. Judy sings "Dear Mr. Gable" to a photo of Clark Gable on her dressing room table. The highly emotional delivery coming from the very adult voice of a very young woman captured widespread attention, and the scene ends on a warm and fuzzy note as Gable himself walks into the room and smiles.

Following this performance Judy launched into nine films with Mickey Rooney, some of them musicals in the Andy Hardy series.

And then came *The Wizard of Oz*.

Shirley Temple was originally chosen for the role of Dorothy, but her studio wouldn't release her. When Judy was chosen she was thrilled. "I had dreamed of Dorothy since the days when my father read me the "Oz" series."

It's interesting to note that all the original selections for major part in *The Wizard of Oz* were replaced for one reason or another, including the witches, the wizard, the hired hands, and Dorothy. Yet we think today: how could it have been any other way? Seven directors worked on the movie, though Victor Fleming received the final credit. Following her success Judy was invited to dip her feet into wet cement at Grauman's Chinese Theatre, and she also won a special Academy Award for Best Juvenile Actor for 1940.

Judy's great signature song was "Over the Rainbow," written by Harold Arlen. She once said, "The very first song to the score of

"Oz" that they played for me was "Over the Rainbow." "I was terribly impressed with Mr. Arlen's genius and very much in awe of him. The song has become a part of my life…I have sung it time and again and it's still the song that's closest to my heart."

Arlen always said the song came to him "out of the blue." He and his wife were driving from their Beverly Hills home to a movie at Graumann's Chinese Theatre. They arrived at the spot where the original Schwab's Drug Store was when this amazing, broad-lined melody came to him. He jotted it down and next day he wrote the middle and the bridge and presented it to lyricist, E. Y. (Yip) Harburg. Harburg didn't like it at first, saying it was for Nelson Eddy maybe but not for a little girl from Kansas. Ira Gershwin thought it needed a quicker tempo, which Arlen gave it. Then Harburg liked it and right away jotted down some lyrics. Yet, this song was extremely close to being cut out of the movie as the studio executives thought it dragged. In the end it was producer Arthur Freed who saved it.

Margaret Hamiliton made several observations in an interview with Gregory Catsos. When asked about injuries on the set, she said Toto was stepped on by a soldier and missed a few weeks of shooting, that both Toto and the trainer were near nervous breakdowns. She felt Bert Lahr was the most uncomfortable because his costume weighed seventy pounds. He seemed shy, quiet and terribly nervous. Billie Burke used her limousine to even avoid walking fifty feet. Jack Haley didn't like small talk and kept to himself on the set whereas Ray Bolger never missed an opportunity to gain attention. After four months of filming and wearing the witch makeup, Margaret's skin pores were clogged and she took on a green tinge from the copper in the makeup after shooting ended. Margaret did burn herself seriously with the fire set by Judy's landing in Munchkin land. She burned her right hand, chin and eyebrows. After that, she had a stand-in do her stunts; and Frank Morgan liked to take a nip from the flask he'd hidden on the set.

Mervyn LeRoy said about Judy Garland, "She was a great talent and I felt that she was right for *The Wizard of Oz* part." He added with a grin, "You know, the rule I always used is don't take anybody you don't think is right. Only take them if they know what they are doing. Garland certainly knew what she was doing and so did Victor Fleming along with the rest of the cast and crew." When asked what motivated him to produce "Wizard" LeRoy said, "It was a good story with good values."

Deanna Durbin had a faster and brighter start in movieland than Judy and their early friendship fizzled after Deanna became the darling of Universal and Judy was known as "the kid we got stuck with when they let Deanna Durbin go." Now Judy was on top. Knowledgeable observers noted early on that even though Deanna was cuter Judy could sing and act much more easily and better. Judy had stewed in 1938 when Deanna and Mickey shared the Academy Award for Best Juvenile Actor. Deanna had an early blooming. She married bandleader Artie Shaw, but weight problems and changes in music fashions brought about her retirement at age twenty-seven while Judy was still hot.

Yet Judy's early years in Hollywood were far from easy ones.

"I think if it hadn't been for Mickey I never could have lived through those days. It was he who gave me my first understanding of what acting was all about. Although I'd been in vaudeville ten years, I'd never read a line. I thought my first pictures were terrible, until Mickey took me in hand. Just before we started my first "Andy Hardy" picture, he put his arm around me and said, 'Honey, you've got to believe in what you're doing. Make like your singing as though you meant it. Live the part.' I followed his advice and began to sing the words as though they were my own. And when I did this, I began to understand timing, gestures and coordination. Most important of all, I learned to relax."

In 1939 Mickey and Judy co-starred in the smash hit *Babes in Arms,* directed and choreographed by Busby Berkeley. They followed it up with *Strike Up the Band* (1940), *Babes on Broadway* (1940) and *Girl Crazy,* all of which reflect a world far removed from the cynicism of Berkeley's great Depression musicals. Garland went on to appear in two more Berkeley musicals, *For Me and My Gal* (1942) with Gene Kelly, and *Ziegfeld Girl* (1941) but she didn't like working for him— he worked her too hard.

In 1941, rebelling against both maternal and studio rule, Judy unexpectedly married band leader David Rose, who was twelve years her senior. The relationship soon foundered and they divorced in 1945. Her next paramour/husband was Vincent Minnelli, who first directed her in *Meet Me in St. Louis* (1944). Judy was twenty-two at the time and in top singing form. Among the film's hit tunes are the title song, "The Trolley Song," "The Boy Next Door," and "Have Yourself a Merry Little Christmas." Minnelli went on to direct Judy in *The Clock* (1945) (which proved she could act without the crutch of song and dance), *The Ziegfeld Follies* (1946) and in *The Pirate* (1948) pairing Judy again with Kelly. The couple also had a daughter, Liza, in 1946.

Besides knowing oodles of popular songs that were not movie related, Judy made certain songs her own by delivering it in a movie.

In *The Harvey Girls* (1946) she sang "The Atchison, Topeka & the Sante Fe," which won the Academy Award for Best Song. *Easter Parade* (1948), with Judy co-starring with Fred Astaire, was a truly magical film, full of Irving Berlin songs. (Astaire had been brought in when Kelly hurt his ankle.) She did a dynamite rendition of "Get Happy" in *Summerstock* (1950). No one else could have delivered a more emotionally forceful, happy song than Judy in her tuxedo-like suit with cutaway pants and fedora hat tipped jauntily over the eyes. Nervous exhaustion forced her out of filming *Annie Get Your Gun* (1950). She was scheduled to co-star with Howard Keel, who did very well in his part as Frank Butler. Betty Hutton replaced Judy.

When MGM allowed her to terminate her contract in 1950 after being unable and unwilling to do *Royal Wedding* (1952), her goal was reestablishing her credibility with *A Star Is Born* (1954), produced by her new husband, Sid Luft, with Warner Bros. The film was hugely successful and it largely restored Garland's respectability and star power. She was nominated for Best Actress and many people felt it was her very best performance. Her lead song was "The Man That Got Away" by Harold Arlen. James Mason was co-star.

With this film Judy felt she had demonstrated that her reputation as an unreliable performer was no longer warranted. Yet during an interview at that time she observed "…my lack of stage education seems to have given me a great big inferiority complex, which I've never lost. I was never sure. I never knew when I was doing it right— and I still don't. In the movies I never could be sure of how things were going until I saw the picture. And when I opened at the Palace Theatre in New York five years ago, I might have appeared confident and in charge of situation. But the real me was suffering and writhing the whole time, certain I would be unable to sing a note, certain no one would like me, positive that I was, as so many people had said, finished."

In any case, new film offers were few and far between, and Judy set out on a successful concert career, both in England and the United States. Her 1961 recording "Judy Garland at Carnegie Hall" earned five Grammy awards and stayed on top of Billboards charts for two months.

Her television series (1963-1964) was a critical success, but had the misfortune to be scheduled against the popular *Bonanza* series, and it lasted only a year.

Garland divorced Luft in 1965. Two subsequent marriages were short-lived. She died on June 22, 1969, from an overdose of sleeping pills. It was thought to be an accidental suicide.

Little Frances Gumm, singing "Jingle Bells" on the stage in Grand Rapids, Minnesota, grew up to become one of the most widely-loved performers of her time. " Producer Joe Pasternak once called her an "angel with spurs." Director Melvyn LeRoy said, "That little girl's vocal chords are her heartstrings." And Bing Crosby summed up the highs and lows of her life and career with the observation, "There wasn't a thing that gal couldn't do—except look after herself."

Judy Garland's body lies in a large crypt in the main mausoleum at Ferncliff Cemetery in Hartsdale, New York. Some of the celebrities attending the funeral were Spencer Tracy, Katherine Hepburn, Lana Turner, Lauren Bacall, Sammy Davis, Jr., Patricia Kennedy Lawford, and New York City Mayor and Mrs. John Lindsay. James Mason delivered a touching eulogy saying, "The thing about Judy was that she was so alive. You could close your eyes and you see a small vivid woman sometimes fat, sometimes thin, but vivid. Vivacity, vitality… that's what our Judy had, and still has as far as I'm concerned." Ray Bolger said, "Judy didn't die. She just wore out."

Larry Gates

Born 24 September 1915, St. Paul, MN. Died 12 December 1996, Sharon, CT.

Do engineers have talent? Sometimes, but… would a talent scout recruit actors from a pool of chemical engineers? Not too likely. Versatile Larry Gates was a chemical engineer, a field engineer, and a school teacher before turning to the arts. He had a thirteen-year run on TV's *The Guiding Light*, plus two dozen notable TV appearances. He logged fifty years in the theatre, and rounded off his career by appearing in forty movies!!

Actually, Larry felt the bite of the theater bug even while at the University of Minnesota studying chemical engineering. As a student he took part in plays staged at Scott Hall. After working in the engineering field for two years, he went to New York in 1938 to make it on Broadway. Yet he made his start at the Barter Theater in Abingdon, Virginia, of all places. He was reading from *A Christmas Carol* when he tripped, dropped his book and fell on his face. He then picked himself up and continued reading while all bystanders were in thunderous laughter. One bystander was Laurette Taylor, who said, "Young man, you're stark raving mad, but you're an actor if I ever saw one." The next year Larry made his New York debut in *Speak of the Devil* as the Archangel Gabriel. Guess what branch of service Larry entered during World War II. Here's a shock. He actually served in the Corps of Engineers. (Now how did the army get that connection right?) Upon returning, he went touring with the Mary Webster Shakespeare Company until, in 1951, he was cast in *Bell, Book and Candle* opposite Rex Harrison and Lilli Palmer. Two years later he appeared with them again in Peter Ustinov's *Love of Four Colonels*.

In time Gates became known as an actor's actor. He could project both a gentleness and a bluff heartiness. He played Falstaff one week and King Lear the next with equal ease, or appear in a Moliere comedy this week and in the heavy courtroom drama *A Case of Libel* the next. (In fact, he won a Tony Award in 1963 for his performance in that play.) His playing of Polonius for the New York Shakespeare Festival noted that his physical and emotional performance was very reminiscent of Hubert Humphrey espousing the politics of joy and pragmatism. That was in 1975 after a full year of Minnesota acting.

Larry broke into films in 1952 with *Above and Beyond*. Other notable films include *Invasion of the Body Snatchers* (1955), *Cat on a Hot Tin Roof* (1958), *Some Came Running* (1958), *The Remarkable Mr. Pennypacker* (1959), *The Hoodlum Priest* (1961), *Toys in the Attic* (1963), *The Sand Pebbles* (1966), and *In the Heat of the Night* (1967).

In 1973 Larry arrived in the Twin Cities under contract to the Guthrie Theatre. He appeared in *Waiting for Godot* and *Juno and the Paycock*. He played the title role in *King Lear* at the University of Minnesota as a guest actor in February, 1974. Then he was back at the Guthrie for two more productions, playing Orgon in Moliere's *Tartuffe* and Sir Oliver Surface in *School for Scandal*.

In another homecoming contact he appeared in *Airport* (1970) which was filmed mostly in the Twin Cities. It was his twenty-eighth film. It won the Best Picture Oscar that year, and was nominated for eight awards in all. It cost $10 million to make and earned $45 million, making people aware of Minnesota as a viable site for movie making. Halliwell's nutshell critique says, "Glossy, undeniably entertaining, all-star version of a popular novel, with cardboard characters skillfully deployed in Hollywood's very best style."

Larry was an outspoken representative of Actors Equity during the 1950s blacklisting days. He opposed loyalty oaths and the blacklisting process saying, "When I see something wrong I'm going to raise hell. That's the way I'm put together."

In 1985 Larry won an Emmy for his role as the prosecuting attorney on *The Guiding Light*. He appeared frequently on live television shows in the 1950s and made two dozen notable appearances on TV between 1951 and 1977. He played President Herbert Hoover in the highly acclaimed TV mini-series, *Backstairs at the White House*. He appeared on Broadway in the Sam Waterston production of *Hamlet*.

Gladys George

(Gladys Anna Clare)
Born 13 September 1900,
Patten, ME
Died 8 December 1954,
Los Angeles, CA

Gladys George, another adopted Minnesotan, was a leading lady at the old Shubert Theatre as a member of the A. G. "Buzz" Bainbridge Players, a stock company. The Shubert Theatre was on 7th Street, a half block west of South Hennepin Avenue. (The Theatre was moved in 2000 to Hennepin Avenue between Fifth and Sixth Streets.) Like Henry Fonda, Marlon Brando, Hume Cronyn, Victor Jory, Jessica Tandy, and Nick Nolte, Gladys spent time (three years) here, qualifying her as having a touch of roots in Minnesota.

Gladys began her career as a "child marvel" in a medicine show. Her debut took place in Waterbury, Connecticut, when she was three; she played the part of a boy in *Back Among the Home Folks*. She changed her name at age six from Clare to George because George was the name of her favorite grandfather. Her parents were show people and, as a result of touring with them, Gladys had appeared on stage in every state in the union by the age of fifteen. By age eighteen she was billed as a leading lady at the Alcazar Theatre in San Francisco, where Milaca's Belle Bennett was a cast mate. Like Judy Garland, Mickey Rooney, and so many other show folk, she was virtually born in a theater trunk. As a young trooper in small towns she would wear a sandwich board, which said, "Wouldn't you like to see me tonight at the _____ Theatre?"

Her father hailed from England where he had appeared in plays with Sir Henry Irving. Her theater schooling came from her parents. She toured with De Wolf Hopper and James K. Hackett among others. She had a brief foray into silent movies from 1919 into 1921 as a leading lady in seven films for Thomas Meighan and Charles Ray, but otherwise she was a stage actress until the-mid 1930s. She made it to Broadway via Minneapolis, arriving here for the 1930 season and leaving in 1933, always a leading lady. Victor Jory gets the credit for bringing Gladys to Minneapolis after their working together in Salt Lake City stock theater. Buzz Bainbridge saw in her what Jory saw and she became the leading lady. She made several returns to Minneapolis during the 1930s where she always drew rave notices, a habit carried on to Broadway as well.

Her debut at the Shubert was in *Night Hostess*. She impressed the audience immediately as a "dazzling blond" with talent to match on this October night in 1930. That was followed by *The Woman of Bronze*, *The Nut Farm*, *Connie Goes Home*, *Puppy Love* and *The Squall*. The next season brought *The Marquise* by Noel Coward, *Her First Affaire*, *The Brat*, *In the Wrong Bed*, *Fair and Warmer*, *Sis Hopkins* and *Scrambled Wives*.

Each play ran a week. Of note is that the star of *The Squall* was Blanche Yurka, who hailed from St. Paul, and opposite her in *The Woman of Bronze* was St. Paulite Walter Greaza, who had recently returning from his Broadway play debut, *Remote Control*. Walter and Gladys shared the spotlight in the next three plays: *Little Miss Trigger*, *What a Woman Wants*, and *Indiscretion*.

Gladys and Victor Jory addressed members of the Phi Delta Theta Fraternity of the University of Minnesota Alumni Association at a Christmas Eve luncheon, 1931. Gladys admitted that she had recently experienced stage fright in the first act of an opening-night performance of Eugene O'Neill's play *Strange Interlude*. Her heart began to beat double-time, a lump came into her throat, and she could hardly speak. Fear overtook her as she thought about the seven acts to follow, but by the opening of act two she was fine.

While in Minneapolis Gladys lived at the Oak Grove Hotel, a block east of Hennepin Avenue and a block south of Loring Park. One day a reporter called on her and asked about the harshness of her voice at the end of the 1930-1931 season. She received him in black silk, lounging pajamas and tiny mule slippers. Her wet golden hair was plastered to her head. She admitted that during **The Squall** she had been suffering with a cold for three weeks at the time. She asked if he noticed a softer sound now, which he said he did and asked how that happened. "I did do something and I'll let you in a little secret," she said. "If my voice is softer, or if it appears that way, it's all because of the vocal (singing) lessons I took last summer while resting."

In Hollywood she made her new debut with Franchot Tone in *Straight Is the Way* (1934), a low budget film that did not generate much excitement. Gladys returned to Broadway to star in *Personal Appearance* for eighty-five weeks. The play's subtitle is "How Far Is the Barn?" This very successful comedy is in the genre of *Once in a Lifetime* and *Merton of the Movies*. Gladys plays a film queen on a personal appearance tour of the country until her motor car breaks down in Pennsylvania. Gladys' character uses lots of malapropisms such as "I must commute with myself." She is attracted to a gas station attendant, and feels the young man could become a film star, but her press agent repeatedly thwarts her efforts. When she says that all she wants is to be the simple homebody she truly is, manage a household and cook, the audience laughs hysterically.

Fresh from Broadway success, Gladys landed the leading role in *Valiant is the Word for Carrie* (1936). She played a childless woman who devotes her life to orphans, for which she gained a nomination for Best Actress by the Academy. In *Madame X* (1937), she turned in another excellent performance, this time under the wings of MGM, which had originally signed her but ignored her.

In *Love Is a Headache* (1938) she co-starred for the third time with Franchot Tone. Her next film was *Marie Antoinette* (1938) with Norma Shearer leading an all-star cast with Gladys in support. She lent support to Jimmy Cagney and Humphrey Bogart in *The Roaring Twenties* (1939), a superb film directed by Raoul Walsh. She co-starred with St. Paul's Richard Dix in *Here I Am a Stranger* (1939), a very popular film of that day, and she also starred in the remake of *The Way of All Flesh* (1940).

But Gladys will always be best known for *The Maltese Falcon* (1941). Her cameo as Iva Archer is melodrama at its best. She reinforced her new image as a husky-voiced, hard-bitten, heart-of-gold blond in *The Hard Way* (1942). In 1946 she played the mother of a returning veteran in *The Best Years of Our Lives* (1946), which won seven Oscars.

George continued to make films well into the 1950s. Her final appearance was in *It Happens Every Thursday* (1953). She was married four times, and died in 1954 at the age of fifty-four.

Peter Michael Goetz

*Born 10 December, 1941,
Buffalo, NY*

One day in 1961 while attending summer school at Southern Illinois University, Peter Goetz was strolling on campus near the theater building when a door burst open and a man Peter didn't know charged toward him. As he advanced, he spit out the question, "Are you free nights for the next two weeks to be a play?" Peter hesitated then said, "Yea, I guess so." Since that day Peter has been on stage every day of his life, moving from academic theater to ten years work at the Guthrie Theater and Chanhassen Dinner Theatre, to New York stages, Hollywood movies, and TV.

Peter won a McKnight Fellowship at the University of Minnesota. As part of the deal he was assured of a year's apprenticeship at the Guthrie when he finished his Ph.D. in Theatre Arts. Peter credits faculty members Charles Nolte, Doc Whiting, and Robert Moulton for recruiting him for the fellowship program. He was such a workhorse that he hardly had time to see his wife, Connie, during this hullabaloo of academia.

Peter is an "adopted Minnesotan," in that he was born in Buffalo, New York, in the heart of the snow belt of the eastern Great Lakes. During his time at the U he and Connie lived at 4224 France Avenue, and then at 2323 Clinton Avenue just to be closer to the University. During the Guthrie years the couple lived at 55th and Clinton for ten years, which adds up to thirteen years of residency in all, thus qualifying him as a genuine Gopher. Even his shy, self-effacing manner is very Minnesotan.

To watch Peter the actor at work is fascinating. In the winter of 1969 he played the part of Falstaff in Shakespeare's *Henry IV, Part I*. He had never read the play before and during the first read-through it really showed. He drew some laughs where he was not playing for them but gave a pretty lifeless reading overall. However, during the next five weeks he transformed himself completely into Falstaff—the boasting, loud, rude, lusty, overweight rogue that has become an archetype of all red-faced "rounders" that eat, drink, and chase Mary.

At the Guthrie Peter drew immediate praise for his work in Harold Pinter's *The Homecoming* and also as Lenny in John Steinbeck's play of the book *Of Mice and Men*. He took a year off in November of 1971 to play the lead role of Tevye in *Fiddler on the Roof*, which ran for 53 weeks at the Chanhassen Dinner Theatre.

Since his mornings were free, Goetz broke into the radio and TV voice-over commercial business, in which he prospered quite nicely. By the time he left the Guthrie and the Twin Cities he was earning $100,000 annually from commercial work, but he felt the call of the Big Apple and went to slay bigger dragons in a much bigger arena, the Broadway beat.

Right away Peter was cast in the film, *Act of Love* (1980, TV, as Dr. Warren FitzPatrick). Two films followed the next year and two more in 1982 including *The World According to Garp* (as John Wolfe). This film introduced him to Minneapolis-born, Oscar-winning director, George Roy Hill, the film's comic star, Robin Williams, and adopted Minnesotan Jessica Tandy. In the same year Peter made his TV debut in *The Lou Grant Show*. He also appeared in *St. Elsewhere, Twilight Zone, Matlock, Spenser for Hire, Golden Girls,* and *L.A. Law* among many TV appearances. Peter also pursued the avant-garde brand of TV in three episodes of *Twin Peaks* in the spring of 1990.

In 1986 Peter thought he could settle into a TV series without all the hustling from pillar to post. *The Cavanaughs,* is a sit-com about a political family of three generations in elective office. Peter played Chuck Cavanaugh, the middle generation. The settling-in was not to last and for the next twenty-five years Peter fell into a pattern of sorts, appearing in three events a year, usually two movies and one TV show. Specifically, Peter has done some forty-five movies and nearly as many TV guest appearances. Of special note is his role in Steve Martin's marvelously warm comedy, *Father of the Bride* (1991, as John MacKenzie, the father of the groom). He reprised this role in 1995.

Peter is often cast as white-collar professionals: doctors, judges, lawyers, military officers and professors. Yet, he did a simple, emotional performance as a disappointed, blue-collar father in an episode of *Touched by an Angel,* "The Violin Lesson," (1994). The producer of the series is also a Minnesotan, Ken Lazebnik, a former director of Shakespeare-in-the-Park in the Twin Cities and a former company member of The Mixed Blood Theatre.)

In an interview Peter once said, "I always need my theater fix." At the time he was appearing at the Lyceum Theater on Broadway in *The Government Inspector* with Tony Randall. "This is perfect because it's a short commitment, three months. What's interesting is that Charles

Nolte directed this play when I was a student at the University, and I'm actually playing the same role this time."

He credits the U for its fine training, giving him the confidence to audition for the many, varied parts he won because he was well-prepared. Goetz has been helping Minnesota alumni pursue their careers in Hollywood. "We have an alumni network where we work as mentors. We'll see them if they're in a particular production or take them to lunch and answer any questions they have." There are many reunions for alumni in Los Angeles as the Minnesota Film Board knows through its large "Ice Pack" directory of transplanted players in L. A. or New York.

Peter has learned things about himself along the way, too. "I'm very much a family man. I'm not a compulsive worker. Some people act because they don't function real well in society and have nothing else. I think the balance helps me." When his time was divided between plays and films, this separation really bothered him, so in 1987 he moved his family to Malibu. At the time he was shooting in Hollywood and his family was living in New York.

He describes himself as a "working actor," a label he is proud of. "I've never had to be a waiter. I always stress the 'working actor' because you have to work at it." Some other notable films for Goetz are: *Prince of the City* (1981), *Glory* (1989), *The Age of Innocence* (1993), and *Missing Parents* (1995, Fox-TV).

In 2004 Peter returned to the Twin Cities to play Scrooge in a three-month stint in the annual Guthrie production of *The Christmas Carol*.

Peter Graves

(Peter Aurness)
Born 18 March 1926,
Minneapolis, MN.

Peter Graves has accomplished a mission nearly impossible in Hollywood—he has been married for over fifty years to the same woman. That woman's name is Joan Endress. Peter has made his name very solidly in television by virtue of his portrayal of project-leader Jim Phelps in *Mission Impossible*, but he has made a large mark in movies, too. For example, he was unforgettable in *Stalag 17* (1954) playing Price, the German spy in a barracks of captured American sergeants.

These Viking-sized brothers, Pete and Jim (*Gunsmoke's* Matt Dillon), grew up at 2324 Cromwell Drive in Southwest Minneapolis near Penn Avenue South and Minnehaha Creek. Their playground was the woods extending from their back yard to the creek and the open farmland just south of 54th Street.

Peter graduated from Southwest High School in 1944. He was the captain of the track team and high hurdler. In his junior year Peter won the state title in high hurdles. A caption next to his yearbook picture says, "That man has talent to spare." He played the clarinet and saxophone in a 15-piece jazz and dance band directed by piano player Jack Smight, a boy from Cretin School in St. Paul who would grow up to be a major TV and film director. Pete and Jack became close friends and performed together in plays and summer stock. Upon graduation in 1944, Peter joined the United States Army, where he played in the band. In 1945 he was discharged, and spent the next four years at the University of Minnesota on the G. I. Bill.

While at the U Pete met up with Jack Smight again—they were both drama majors—and Peter also met a St. Paul coed named Joan Endress, who dazzled him. She recalls that he was "the most handsome man I'd ever met."

In 1949 Pete and Jack went to Hollywood. Older brother Jim Arness advised them to return home immediately, but they stuck around and started to look for work. Jack's first job was as a car hop in a drive-in. Pete drove a taxi. Why did he go to Los Angeles right out of college? The Aurness family used to take vacations there "and [I] knew that's where I wanted to go and what I wanted to do. So I went in a hurry. I didn't even wait for my degree; I was a couple quarters short."

Soon both of their girlfriends came out to join them. Pete and Joan married in California on December 16, 1950. They have three daughters, Kelly Jean, Claudia King and Amanda Lee. Joyce Cunning and Jack married soon after he was hired as a floor director for *The Colgate Comedy Hour.* "We both married Minnesota girls," Peter said but Jack added, "The irony is that I used to date his wife and he used to date mine." Peter had decided to adopt his mother's maiden name, Graves, while his brother, Jim, just dropped the "u" from Aurness.

Along the way the Aurness brothers became good friends with Dave Moore, long-time WCCO-TV anchor newsman. In fact, their parents had been good friends. (Dave Moore studied theater and radio at the University of Minnesota and acted a bit in local theater, particularly at The Old Log in Excelsior in such plays as *Mister Roberts*.

It is a nice coincidence that the Aurness brothers appeared in many films in the early 1950s but each was given a starring role in a TV series that started in 1955. Peter's show was *Fury,* which had six highly successful seasons. Jim played Marshal Matt Dillon in *Gunsmoke* for twenty seasons, with reruns continuing for many more years. He also appeared in several made-for-TV *Gunsmoke* films.

With his striking good looks, Peter landed some film roles as soon as he arrived in Hollywood. *Rogue River* (1950) was his debut. He was a featured player in *Fort Defiance* (1951) starring Ben Johnson, and in *The Red Planet Mars* (1952).

Three films later he appeared in a smash hit for Paramount Studios, *Stalag 17* (1953) which put Graves on the map as a serious actor. The film starred William Holden, who won the Academy Award for Best Actor. Billy Wilder wrote and directed this dark comedy about a spy among inmates in a German prisoner-of-war camp. Graves' nuances were perfect as no one is to tip his hand in a mystery and he didn't. Billy had only twenty pages of script in the beginning, which took two weeks to shoot. Then he'd write the scenes each day as they came up. Everyone would appear in the morning, gather around a table, discuss what he'd written, rehearse, and maybe shoot the scene. The method worked beautifully AND won Oscars.

Life Magazine said of this film, "Raucous and tense, heartless and sentimental, always fast-paced, it has already been assigned by critics to places on their lists of the year's ten best movies." Halliwell describes it as "High jinks, violence and mystery in a sharply calculated mixture." For Peter, there was never such an unstructured filmmaking as this one. Billy Wilder made this work but many of the cast were really insecure without a real script to study and work from.

Pete was suddenly in demand. He made eight movies that were released in 1955 beginning with *The Night of the Hunter* and ending with *The Court Martial of Billy Mitchell*. The same year he started working on the Saturday morning kids' TV show, *Fury.*

Fury starred Graves as Jim Newton and Minnesota-born Bill Fawcett as Pete, the hired hand. This popular series, which ran for 114 episodes, told the story of an orphaned city boy who's taken to the safety of the Broken Wheel Ranch, and put under the care of an adoptive father (Graves) who'd recently lost his wife and kids in an accident.

The pace for making these shows was fast. Crews worked ten-hour days and six-day weeks. Many of the technicians were veterans of low-budget Western movie sets. Pete said, "All the knowledge that had been gained in the history of motion pictures was used on our TV shows. We had to make our stories in a hurry for very little money, and we had the people to do it." Ten years later *Mission Impossible* put Peter Graves on the world map, so to speak. Millions of TV viewers came to know and respect this man, known in the series as Jim Phelps, who headed the commando operation/force. The show ran on CBS from 1967, with Graves coming on board in the second season and continued through the sixth and final season. He was the only player brought back for the remake in 1988 to 1990 on ABC.

In *Airplane* (1980) Peter made a highly successful but potentially risky comedy. He was reluctant at first, because his on-screen reputation for probity was to be used as comic fodder in a grand parody of the movie *Airport* (1970). Though Graves was concerned that his career was about to go up in smoke, in the end he decided the role would be a healthy challenge. The film was so popular that a sequel appeared two years later, *Airplane II - The Sequel* (1982).

Pete appeared in the TV mini-series *The Winds of War* (1983) starring Robert Mitchum. It was an ambitious undertaking, with 1,785 scenes shot in 267 locations in 6 countries over a 14-month span. He reprised his role in 1989 in the sequel mini-series, *War in Remembrance*.

Lately, Peter is seen as the host of the A&E Biographies (1987-1994 and sporadically after that) such as *Tarzan: The Legacy of Edgar Rice Burroughs* (1996); *Sophia Loren: Actress Italian Style* (1999); and *Nick Nolte* to name just a few. He still makes movies and appears on TV occasionally, and he is still married to Joan, his college sweetheart from St. Paul. They have six grandchildren. Pete likes swimming, skiing, tennis, history, and music.

"It's all been damn interesting," says Peter Graves. "What I had learned at the University I had learned well. Doc [Frank] Whiting headed the theater department and was a wonderful teacher. I got a basic background in theater and got to perform and be around all the great literature. That exposure and study was a jewel."

Coleen Gray

(Doris Jensen)
Born 23 October, 1922,
Staplehurst, NE.

Raised in Hutchinson, Minnesota, Coleen Gray graduated from Hutchinson High School in 1939, went on to Hamline University in St. Paul, and then went further than that—she went on to make forty-five movies over the next forty-two years. Her "Hutch" classmates always remembered Doris Jensen, "the one who always got a lead part, who stood out with a beautiful voice from her early years." In the senior class play, *Jane Eyre,* she played the featured part of Nora.

Coleen's parents, Mr. & Mrs. Arthur Jensen, were Danish farmers and strict Lutherans who did not like movies or dances and forbid their children to attend them. "That's when and why I first learned to lie," recalled Coleen to author Richard Lamparski fifty years later. Good acting, in a way, is similar to knowing how to lie. Coleen and her brother Merle usually said they were at sporting events, an approved activity.

Lamparski quotes, "By the time I was in junior high school and was a teenager, I decided that Loretta Young was my favorite movie star. When my seventh grade teacher asked me to state my life goals, I stood and said that I wanted to be a movie star. The class absolutely dissolved in laughter so I learned to keep my ambitions to myself." The boy Coleen dated at Hamline was drafted and she followed him to Southern California. After they broke up she decided to remain in Los Angeles. She joined a little theater group there and appeared in three productions. An agent was impressed with her work and he offered to represent her. He managed a deal with Twentieth-Century Fox Studios, and that's how Doris Jensen became Coleen Gray.

Coleen's first film, *Pin Up Girl* (1944), starred a Betty Grable who was fresh out of college. She continued to land parts in high-quality films including *State Fair* (1945); *Kiss of Death* (1947) with Victor Mature and Minnesota's Richard Widmark; *Nightmare Alley* (1947), her best film, directed by Edmund Goulding; *Red River* (1948) with John Wayne, Joanne Dru and Montgomery Clift, directed by Howard Hawks; and *Riding High* (1950) starring Bing Crosby, directed by Frank Capra.

In *Nightmare Alley*, her fifth film, Coleen showed remarkable talent as a pixieish, coy, and alluring young woman. One critic observed, "She was a petite actress…like a carny temptress…suggesting a mischievous, feline quality which should have been exploited by other movie producers."

Following these successes Coleen co-starred with William Holden, one of the main heart-throbs of the day, in *Father Is a Bachelor* (1950); with George Raft in *Lucky Nick Cain* (1951, as Kay Wonderly); Dennis O'Keefe in *The Fake* (1953, as Mary Mason); Robert Stack and St. Paul's Richard Arlen in *Sabre Jet* (1953, as Jane Carter); Sterling Hayden in *Arrow in the Dust* (1954, as Christella Burke); and with Hayden again in the two-starred film, *The Killing* (1956), written and directed by Stanley Kubrick long considered a cult classic.

She co-starred in three films with John Payne and three with Stephen McNally. Other films of note were *The Twinkle in God's Eye* (1955) with Mickey Rooney, who turned in a wonderful performance as the son of a parson who builds a church in a town where Indians had killed his father; *Death of a Scoundrel* (1956): and *The Vampire* (1957) which is thought by some to be a key cult film. In general, however, the quality of her films had been going downhill, and in 1960 she starred in a movie that critics wished she had never made, *The Leech Woman.*

Coleen also appeared often on TV, beginning with *Your Show of Shows* in 1950 with Sid Caesar and Imogene Coca, and ending in 1986 with *Tales of the Darkside.* Along the way she had guest appearances in *Perry Mason, Bonanza, Family Affair, Mannix, Maverick, Rawhide, Alfred Hitchcock Presents, Have Gun, Will Travel,* and *My Three Sons.*

In 1951 Coleen came to Minneapolis to join in the Aquatennial Fete. On this visit Coleen was also scheduled to appear at a reunion of Hamline University, her St. Paul alma mater which Betty Hohn/Kathryn Adams also attended. Coleen was married to Rodney Amateau from 1945 to 1949. The had a daughter, Susan; a second marriage, to William Bridlack, an executive from Lockheed, produced a son, Peter. Bridlack died in 1978. The next year Colleen married Fritz Zeiser, a widower, and that marriage is still going strong. They attend Hutchinson reunions together regularly.

"When I think of Hutchinson," Gray recently mused, "it's usually in terms of school experience. How privileged we were to grow up where and when we did, with good teachers who we could respect and obey. The values that were instilled in us have made their imprint on us. And still we had a jolly good time."

Walter Greaza

Born 1 January, 1897,
St. Paul, MN.
Died 1 June, 1973,
Kew Gardens, CA.

Walter (last name is pronounced Gree-ZAY), like many actors of his generation, honed his craft in the theater and on radio before appearing in films and television shows as a seasoned character actor. He was a regular member and featured player in the Shubert Theater's Stock Company, The Bainbridge Players, during the 1920s and 1930s, along with fellow St. Paulites Larry Keating and Blanche Yurka, Gladys George, Victor Jory, Ruth Lee, and Dorritt Kelton. They performed primarily at the Shubert Theatre on 7th Street just west of Hennepin Avenue South in downtown Minneapolis.

Walter's father, Albert, was a department manager for the Field, Schlick & Co. The Greaza family lived in Highwood Hills, a crooked, finger-shaped section of southeast St. Paul along Highway 61 and the Mississippi River. He attended Mounds Park Elementary School and after high school he entered the University of Minnesota. It was there that he really honed his craft, appearing in every production he could.

After a stint in the navy at the end of World War I, Walter joined the Bainbridge Players and also became a vaudevillian on the Pantages Circuit. Mr. Greaza perhaps set a record from 1926 to 1928 for stock company performances by appearing for eighty-one consecutive weeks in local houses in Jamaica, Brooklyn and the Bronx. In 1929 he was on Broadway appearing in *Remote Control*, but the next year he was back at the Shubert Theater playing opposite Gladys George in four successive plays—*The Woman of Bronze, Little Miss Trigger, What a Woman Wants* and *Indiscretion*. Each production ran for a week.

Throughout the thirties and forties Greaza appeared in plays too numerous to mention. In 1944 he played the lead in the Elmer Rice play, *Judgment Day*. Rice considered Greaza "one of his most useful and reliable actors." He also appeared in Rice's *We, the People* and *The Trial of Mary Dugan* with Pierre Watkin, another St. Paulite from the Arthur Casey (theatrical) Company. (The Casey Company performed mostly at the President Theatre, formerly the Orpheum).

During the 1940s Walter served for eight years as assistant executive secretary for Actor's Equity. He also served on the board of Shepherd of the Lambs for three years as secretary. He was on the board of the Actors Fund of America and the Percy Williams Home for Actors and served briefly as national administrative director of the American Guild of Variety Artists.

Other plays Walter appeared in were Theatre Guild productions of *Wednesday's Child, If This Be Treason,* and *Ceiling Zero* for Brock Pemberton, a producer/theater manager. Just before the opening of another Pemberton production, *Now You've Done It,* the lead actor was stricken with acute appendicitis. The show was canceled for one week. Greaza learned the part and the show went up. It was considered to be a record of sorts at the time for Broadway.

While he was doing all his service-related work, Walter did find the time to play the role of Inspector Ross on the radio show *Crime Doctor* for nine years and also as the editor on *Big Town.* He was also on *The Kate Smith Hour.*

Though his movies and TV appearances were not numerous, they are fairly significant. His first film role was as a psychiatrist in Jimmy Cagney's *13 Rue Madeleine* (1946). Two years later he acted in Alan Ladd's *The Great Gatsby* (1949). His face and voice lent themselves naturally to mystery and suspense movies, and he used them to good effect in *Boomerang* (1947) in which Dana Andrews investigates a murder in a New England small town. Other similar films in which he appears are *Call Northside 777* (1948), and *The Street with No Name* (1948).

He became The Chief for a five-year run in the TV series, *Treasury Men in Action* (1950-55). When this show folded he joined the cast of *The Edge of Night* as Winston Grimsley and kept the part until his death seventeen years later. He can also be seen on *Sgt. Bilko, The Milton Berle Show,* and *The Jackie Gleason Show."*

Walter Greaza's first wife, singer and dancer Mary Young, died in 1947. His second wife was actress Helen Ambrose who died in 1966. Walter died in semi-retirement in his home in Forest Hills, Queens, New York. He had stopped all acting except his long-running part on *The Edge of Night.*

Lois Hall

Born 23 August, 1926,
Grand Rapids, MN.

Lois Hall hails from the same hometown, Grand Rapids, as her slightly more famous fellow-actress Judy Garland. And like Judy Garland before her, the family left their home for California where the prospects seemed brighter. It was 1933—the depths of the Great Depression—when the family relocated to Long Beach. Lois was seven and her sister, Ruth, was eight. The Golden State continued to offer the tantalizing allure of prosperity that all of America had once presented to immigrants looking for better opportunities in life. Also, Lois's mom suffered badly from arthritis and California's milder, drier climate would be good for her. They sold everything they couldn't load into the car, including Lois's new double-bladed beginner's skates, and headed west.

In Minnesota Lois and Ruth had attended the one-room country schoolhouse (which doubled as the Methodist Church on Sundays) in Pengilly, also known as Swan Lake. Her father, Ralph, had built a brick factory along with his father, but the enterprise failed and he took up farming and also ran a general store/post office/gas station combo. Ralph's mother, Edith, was the town's grandmother. During World War II she corresponded with all the servicemen from Pengilly.

In summer Lois and Ruthie played in the woods with their dog, Chummy. They carried around garter snakes in their kimonos; they went fishing with their father in their canoe; they watched him skin deer, fillet fish, and pluck feathers off ducks he'd shot. On July Fourth the family went into Grand Rapids to watch the parade. Later that night all the "cottagers" (Hibbing People) would build bonfires, roast marshmallows and "weenies," sing songs, and shoot fireworks.

On Saturdays they went to the matinées, especially if it was a Tarzan movie. The girls learned to swing from tree to tree and give a robust elephant call—just like Tarzan. Years later, in her first leading role, she would do those same things in *Daughter of the Jungle* (1949). The next year she co-starred with Buster Crabbe in *Pirates of the High Seas* (1950). Lois had seen Crabbe in a few Tarzan films, and when she was introduced to him on the set she blurted out, "It's so nice to meet you. I used to watch you when I was a little kid." Ouch!

Lois had her first taste of theater experience at Wilson High School in Long Beach, where she volunteered as a set designer, stage manager, and eventually head electrician. Later the Pasadena Playhouse gave her a scholarship to do the essential yet underrated backstage jobs of painting scenery and handling props. Then, the "acting bug" bit her.

Hall was twenty-two when she appeared in her first movie, *Every Girl Should Be Married* (1948), starring Cary Grant and Betsy Drake. Her role was nothing more than a gag walk-on, really—she enters a nightclub amidst bells, whistles, and a flourishing band while Grant clowns as a waiter. The same year she appeared briefly in *Family Honeymoon* (1948) starring Claudette Colbert and Fred MacMurray. Before long she was churning out B-budget comedies and adventure/westerns one after the other, enabling her to appear in nearly thirty movies in five years' time. A few of them are significant, such as the Marx Brothers' *Love Happy* (1950), which introduced Marilyn Monroe to American and world audiences. Other films include *The Petty Girl* (1950), *My Blue Heaven* (1950), *Kill the Umpire* (1950), an independent film called *The Congregation* (1952) co-starring Peter Graves, *Carrie* (1952) starring Laurence Olivier, Jennifer Jones and Eddie Albert, and *Seven Brides for Seven Brothers* (1954), which garnered five Oscar nominations and won for Best Music.

But Lois is best known today for the Westerns she made during the late 1940s and early 1950s. She was the leading lady for Johnny Mack Brown in *Colorado Ambush* (1951), *Blazing Bullets* (1951) and *Texas City* (1952); for Whip Wilson in *Cherokee Uprising* (1950) and *Night Raiders* 1952); for Charles Starrett in *Horsemen of the Sierras* (1949), *Texas Dynamo* (1950) and *Frontier Outpost* (1950); and for Jimmy Wakely in *Roaring Westward* (1949). She was the second female lead in *Slaughter Trail* (1951) starring Gig Young. When TV came into being Lois rode the ranges again in two "Lone Rangers", three "Annie Oakleys," three "Cisco Kids," a "Wild Bill Hickok," a "Kit Carson," six "Range Riders" and three "Rawhide Rileys."

Lois married Maurice Willows in 1953. They had a daughter, Deborah, in 1956, then moved to the desert for solitude. They later moved to Hawaii for seven years, where their second daughter, Kimberley, was born in 1960. Upon returning to Beverly Hills, their third daughter, Christina, was born in 1967.

Just before moving into the desert, Hall appeared in three TV shows: *The Adventures of Superman* (1954); *Highway Patrol* (1955); and *Annie Oakley* (1955). She had by this time made nineteen TV appearances.

Lois worked with Oscar-winning director George Roy Hill in *Hawaii* (1965). Hill, who grew up on 51st and Bryant Avenue South in Minneapolis and graduated from Blake School in 1939, later won an Oscar for *The Sting* (1973). About Hill Lois says that, "I didn't get to know him very well as I had only a small part as the wife of a missionary but he seemed like a very nice and knowledgeable man. I know now that we shared the same taste for shopping in thrift stores and bragging about how little we paid for this or that frock."

Lois and her husband, Maurie Willows, were active in the Baha'i faith throughout most of their forty-two year marriage. She was the long-term secretary of the Baha'i administration in Los Angeles, and for many years she committed forty hours per week to advancing the cause of inter-religious dialogue and working with the Human Relations Council for the City of Los Angeles. She arranged cross-cultural events and she scheduled and set up after-school tutoring and enrichment classes for at-risk young people. For many years she held weekly introductory meetings in her home about the Baha'i faith.

Lois acts once in a while just to keep her hand in the movie/TV biz. You might catch sight of her in an episode of *Marcus Welby, M.D.* or *Star Trek: the Next Generation,"* for example. Of the nine movies she made between 1980 and 2002, after a twenty-six year hiatus, only Kenneth Branaugh's **Dead Again** (1991, as Sister Constance) is really notable.

In her prime Lois Hall was as pretty as they come. In proof of her etherial beauty if required, just consider than she was chosen for the role of The Lady of the Lake in the film series, *The Adventures of Sir Galahad* (1949). She also did a screen test with George Reeves. Now she does action adventures with her three grandchildren: Jessica, Brennan, and Hunter.

William S. Hart

Born 6 December, 1862,
Newburgh, NY.
Died 23 June, 1946,
Newhall, CA.

William Surrey Hart was the first true cowboy movie star. Though he was born in New York, Hart's family moved frequently, and after short stops in Oswego, Illinois, and Portland and Rockford, Iowa, they arrived in Minneapolis in the winter of 1868-69. Hart learned to ride horses and speak the Sioux Indian language while in Minnesota.

Bill's father, Nicholas, was born in Liverpool, England, about 1833. His mother, Rose, was born of good family in Northern Ireland. Bill also had an older sister, two younger sisters, and a baby brother, who soon died in infancy.

During their stay in Minneapolis the Hart family lived in two rooms above a saloon at the Nicollet House on Hennepin Avenue South near the St. Anthony Falls. In those days there were usually plenty of horses tethered in front of the Nicollet House. The sidewalks were made of wood and Indians walked the streets; some women had baskets of goods on their backs for sale. There were also many teams of oxen and bulls passing by, and lumberjacks were everywhere.

However, Nick Hart hadn't come to Minneapolis to work in the lumber mills. He was a millwright (machinist) for flour mills and Minneapolis was then the flour-milling capital of the world. In the spring of 1869 the family traveled seventy-five miles south on the Mississippi to Trimball, Wisconsin, where Nick installed some machinery for a new mill. At the time Trimball consisted of a store-post office and three houses. (The town no longer exists.) While there, the family befriended a Sioux woman and Bill soon learned the rudiments of the Sioux language from her twelve-year daughter. In time he developed many friends among the Sioux boys, who were astonished that he could speak to them.

Once the machinery had been installed the family moved across the river to Red Wing, where they experienced some very hard times—the baby boy died there and is buried in Red Wing—then continued west to the town of Oronoco, which at the time numbered about fifty persons occupying a dozen houses. Nick Hart installed machinery there for six months.

The family continued their peregrinations in search of work, moving to Prescott, Wisconsin, then back to Oronoco, where Bill sometimes sang at community Christmas gatherings. It was said that he "sang like a girl" at that tender age though everyone thought it was a very pleasing voice. He would also act in stage plays in a vacant barn which included songs that his father wrote for the occasion. In the fall of 1876 Bill entertained at a meeting of the Independent Order of Good Templars of Oronoco.

Hart's mother was in frail health, and after she had delivered another baby boy her husband put her on a train for her hometown of Newburgh along with the three girls and the baby.

Young Bill Hart played hooky as often as he attended classes, and since his father worked all day Bill was completely on his own. His father once took him to Minneapolis to buy a pair of boots, and he became so fond of them that he even wore them to bed. He had learned how to ice fish from his Sioux friends, and once he fell through the ice, boots and all. Some Indian friends dragged him from the water, thus saving his life. That evening he put the boots by the fire, and he was crestfallen to find the following morning that they had shrunk to the size of baby shoes!

In the following years Bill and his father resettled first in Abilene, Kansas (probably around 1874), and then in Dakota Territory, where Bill witnessed his first gunfight. From there the pair traveled by stagecoach to Yankton where they bought three saddle horses and two packhorses, then pushed further westward into Indian Territory.

One morning after they had passed Fort Randall, a Sioux war party raided them. Through field glasses Nick spotted what appeared to be riderless horses approaching. When the horses were only six hundred yards away whooping Indians rose from the withers of each horse. The party circled around Bill and his father to assess their strength, then rode straight toward them. As they approached Bill started shouting in Sioux, which made the lead Indian raise his right hand to halt the attack. Bill had never seen full war paint on warrior Indians before, but he didn't feel any danger because he had always liked the Sioux. The warriors may have sense this. In any case, after a bit of conversation they left, seemingly amused by the incident.

After reaching the Missouri River, Nick and Bill turned back to Minnesota, travelling by train to Rochester and then by mill team back to Oronoco. The great news that Christmas (1875) was that Bill's mother was strong and healthy again and would rejoin the family with his sisters and baby brother.

Nick built a new log home two miles outside of town. The family arrived by a six-horse team. Bill had not seen his mother for three years yet here she was suddenly hugging him. He was light-headed. The table was set with lighted candles, the kettle was steaming and the fireplace was crackling and throwing sparks. This was Bill's favorite Christmas memory. There was such joy in the pioneer cabin that night.

That spring the family moved a few miles to Zumbro Falls, where Bill's father finally realized his dream of becoming a partner in a flourmill. During the family's months in Zumbro Falls a troop of circus performers arrived in town with their props—cannon balls, hoops of fire, trapezes, etc.—in two prairie schooners. Bill was hired as manager almost before the wagons came to a stop. He spent two days riding everywhere within thirty miles of Zumbro Falls to let the people know about the great event about to occur. The show included a tightrope walk across the Zumbro River on a slack wire and a musical performance during which the fat circus owner played violin, banjo, cornet, and tambourine while his wife sang popular southern songs in black face, and then "The Last Rose of Summer" and "Ben Bolt" in a sweet, wholesome voice. A few contortions and gymnastic feats by the tightrope-walker wound up the show.

Bill's mother, Rose, was ill again so the entire family except Nick took the train back to Newburgh, New York. It would be many years before William S. Hart, a Shakespearean actor, would return to the Midwest on theater tours.

Bill celebrated his fifteenth birthday in New York City and he noted that he weighed one hundred fifty-three pounds. He also learned that people couldn't understand him very well as his speech seemed strange and his stories of the West even stranger. He became a messenger boy and sometimes met important theater people. In fact, early on he met two of the great leaders of the stage, Edwin Booth and Lawrence Barrett. Over the years he worked his way up the ranks from "spear carriers" to bit parts and on to minor characters, and by 1895 he was a leading man in the final tour of Madame Modjeska's company, earning a hundred dollars a week. Bill was thirty-two.

He joined another company and befriended an actor named William Farnum. Because they were the only two non-drinkers in the cast they spent a lot of time together, and eventually became lifelong friends.

Bill joined the cast of *The Great Northwest*. One scene required him to ride a horse through a staged fire into the arms of his love. The horse had a different idea—it bolted into the audience, not quite clearing the orchestra pit. Bill leapt off the horse as it backrolled into the pit, plummeting through mid-air over his surprised mother and sisters, who were in the audience that night.

Lily Langtry and Joseph Jefferson were Bill's main competitors on the Broadway stage in those years. He scored successes as the lead in *The Man in the Iron Mask* and as Messala in *Ben Hur*. His career move into films was made easier by the fact that many of them were westerns filmed in New Jersey. Not surprisingly, they were almost invariably unrealistic. A vision and a mission were emerging. Bill would help the nascent movie industry make realistic westerns.

Bill's cinema career began in earnest in 1914, when he was fifty-one years old. Thomas Ince, a founder of Triangle Pictures, became his mentor. Ince had begun as an actor and director at Biograph Studios and later formed his own Essanay Studios, where he made hundreds of lucrative westerns between 1908 and 1915. He is considered by film historians to be the prototype of the creative producer.

In 1915 D. W. Griffith formed the Triangle Film Corporation along with Ince and Mack Sennett. Griffith, the most talented director of the time, had just released **Birth of a Nation** that year, and its remarkable score and imagery immediately brought greater stature to the fledgling industry. Sennett, meanwhile, had become known for the frantic comedies he produced, especially the Keystone Cops. Ince was known for making straightforward movies of tight construction, believable characters, and clear, fast action. Director John Ford credits Ince with understanding how to make a picture move. It was Ince who discovered Douglas Fairbanks, Sr.

No one made better westerns than Ince, and William S. Hart was his star. The typical Ince production offers a realistic portrayal of an individual of strength and purpose whose sins are redeemed by the love of a good woman. The didactic nature of these productions may be suggested by some of the titles: *The Cradle of Courage, The Testing Block* (both 1920), *Square Deal Sanderson* (1919), *Selfish Yates* (1918) and *Truthful Tulliver* (1916). Ince and Hart left Triangle in 1917 to join forces with Adolph Zukor at the Famous Players-Lasky Studio until his last regular film, which many people consider his best, *Tumbleweeds* (1925) made with United Artists. Thomas Ince died in 1924.

Including three cameo appearances late in life Bill Hart acted in seventy-eight movies, often with his favorite co-star, a pinto pony named "Paint." He also directed forty-nine films, produced sixteen, and wrote ten, in the course of a career that spanned twenty-four years. He was a great sensation for six years, but as the film industry developed, he was left behind, and by 1920 he was widely considered to be passé.

Some of Hart's best movies are: *The Disciple* (1915), *The Captive God* (1916), *The Return of Draw Egan* (1916), *Hell's Hinges* (1917), *Blue Blazes Rawden* (1918), *Riddle Gawne* (1918), *The Border Wireless* (1918), *Wagon Tracks* (1918), *The Poppy Girl's Husband* (1919), *The Toll Gate* (1920), *Sand* (1920), *O'Malley of the Mounted* (1921), *White Oak* (1921), *Travellin' On* (1922), *Hollywood* (1923), *Wild Bill Hickok* (1923), and *Singer Jim McKee.*

Bill was tall at 6'2" and his nickname was Two-Gun Bill. He married once late in life to Winifred Westover. The couple had one child, William S. Hart, Jr. though they divorced in 1927 after only two years of marriage. Hart built a Spanish-style museum/home in Newhall, California, where he displayed his many mementoes of Western lore, including paintings by noted western artists Charles Russell and James Montgomery Flagg. Bill wrote two books, an autobiography, *My Life East and West* (1929) and *Hoof-Beats* (1933). At his funeral Rudy Vallee sang his two favorite songs, "The Long, Long Trail" and "The Last Roundup."

Josh Hartnett

Born 21 July, 1978,
San Francisco, CA.

A 1996 graduate of Minneapolis South High School, Josh's career began as a teenager in *Mallrats* (1995), shot at the Mall of America in Bloomington, Minnesota. He hit the big-time with a major box-office success, *Pearl Harbor* (2001), followed by a major critical success, *Black Hawk Down* (2001).

Josh is 6'3" and ruggedly handsome. He grew up in St. Paul and attended Cretin-Derham Hall there before moving across the Mississippi River to Minneapolis South High, an Open and Magnet School. At South he met actress Rachael Leigh Cook, a year younger. He played Huckleberry Finn in the Youth Performance Company's production of *The Adventures of Tom Sawyer*, and recently identified the role of Huck Finn as closest to his heart.

Josh played football at Cretin but dropped out when he injured his left knee at age fifteen and took up the theater as an alternative. He's 100% Swedish-American. When his parents divorced and his mother moved back to San Francisco, he opted to stay here with his father, Daniel Hartnett, and stepmother, Molly. He has a sister, Jessica, and two brothers, Jake and Joe, all younger.

Right after high school graduation, Josh bolted out of Minneapolis to attend Syracuse University in Purchase, New York. In 1997 he was given the role of Michael Fitzgerald in the TV series *Cracker*, which had a short run. After a few parts in plays and television commercials, Josh made his first film, a slasher sequel called **Halloween H20** (1998).

In the next three years he appeared in eight films, including **The Faculty, Here on Earth, Blow Dry, Town and Country, The Virgin Suicides**, a version of *Othello* called "O" that's set in an American high school, and the two blockbuster war movies mentioned above.

Hartnett was the first actor Michael Bay, the director of **Pearl Harbor**, auditioned for the part of Danny Walker. "In came this fresh-faced grunge kid from the Midwest," Bay said, "with a few credits to his name. I was impressed, but I thought, I am not hiring the first kid." Three months and 1,000 actors later, Bay called Josh back for another screen test. "He had comic timing, sincerity and a genuine shyness that really worked."

Pearl Harbor was widely panned by the critics, but Hartnett's next film, **Black Hawk Down** (2001) received rave reviews. It depicts in excruciating detail a single heroic but unglamorous episode in America's involvement in Somalia. The film was described by the director, Ridley Scott, as "anti-war but pro-military."

Josh moved back to Minnesota in 2002 to escape the madness of the celebrity lifestyle. In February of 2003 he was offered the role of Superman/Clark Kent by Brett Ratner and Warner Brothers for the 2004 film, but he was reluctant to commit to the sequels and turned the role down. Since that time he has appeared in a few films, including the recent **The Black Dahlia (2006)**, and several more are in production. Colleague and co-star Ben Affleck has expressed amazement that Josh still holds doors open for others and runs his own errands. He expects that to stop sometime soon. Don't bet on it, Ben. Josh was raised with that "Minnesotan nice" and it is genuine.

Tippi Hedren

(Nathalia Kay Hedren)
Born 19 January, 1931,
New Ulm, MN.

Tippi attended Minneapolis West High School before being whisked out of her junior year in the fall of 1946 when the family moved to California—her father needed the warm climate for his health. She appears in the West High yearbook that year as a sophomore. Her parents, both of Scandinavian descent, are Bernard (Ben) Carl Hedren and Dorothea Henrietta Eckhart. She also has a sister, Patty Davis. Though born in New Ulm's Loretto Hospital, she was raised for six years in Lafayette, Minnesota. At the age of thirteen she was chosen as a teen fashion model for Donaldson's Department Store.

Tippi continued teen modeling in Los Angeles while going to Pasadena City College, where she studied acting with Claudia Franck and Gertrude Folger. She jumped into her first film as a model, specifically in an uncredited role as the Ice Box Petty Girl in *The Petty Girl* (1950). (Lois Hall, from Grand Rapids, Minnesota, played the Coca Cola Petty Girl in the same film.)

From 1952 to 1960 Tippi lived in New York doing high-fashion modeling with Eileen Ford. She met and married actor Peter Griffith there. Their daughter, Melanie Griffith, following in her mother's footsteps, has also made a name for herself as an actress.

Tippi did numerous TV commercials and dramas in the early, live television days, and also appeared in several plays. Her big break came in 1961 when Alfred Hitchcock happened to spot her in an advertisement on NBC's *Today Show,* invited her to Hollywood, and cast her in the starring role of his psychological thriller *The Birds* (1963).

Although the film is pretty tame by today's standards, at the time it's depiction of a small coastal California town being persecuted by a flock of crows was considered a masterpiece of terror and visual shock. Hitchcock compared Hedren to Grace Kelly in both her frigid, fragile beauty and her vulnerable core.

Hedren was voted a "Star of Tomorrow" by the Hollywood Foreign Press Association at their annual awards banquet that year, and in her next Hitchcock film, *Marnie* (1964) she proved herself worthy of the honor by delivering a subtly-nuanced performance opposite

Sean Connery. *Marnie* is a suspenseful work, but it also explores the troubled sexual relationship of a married couple—not a popular subject in those days. Though more complicated and interesting than its predecessor in many ways, it was less striking technically, and also less successful.

Hedren began her second marriage in 1964, this time to Noel Marshall. Her marriage to Peter Griffith had ended in 1961. (Her marriage to Marshall ended in divorce in 1982.)

Next in a string of interesting but bizarre productions that seemed to characterize her career, Tippi appeared in Charlie Chaplin's last (and weakest) film, *The Countess from Hong Kong* (1967) along with Marlon Brando and Sophia Loren. A few years later she starred with James Whitmore in *The Harrad Experiment* (1973), which is based in the career of sexologist Alfred Kinsey. The same year she co-starred in *Mr. Kingstreet's War* (1973) which is notable for introducing her daughter, Melanie Griffith, to screen audiences around the world.

This film also triggered Tippi's interest in animal-rights issues. The cats used in the film were going to be left to languish in small cages once the filming was over. Hedren was outraged by the fact, and bought a ranch near Los Angeles to establish a more comfortable home for these and other animals. She named the ranch Shambala.

In 1981 Tippi produced, and starred with her husband Noel Marshall in a film about animal rights called *Roar*. (By this time the couple had relocated more than 150 lions and other animals on their ranch.) The film cost seventeen million to produce, and it contains wonderful wildlife footage, but the plot is predictable and the ending is truly over the top.

Tippi also created the Roar Foundation to continue her charitable work for animals, and she has worked on many other relief efforts over the years. For her tireless efforts along these lines she was given the "Humanitarian Award" from the Baha'i faith. Meanwhile, her contributions to world cinema have brought her a Life Achievement Award in France at the Beauvais Film Festival Cinemalia (1994) among other honors.

Tippi was a member of the USO tours to Vietnam and in 2003 she received a star on the Hollywood Walk of Fame

Among recent film appears are a minor part in *Sixth Sense* (1995), and the role of an elderly environmentalist in *I (Heart) Huckabees* (2004).

James Hong

Born 22 February, 1929,
Minneapolis, MN.

You've heard of "road" movies? Well, James Hong *built* roads at the same time that he was making movies. Hong studied civil engineering at the University of Minnesota from 1947 to 1950 but transferred to the University of Southern California where he graduated in 1953. For a year and a half he worked as a road engineer with the County of Los Angeles, but all the while the lure of movies and the desire to act was gnawing at him, and he often took sick leaves and vacation time to do films. Eventually, he was able to quit the road work and do film acting full-time.

James was raised at 220 S. 8th Street in downtown Minneapolis in back of his family's food supply business, the F W Hong Co. He has a sister named Jean L. Hong. James's father, Frank, was afraid of his son becoming too "Americanized" so he sent James at age five to Hong Kong for Chinese elementary education. With the outbreak of World War II, James returned home in 1939 to resume school in Minneapolis. Though he started American school at age ten without speaking any English, he soon made up the language deficit. In the late 1940s the family rented space at 4451 Pillsbury Avenue while James and Jean were University students. In order to please his parents James took up engineering studies.

James got his start in show business performing in a nightclub comedy duo. His flair for comedy led to an appearance as a contestant on TV's *You Bet Your Life* during which he did a memorable impersonation of host Groucho Marx. This led to a contract with a popular San Francisco club called The Forbidden City. Meanwhile, James worked in the Los Angeles area as a civil engineer. But in 1954 James was invited to appear in three feature films. He quit the engineering job and has never looked back.

Hong's debut film *Soldier of Fortune* (1955) starred Clark Gable and Susan Hayward. He also had a small part in *Love Is a Many Splendored Thing* (1955) starring Jennifer Jones and William Holden. Nightclub work from San Francisco and Hawaii brought him the contract to play Barry Chan, No. 1 son, to J. Carroll Naish's Charlie Chan in the 1957 TV series, *The New Adventures of Charlie Chan,* and from that time on, James has racked up more movie and TV credits than any other Minnesotan except George Chesebro.

His early films offered appearances with little dialogue, for example, as the head waiter in *Flower Drum Song* (1961). He met up with his engineering-actor colleague from Minnesota, Larry Gates, in *The Sand Pebbles* (1966). James appeared as a Japanese general in the spoof, *Airplane* (1980). Among his other noteworthy appearances are in *Blade Runner* (1982, as Hannibal Chew), *Yes, Giorgio* (1982), and *Breathless* (1983). He is also featured in *Big Trouble in Little China* (1986), *Tango & Cash* (1989), *The Secret Agent Club* (1996), *Red Corner* (1997); *Broken Vessels* (1998) and *Mulan* (1998) as a voice-over for Chi-Fu.

Hong is one of the founders of East-West Players, the oldest Asian-American Theatre in Los Angeles. He was a charter member and President of the Association of Asian-Pacific-American Artists. A man of several talents, James wrote and directed *The Vineyard* (1989), and produced and directed *Teen Lust* (1978). In 1990 he reprised his *Chinatown* butler role in *The Two Jakes*. Probably his biggest screen role came in *The Shadow* (1994) as Lamont Cranston's brainy assistant, Li Peng.

Over the years James has appeared in so many TV shows that his resumé is a veritable history of the medium. It includes *Dragnet, Bonanza, Hawaiian Eye, Hawaii-Five-O, Perry Mason, The Man from U.N.C.L.E., I Spy, Gomer Pyle, U.S.M.C., and Mission Impossible.* Recent series include *Kung Fu, All in the Family, Dynasty, Dallas, Here's Lucy, Seinfeld, X-Files, Chicago Hope, Friends, The Drew Carey Show, Taxi, Lou Grant, St. Elsewhere, MacGyver,* and *The West Wing.* All in all, James has acted in more than one hundred different TV shows over a fifty-year period. Versatility has been the key to James' busy career, with roles ranging from U.N. Secretary General U Thant to the Dalai Lama to a nerd master in *Nerds in Paradise*.

Ernie Hudson

Born 17 December 1945,
Benton Harbor, MI.

Ernie is another "adopted Minnesotan" who came to the University of Minnesota to do his doctorate degree, just as Peter Michael Goetz, Warren Frost, and George Muschamp had a decade earlier.

Hudson grew up writing short stories, poems, and songs in Benton Harbor, and he always hoped that his words might be spoken one day on a stage where everyone could hear them. Following a stint in the Marines he moved to Detroit and became the resident playwright at Concept East, the oldest Black theater in the country. He also cofounded the Actors' Ensemble Theatre which recruited Black writers to act in and direct their own works. All the while he was pursuing his bachelor's degree at Wayne State.

After graduating Ernie went on to study at Yale and also appeared in the Los Angeles production of Lonnie Elder's musical *Daddy Goodness*. He appeared briefly in Gordon Parks's film **Leadbelly** (1976). Uncomfortable with the fickle tastes of the Hollywood movie machine, in 1975 Hudson came to Minnesota to study for his doctorate. That fall he was cast as Jack Jefferson in *The Great White Hope* at Theatre in the Round Players in Minneapolis. He said that he put "everything he had" into playing Jefferson including shaving his head. In a review Mike Steele of the *Minneapolis Tribune* praised his performance, remarking that "…Hudson radiates presence, cockiness, intensity whether he's lording it over the white world or shuffling despairingly in front of it. It's a touching, whirlwind performance."

Since his days in Minnesota Ernie has appeared in many films and television programs, including *The Main Event* (1979), a romantic comedy starring Barbra Streisand and Ryan O'Neal; *The Jazz Singer* (1980), a remake of the 1927 Al Jolson film, and the plum role of Winston Zeddemore in the mega-hit, **Ghostbusters** (1984).

He is featured in **Weeds** (1987, as a Black Muslim prisoner) and he won plaudits for his role as a retarded handyman in **The Hand that Rocks the Cradle** (1991).

Ernie has been a reserve Deputy Sheriff in the San Bernardino County Sheriff's office since 1990. He has four sons.

J–K

Victor Jory

Born 23 November, 1902,
Dawson City, Yukon Territory,
Canada
Died 12 February, 1982,
Santa Monica, CA.

The best boxer-actor ever to appear in movies was the Canadian Victor Jory, another adopted Minnesotan. Victor was also the US National Guard Wrestling Champion and its Boxing Champion in the early 1920s before turning to dramatic arts. Jory was involved in two of Hollywood's most notorious unscheduled fist-fights. One was with the swashbuckling actor from Australia, Errol Flynn, and the other was with the film director John Huston. Flynn had done a lot of amateur boxing in Australia both inside the rings and out. Huston, an adventurer who joined the United States Cavalry at seventeen in order to fight Pancho Villa with Pershing's Army, had a temper to match his size. He and Flynn were both 6'2" and had long arms but neither of them could drop Jory. Jory played a bad guy quite often in films and even in life he was not someone to take lightly.

Jory's parents, Edwin and Joanna (Snyder), were prospectors. Tired of living in sleeping bags as they panned for gold in the frozen Yukon, the family went south to Los Angeles. They later returned to Dawson City where Victor attended school for a time, and then returned once again to L.A. There, at the Pasadena Playhouse, Victor stepped on a stage for the first time at age sixteen and fell in love with the theater. After a spell of time at the University of California at Berkeley, and another one at the University of Canada, Jory joined a stock company in Vancouver. While there he took up boxing and wrestling on the side and became the Light-Heavyweight Champion of British Columbia. He later became the National Guard Wrestling and Boxing Champion in Monterey, CA. He also taught the pugilistic arts for many years.

Victor spent a few years on tour with various stock acting companies in Los Angeles, Salt Lake City, Denver, and the Ohio circuit of Cincinnati, Cleveland and Dayton. But it wasn't an easy life, the stock companies struggled to stay afloat, and pay was meager.

Victor once found himself in a snowdrift beside the railroad tracks, having been booted off his boxcar by a porter. "Just before darkness I found a haven in a hobo jungle in the timber close to the right of way. There was a big fire and a stew of sorts brewing in a dilapidated bucket. 'What you been doin', buddy?' the head tramp inquired. 'Acting,' I replied. "Stage Actin'?' "Sure.' 'Oh! A sissy, huh?'

While acting in a stock company in Salt Lake City Victor met Gladys George, who was part owner of the company. They and some companions travelled to Denver and when the season closed, the four of them had $29 in cash.

"We bought $29 worth of groceries and moved into a mountain cabin, and what a summer! Beans! Beans! Beans! But it got much worse. The beans were soon gone and I couldn't get a job in Denver. I started hitting the hectic hobo train for the Pacific Coast but caught on with a stock company in Salt Lake after weeks in the hobo jungles. It was one grand fight after another."

Jory eventually organized his own company, took it out on the road, and went broke. At that point he hitchhiked to Minneapolis and landed a job working opposite Edith Taliaferro in the Bainbridge Players.

For the next three years (1928-1930) Jory was a leading man in several plays for the Shubert Theater's Buzz Bainbridge Players headquartered at 7th Street just west of South Hennepin Avenue. Victor enjoyed the meaty roles offered in Eugene O'Neill plays such as *Strange Interlude,* and boasted in 1930 that he had performed in more O'Neill plays than any other American actor. In fact, for *Strange Interlude* he memorized 175 typed pages (called "sides" back then) and was "word perfect" by the Wednesday curtain call. He liked to boast that he had learned the longest part in the shortest time of any actor, though St. Paulite Walter Greaza performed a similar challenge once.

Jory's contract allowed him to pick two plays each season and his choices for 1930 were *All God's Chillun Got Wings* and *The Racket.* He had the lead in *An American Tragedy,* a play based on Theodore Dreiser's great book, and he co-starred with Florence Reed in *The Shanghai Gesture.* Both plays were held over an extra week because of their great popularity. Not every play was quite so heavy-going, though—he starred in *Snow White* with Lois Janes, (who later worked in Victor's TV series, *Manhunt*.)

By the end of Victor's third season with the Bainbridge Players, he boasted (he liked boasting) that he had starred in 118 productions or forty per year. That's a lot of memorizing.

Minneapolis journalist Bradley L. Morison reviewed the Eugene O'Neill play and said, "Much of the credit for a splendid performance of *All God's Chillun Got Wings* must go to Victor Jory, who cast the production and had a great deal to do with the staging of it. His Jim, beyond that, is capitally done, and his characterization is as careful and well-reasoned and intelligent a piece of work as Mr. Jory, in many weeks of excellent performances at the Shubert, has given us."

Gladys George, an "adopted Minnesotan" from Maine, co-starred with Victor in several plays at the Shubert. They also appeared together to address the Phi Delta Theta Fraternity of the University of Minnesota Alumni Association at a Christmas Eve luncheon in 1931. On that occasion they told of their various theater experiences including some embarrassing moments. Jory was working on Broadway by that time, but he was also peddling his new cookbook, *Every Man a Gourmet Chef...and a Few Women*, which was geared toward bringing a little more "drama" to the dinner table.

Jory was a dapper dresser, and a *Minneapolis Journal* writer once described him as "a leading man, a character man, a singer, a clever boxer, a wrestler and a poet." Ten years later it was still thought that Jory had been the most popular leading man ever to work for Buzz Bainbridge. In order to maintain his stature as a leading man, Jory went so far as to keep his marriage a secret. He met his wife, Jean Innes, while working here in the Twin Cities. She was a leading lady for St. Paul's Arthur Casey Company. They were married on December 27, 1928, and the union was only ended by her death in December 1978. They had two children.

Not long after making his move to Broadway, Victor attended an opening night party at the apartment of Judith Anderson, a Shakespearean-trained actress and one of the first women ever to play Hamlet. As it night wore on the crowd thinned out, and Jory, feeling it was his duty to leave, went to say his thank-yous to the hostess. He shook Anderson's hand, but she wouldn't let go of his, asking him to stay a little longer. He stayed all night.

(This is one of many stories that Victor told to Richard Hilger in the summer of 1971 while Jory was teaching an acting workshop in Minneapolis under the auspices of the Concerts and Lectures

Department and the Theatre Department of the University of Minnesota. Hilger, a graduate student in Theatre Arts, became Victor's very willing drinking buddy. After the summer workshop was over, Victor continued for several years to keep Richard posted on his new movie or TV appearances.)

Jory's first major Hollywood role was co-starring with Loretta Young in *The Devil's in Love* (1933). Two years later he played Oberon, the Fairy King, in Shakespeare's classic, *A Midsummer Night's Dream*, along with Jimmy Cagney and Mickey Rooney. He was a marvelous "Injun Joe" in *The Adventures of Tom Sawyer* (1938).

By the next year he had found his Hollywood character niche, typified by his role as the whip-wielding overseer, Jonas Wilkerson, in *Gone with the Wind* (1939)—a grasping, cruel, bitter, vengeful villain, so easy to hate. We love it when Scarlett O'Hara throws some dirt in Wilkerson's face saying, "Here's all of Tara you'll ever get."

Critic Leonard Maltin once remarked that Jory "never lost his big, burly physique. His sinister looks and distinctive voice typed him as a heavy, at which he excelled."

He used his powerful voice to good effect in melodramatic radio roles, and the great actress Elsa Maxwell even went so far as to assert that Jory was "the first radio star to link the spoken voice with sex appeal." Victor also made several children's records including "Peter Pan," "Peter and the Wolf" and "Tubby the Tuba."

Victor had his share of good guy roles, for example in the science-fiction drama *Cat Women of the Moon* (1935) where he plays Kip Reissner, co-pilot and sympathetic lead. He played Helen Keller's father in *The Miracle Worker* (1962).

Also notable among Jory's 150 films are *Each Dawn I Die* (1939), his second film with Cagney, *Meet Nero Wolfe* (1936), *Dodge City* (1939), *Charlie Chan in Rio* (1941) and *The Shadow* (1940). Over the years Jory played doctors, senators, foreigners and Indians. He portrayal of the stoic Indian in *Cheyenne Autumn* (1964) has great intensity. His personal favorite was the role of Jade Torrance in *The Fugitive Kind* (1960) where he co-stars with Marlon Brando, Joanne Woodward, and Anna Magnani.

Victor's first love was theater, however, and some of his memorable Broadway performances must be mentioned. He played Geoffrey opposite Elisabeth Bergner in *The Two Mrs. Carrolls* at the Booth Theater; he played Dale Williams opposite Miriam Hopkins in *The Perfect Marriage* at the Ethel Barrymore Theatre. He joined the American Repertory Theater for the title role in Shakespeare's *Henry VIII* and was Ferrovius in Shaw's *Androcles and the Lion*. He was Anthony

Anderson in Shaw's *The Devil's Disciple* at the New York City Center in January 1950. The list goes on and on. Jory also wrote two plays that were produced on the New York Stage: *Bodies by Fisher* and *Five Who Were Mad.*

Jory's TV debut came in February of 1950, in *The Chevrolet Tele-Theatre.* He appeared often on the *Kraft Television Theatre* (1954-57); and there were many other series appearances over the years, from *Rawhide* to *The Rockford Files.*

The Jorys' son, Jon Jory, became managing director of the Actors Theatre of Louisville where Victor starred in *The Time of Your Life* and directed *On Golden Pond* and *The Oldest Living Graduate.* Their daughter, Jean Anderson, lived in Utah.

Peggy Knudsen

Born 27 April, 1923,
Duluth, MN.
Died 11 July, 1980,
Encino, CA.

Peggy threw herself into Humphrey Bogart's arms in *The Big Sleep* (1946) as Mona, the wild, younger daughter of General Sternwood. As a fireman's daughter in real life, she knew how to fall into someone's arms, perhaps, and why not Bogart's? Lauren Bacall played the wiser, older sister in this classic Howard Hawks detective movie, based on a novel by Raymond Chandler. It was only Peggy's second film appearance. She was also featured in her first film, playing Dierdra in *A Stolen Life* (1946) which starred Bette Davis and Glenn Ford.

What ignited this show business fire? It all started with music and violin lessons. Knudsen had become a frequent performer on Duluth radio even as a teenager. At her school, Stanbrook Hall (Villa Scholastica), she participated in all entertainments and musical activities. She made her acting debut at Duluth's Little Theatre in 1939 at age sixteen in *Susan and God.* By now she was determined to be an actress.

A year later Peggy experienced one of the biggest thrills of her life when she won a contest sponsored by two Duluth newspapers which lead to a meeting with Jackie Coogan, who was passing through town with a touring show. It was the first time she had met a celebrity.

Peggy's mom, Helen, supported her show business dreams, and they left together for Chicago right after her high school graduation to audition for radio shows. "My mother sympathized with my ambition to go on the stage, and she taught me much that helped me when the opportunity came," Peggy later remarked

Chicago was the radio hub of the Midwest at the time, and Peggy dutifully met with agents and made the rounds of radio auditions. It wasn't long before she had won the part of Betty Adams in *Woman in White,* heard weekdays over NBC. After the audition the writer and director of the serial walked up to her and said, "You're the one." Nearly simultaneously she signed a three-year contract with the Mutual Broadcasting System as a singer. Her first gig was soloist with the Anson Week's Orchestra. This brought offers from several nationally known bands, but Peggy was determined to be an actress and she turned them all down.

Howard Keegan, the director of *Woman in White,* said he was anxious to have Peggy do stage work as well as sing and act on radio, in order to develop her talent fully. "We have talented actresses around the studios who have been here for years," he said, "trying to get some place, and young Peggy comes along without a bit of experience, and lands in the top shows. You don't see that happen very often."

Miss Helen Hayes, the First Lady of the Theatre, selected Peggy from several other girls auditioning in the CBS Studio in Chicago to appear with her in the radio play, *The Late Christopher Bean.* She also introduced Peggy to her husband, the famous playwright Charles MacArthur. Working with Helen Hayes was another great thrill.

After a year of working Chicago radio shows, Knudsen returned home briefly just as Phil Spitalny and his All-Girl Orchestra arrived in town. Peggy auditioned for the orchestra and was signed to a featured role as violinist. While the band was performing in New York City Peggy won a role in the Broadway play *My Sister Eileen.* She quit the band and stayed in the show for the remaining run of one year.

At the age of nineteen, and in the midst of a whirlwind performing career that any young woman might envy, Knudsen succumbed to the passionate wooing of Adrian Samish, fourteen years her senior, and the two eloped—against the wishes of Peggy's mother who thought she was too young to marry. A year later little Peg-Peg was born. In 1945 Peggy returned to Duluth to visit and show off her daughter to her many relatives living in the area. During the visit she stayed with her aunt and uncle, Dr. and Mrs. W. E. Hatch, at 201 Garden Street

Peggy then set off confidently for Hollywood and almost immediately signed a contract with Warner Brothers Studio. She had become a shapely, leggy, honey-blond with a hard look, and Warner Brothers liked that look. They strutted her about like a model but after a few films she was relegated to "the other woman" roles.

Among the films in which she appeared are Errol Flynn's *Never Say Goodbye* (1946), and *Humoresque* (1946) starring John Garfield and Joan Crawford. For *Stallion Road* (1947) she was cast opposite Ronald Reagan and Alexis Smith. There was a lot of horse talk in this movie and it made perfect horse sense for those who speak horse. Peggy's next film appearance was a bit part in *My Wild Irish Rose* (1947) which showcased Minnesota's Arlene Dahl.

Following a string of B-budget films with Fox, Peggy did no films at all for a five-year period. Her marriage to Adrian Samish had ended in divorce and in 1949 she married TV director James C. Jordan, son of radio's Jim and Marian Jordan of *Fibber McGee and Molly*. They had two children, Janice and Molly. (They were divorced in 1960.)

In 1955 Knudsen returned to the screen in *Unchained* and was featured in the film *Good Morning, Miss Dove*, a starring vehicle for Jennifer Jones. (St. Paulite Eleanore Griffin wrote the screenplay for this film.) Jones and Knudsen enjoyed one another's company, and when Peggy developed a debilitating arthritic condition which effectively ended her career Jennifer remained a steadfast friend.

Peggy's last film, *Istanbul* (1956), was a reunion with Errol Flynn. Flynn was nearing the end of his career, as boozing had taken its toll, and Peggy's shapely body was stiffening up as arthritis grew more severe. Yet Peggy made nineteen films in the previous ten years and in 1955 she could be seen regularly as April Adams in a TV series *So This Is Hollywood*.

Peggie continued to appear sporadically on TV until 1961. Her debut appearance was in January 1949 on *Your Show Time*, and her final appearance was on *The Adventures of Ozzie & Harriet*.

Peggy's father and mother, Conrad R. Knudsen and Helen Haynes, were both born in Duluth. Conrad had become Duluth's fire chief by the time Peggy graduated from high school. Over the years they lived at the Stratford Apartments at 18th Avenue East and Fourth Street, and also at 506 ½ E. 4th Street. Peggy graduated from Villa Scholastica, Stanbrook Hall, in June, 1941, and always remembered her childhood in Duluth fondly.

Knudsen's show business career was somewhat like a comet that flared brightly but then just fizzled out, largely due to her crippling arthritis. In middle age Peggy did TV commercials for the Arthritis Foundation. Though crippled, she never lost her charm of her vivacious, up-beat attitude toward life.

L

June Lang

Winifred June Vlasek
Born 5 May 1914?,
Minneapolis, MN.

June was a stunning blue-eyed blond—as stunning as any woman could be. She advertised for the State of Minnesota on travel brochures, she was Shirley Temple's mother in *Wee Willie Winkie* (1937), and she made several other movies, but she never became a star. Some historians speculate that her second marriage, to Johnny Roselli, undermined her career. Roselli was a West Coast representative of the Chicago Mob who tried to pass himself off as a film producer. June was not the first to be involved with seamy characters. Thelma Todd's death may well be related to the Mob, and both Veronica Lake and Lana Turner rubbed elbows with mobsters—or so they say.

The year of June's birth remains a matter of dispute. A girl was born to Clarence V. & Edith Irene (Olson) Vlasek on May 5, 1907, at Eitel Hospital on Loring Park. Clarence was listed as an inspector at the Gamble Robinson Fruit Company at the time. Yet June herself claims to have been born on May 5, 1914, while her parents lived at 1904 Park Avenue and her father was a railway inspector. (The 1920 city directory lists the Clarence Vlasek family at 1106 E. 38th Street in the Minneapolis Central High School District. Their last Minneapolis address was 1801 Park Avenue.)

As a child June attended Ruby Helen MacLoon's School for Children. One of her playmates there, Audree Hall, asked her to go along with her to the Marian Lewis dancing class, and two weeks after joining the class the girls made their debut at the Metropolitan Theater in downtown Minneapolis. They were an immediate hit, and the duo was in constant demand by civic organizations as after-dinner entertainment. Her mother was pleased with June's success and enrolled her in the Seton Guild for further instruction in dancing and other performance techniques. In fact, Edith grew so excited by her daughter's prospects that she began to ponder moving the family to California so June could pursue a movie career.

As it happened, the railroad fortuitously transferred Clarence to Los Angeles when June was seven (some reports say she was twelve.) In fact, no one knows for sure when the family moved or how old June was at the time, but in 1931 she appeared in a two-reel Christie comedy, in the chorus of Barbara Stanwyck's film, *The Miracle Woman*, and in *She Wanted a Millionaire* starring Spencer Tracy, Joan Bennett, and Minnesota-born Dorothy Peterson.

June had been chosen among twenty girls for a swimming pool sequence in the third film, but when director John Blystone was filming her close up she insouciantly saluted a waiter that was passing by. Blystone liked the gesture and advised Winfield Sheehan, the Fox Studio Production Chief, to sign June to a short contract with the studio.

During her screen test for *Young Sinners* June sang "I Loved You Wednesday" and knocked 'em cold. In fact, Sheehan liked her well enough to put her through their private dramatic training school for the next three years.

June also attended the Meglin School for Kiddies, a school run by Ethel Meglin for talented children preparing for a life in movies or show business. Shirley Temple went to this school for a time. The kids at Meglin would perform in the various vaudeville houses or nightclubs in the metropolitan area to "strut their stuff" as they became competent in dancing or singing or whatever.

Lang completed Beverly Hills High School (or Hollywood High) in 1933 at age nineteen, perhaps. If this is true, then she did movies while still in high school such as *Chandu the Magician* (in which she spoke her very first lines in a movie). This film, coming out during the fall of her senior year, starred Edmund Lowe and Bela Lugosi.

June appeared briefly in five films in the next two years. The last, an operetta called *Music in the Air* (1934) impressed Sheehan so much that he gave her a seven-year contract at $750 a week. He also changed her name to Lang. When she was brought into this Jerome Kern and Oscar Hammerstein operetta the three principal parts had already been cast with Gloria Swanson, John Boles, and Douglass Montgomery. Many noted ingenues were tested for the fourth major part, a Bavarian peasant girl, but none had the blend of youthful, innocent freshness and dramatic power that June brought to the part.

Fox Casting Director, Ben Lyon, was very sweet on (and much later married to) Minnesota-raised Marian Nixon, who complained to her sweetie that this new Lang girl was a threat to her. Gloria Swanson, too, was aloof and cool to June because June's part grew to greater importance than hers. June felt strange in the singing scenes as her voice was dubbed yet she had to convey the real effect of singing. "It was very hard and took great concentration," she said.

June was in the Laurel and Hardy feature, *Bonnie Scotland* (1935) although, she said, she was never actually filmed with them. June's contract, it turned out, gave the studio the option of renewing the contract. If they didn't, it automatically became null and void. In 1935, they dropped June.

But not for long. One night Lew Schreiber saw June dancing at the Trocadero and was bowled over by her beauty and dancing talent. He telephoned Darryl F. Zanuck and urged him to renew her contract. Zanuck gave in. Director Howard Hawks saw her latest screen-test and cast her in his upcoming movie, *Road to Glory* (1936) as a leading lady opposite Fredric March and Warner Baxter. Both March and Baxter were Academy Award winners and Lang felt as if she was living in an air castle.

Lang later she admitted that she had a "big crush" on Baxter, who co-starred with her again the next year in *White Hunter*. In 1936 she also starred in *The Country Doctor*, a film about Canada's Dionne Quintuplets. Michael Whalen played June's husband and the tabloids suggested that they were becoming an item. June was the second lead in *Captain January* (1936) a Hal Roach film about colonizing Australia.

It was asserted by sculptor Albert Stewart that Lang had a "modernistic figure," and he used her as a model for the war bride in the New York Peace Memorial. At the time she weighed 104 pounds and was 5'3 ½" tall.

June's father came back to the Twin Cities for a visit, and the *Minneapolis Tribune* quoted him as saying that all the stories about wild drinking parties in the homes of Hollywood movie stars "are a lot of bunk." He continued, "The stars like a quiet home life just the same as the people in Minneapolis do. Many of them are in bed at 9 o'clock every night when they're working on a picture." He talked about his daughter's intensive training at the Fox Studio school where she studied voice culture, dramatics, dancing, diction, make-up, and a dozen other subjects. He added, "She has had her chance and has made good."

June herself was also scheduled for a summer visit to Minneapolis in 1936. She acknowledged that she had had a few romances, but nothing for her parents, with whom she lived, to worry about. In fact, most of her dates were arranged by the studio's public relations department as a means of molding her public image.

Yet only a year later, on May 29, 1937, June married actors' agent, Vic Orsatti. Since it was unusual to have a church wedding instead of the customary eloping to Mexico or Nevada, many film notables showed up, including producer Joseph Schenk, who gave away the bride (Why not her own father?) and Alice Faye, Claire Trevor, and Ginger Rogers were the bridesmaids.

Vic and June returned from honeymooning in Honolulu to find June's parents ensconced in the next bedroom. Vic protested but to no avail. Clarence and Edith were determined to go wherever June went and Vic therefore filed for divorce after only 45 days of marriage, citing "outside influences."

Following that bizarre domestic episode June returned to filmmaking. She had the title role in *Nancy Steele Is Missing* (1937) and co-starred with Gypsy Rose Lee and Eddie Cantor in *Ali Baba Goes to Town* (1937). When Jean Harlow died she was included in the short list of those who might take her place as The Blond Bombshell.

Perhaps the highlight of June's career was playing Shirley Temple's mother in *Wee Willie Winkie* (1937), though some people thought she did not look old enough to be a mother. In any case, it was the most-watched and most popular movie June would ever be in. Shirley was at her peak which guaranteed huge box office appeal.

June would often play hide-'n-seek with Shirley, who would caution her, "Now don't you make a sound—this is fun." John Ford, the director, was very understanding. Shirley just loved to be looked for— and she was always hiding when they would need her for a shot.

In 1937 Lang returned to Minnesota for a week of festivities associated with its Centennial Celebration. The Shriners made her an "Honorary Captain" in the Zurah Shrine Patrol and Drum Corps as they marched the two blocks from the Great Northern Depot to the Nicollet Hotel. The police couldn't contain the huge crowd which bustled past the barriers to get close to the returning celebrity who had left the state when she was "seven."

Lang's week-long stay was filled with luncheons and dinners including the mayor's dinner at the Nicollet Hotel. She also attended a dance at the Armory and presented awards to winners in the Northwest Parade. It was on this visit that June posed for the *Minnesota Official Tourist Guide Book*. She is seen fishing, holding a tennis racket, standing near a campfire, and bicycling on a sandy beach.

After making *Meet the Girls* (1938), Lang was commissioned to go to England to film *So This Is London.* However, as war in Europe became imminent she wanted to leave, and William Waldorf (Lord) Astor not only advised her to go home but booked the very last cabin on the Queen Mary for her. When Zanuck heard that she'd abandoned the film right in the middle of shooting, he tore up June's contract and from that moment on she was effectively black-balled by all the major studios.

That same year she married Mob boss Johnny Roselli, though at the time neither she nor anyone else in Hollywood actually knew who he was. When she found out she pleaded with him to "go straight" and divorced him a year later when it became obvious that he wouldn't.

(Roselli had cut his teeth in Chicago working for Al Capone, and was a close friend of Frank Costello, head of one of the five Mafia families in New York. His name appears often in accounts of both government attempts to assassinate Fidel Castro and the Kennedy assassination. He disappeared in July 1976 a few days before he was scheduled to testify before the Select Committee on Intelligence Activities. Ten days later his body was found in a steel drum off the coast of Florida.)

At this point in her career June Lang was reduced to appearing in independent productions like *Captain Fury* (1939) and *Zenobia* (1939), which were both shot at the Hal Roach Studios. She returned to Fox Studios for *Footlight Serenade* (1942), *City of Silent Men* (1942), *Stage Door Canteen* (1943), and *Up in Arms* (1944) starring Danny Kaye.

In 1944 June married Lt. William Morgan, her third husband. The couple had a daughter, Patricia Morgan, a few years later. They were divorced in 1952.

Lang made her last film, *Lighthouse,* in 1947.

Late in her career June promoted Lux soap, Kellogg's cereal, and various beauty products. She also appeared on a few TV shows, including *Peyton Place, 77 Sunset Strip, Felony Squad, Fireside Theatre,* and *City Detective.*

In retirement Lang appeared occasionally in commercials and on local TV talk shows. She lived quietly in a one-story stucco house in North Hollywood until her death in 2005.

Jessica Lange

*Born 20 April 1949,
Cloquet, MN.*

In her graduation yearbook at Cloquet, Class of 1967, Jessica was described as "artistic, dramatic, and fun is she, a new girl Cloquet is glad to see." She was the lead in the senior class spring play, and was also scheduled to star in *Rebel without a Cause* but the play was cancelled. She was a member of Pep Club, Book Club, the Sno-Ball Committee and other party-oriented groups, but she was also a reporter for the school paper and a member of the National Honor Society.

Jessica's father, Al, was a history teacher on occasion and a traveling salesman at other times. Because of his unsteady employment, the family moved twelve times during Jessica's school years. She has two older sisters and a younger brother, George, a pilot.

Perhaps because of her transient upbringing, Lange became fascinated with the world of films. Her special obsession was *Gone with the Wind*—she saw the film more than once and read the book at least four times. Whenever she was sick, she would reenact Melanie's deathbed scene. Yet it never occurred to her to pursue a career in acting. Painting was her focus.

Lange had won a scholarship to study art at the University of Minnesota, but she fell in love with a Spanish photographer and experimental filmmaker named Paco Grande and dropped out of school after five months. For the next two years the couple travelled extensively by motorcycle through Europe, and then around the United States in an old Econoline van. They got married in 1970. She once told David Rosenthal in an interview for *Rolling Stone*, "With my husband, when we were together during the early years, the really strong years, we were inseparable. We lived, literally, in this truck together, and we'd go for days without speaking to anybody else except maybe a gas station attendant."

When the couple broke up in 1971 Jessica returned to Paris with a suitcase of belongings and $300. For the next two years she studied art and mime and supported herself as an artist's model. She studied with the master of classical mime, Etienne DeCroux, the teacher of Marcel Marceau.

Paris had a sexually liberating effect on Jessica, just as it had on Henry Miller. "I've always been drawn to men who have this powerful presence, the power to obsess you." In Paris she met several, including one of the world's foremost fashion illustrators, Antonio Lopez. It was Lopez who hooked up Lange with movie producer Dino De Laurentiis, who was looking for an "unknown" to play the lead in a remake of *King Kong* (1976).

At the time Lange was living in New York City, working as a waitress at the Lion's Head Saloon in Greenwich Village. She flew with another model to California, very confident that she'd get the part, even though it was her first movie audition. "Foolhardily, I believed I could do anything. I walked into this cattle call, weighing 114 pounds, looking different than the other girls—a lot of big, buxom blondes. Just from the sight they weren't interested in me. By the time it was my turn, the director had already gone. I did a screen test with the assistant director, who called the director and said, 'You better come down here and see this screen test,' and I did it all over again because they called Dino.

"Now I'm thinking, of course I've got the part. So I took off to see my sister, then came directly to Minnesota for Christmas [1974]. They were frantically looking for me because they'd just found this girl to star in their $25 million dollar movie and I had disappeared. But I had things to do. I knew they'd find me sooner or later."

Filming took nine months on Hollywood back lots and it was a lonely time for Lange. The film was widely derided and Jessica was especially singled out for derision. Because of the poor reviews she did not work in films for two years after that but she said, "I never accepted failure at anything. There was no doubt I was going to succeed."

Yet even at the time critic Pauline Kael discerned that the film's main spark came mainly from "…the impudent new conception of the screaming-in-fear blonde and Jessica Lange's fast yet dreamy comic style." Kael noted that Lange's character is "as childlike as Kong himself," [with] "one-liners so dumb that the audience laughs and moans at the same time, yet they're in character, and when Jessica Lange says them she holds the eye, and you like her, the way people liked Carole Lombard."

Jessica was appalled at the lies told in plugging the film, but since she was no longer employed, it was a relief that De Laurentiis had signed her to a seven-year contract. (At the end of the third year both agreed to stop payments.)

Jessica really pushed hard for the role opposite Jack Nicholson in *Goin' South* for Paramount Studio in 1978 but lost out to Mary Steenburgen. Nicholson sent her a bouquet of roses and a note which read, "I'm sure we'll work together some time soon. We will have lots of fun and make lots of money. Love, Jack."

Bob Fosse, a friend and lover, helped save the day a bit with writing her into his film, *All That Jazz* (1978). She played the Angel of Death, Angelique, in a Fellini-like style. It was a small but very showy part. This was followed by *How to Beat the High Co$t of Living* (1980), a comedy about three financially-stressed housewives who go shoplifting in order to make ends meet. It was nice and enjoyable but did nothing for Jessica's career.

The next year Lange's name came up as a candidate to play opposite Nicholson in a remake of *The Postman Always Rings Twice* (1981). Director Bob Rafelson visited her in North Carolina to see if she was right for this role. He found her to be "an incredibly sensual woman who made no effort at all to be sensual." He wondered if he "could get this woman to be on-screen the way she was in repose, [then] she would be utterly striking." He tested more an a hundred other actresses but Jessica was the only one who could make the transition between being nice and being manipulative with such ease.

This quality came out loud and clear in the film, and critics were unanimous in their praise of her performance. Nicholson himself nick-named her "blinky" and said to *New York* Magazine that "she can hardly see without her glasses, can hardly see herself in a mirror—that's why she isn't narcissistic." He went on the describe her as "a delicate fawn crossed with a Buick."

It was a truly bizarre coincidence that before shooting began Nicholson gave Jessica a copy of Cloquet-born Barbara Payton's book, *I Am Not Ashamed*, which he thought might "prep" her for playing a woman who was sliding down the rat hole of life yet hanging passionately onto what she could.

The next year Lange impressed the critics again with her portrayal of actress Frances Farmer in *Frances* (1982), a role she had wanted to play since learning about Farmer in an acting class in 1974. Farmer was a promising stage and screen actress whose rebellious spirit and lack of discipline lead to a stagnating career, alcoholic, and a nervous breakdown. Jessica captured the nuances and contradictions of Farmer's character beautifully and was nominated for an Oscar for Best Actress. Others who wanted this role were Jane Fonda, Diane Keaton, Goldie Hawn and Tuesday Weld.

Following the advice of Kim Stanley, who played Frances' mother in the film, Jessica immediately followed up the dark forcefulness of her performance in *Frances* with a comic role. The film was *Tootsie*

(1982) and it, too, was a critical success. Lange was nominated for Academy Awards for both roles that year—a rare occurrence. Everyone could see the tremendous range of talent that Miss Lange possessed, and viewers and critics alike were bowled over by it.

Dustin Hoffman stars in the picture as a man desperately in need of a job. His wins a role on a soap opera only by auditioning as a woman. Lange is also in the cast, and he develops a strong "sisterly" rapport with her on the set. But he's actually interested in something else entirely. The comic aspects of this mistaken-identity plot are deftly mined, and there are also a number of thought-provoking gender issues involved.

The American Film Institute lists *Tootsie* as 62nd on their list of the 100 Best American Movies. It earned $126,000,000 in its first three months and won ten Oscar nominations. Jessica went home with the Best Supporting Actress Award. She had earlier won best supporting awards from the New York Film Critics and the National Society of Film Critics.

Andrew Sarris reported in the *Village Voice* that Lange, "was more of a knockout than Frances Farmer ever was, that she was everything Marilyn Monroe was supposed to be in *Some Like It Hot*, and a great deal more besides, that she lit up the screen with so much beauty and intelligence that she and Dustin Hoffman were able to transform what might have petered out into a tired reprise of *Charley's Aunt* into a thoroughly modernist, thoroughly feminist parable of emotional growth and enlightenment."

Though legally married to Paco Grande until 1982, Lange was living much of the time with American Ballet Theatre star dancer and director, Mikhail Baryshnikov, with whom she had a daughter, Shura. In those days she divided her time between New York with Misha, her apartment in L. A., a lakefront cabin in Nickerson, Minnesota, near her parents' cabin, and a retreat near Taos, New Mexico.

Jessica not only starred in but also produced her next film *Country* (1984), which co-starred the new man in her life, Sam Shepard. Sam met Jessica during the filming of *Frances* but he was married at the time and Jessica had a new baby, so he made himself scarce whenever he could. In *Country* they play a struggling farm couple and Jessica says, "This was very dear to me at the time. It dealt with the Midwest and that kind of disappearing rural life in America. It was a very personal film." Again she garnered an Oscar nomination for Best Actress.

Another Oscar nomination came from portraying Patsy Cline in *Sweet Dreams* (1985), "one of my favorites," she confesses.

She is teamed up with Diane Keaton and Sissy Spacek as eccentric Southern sisters in *Crimes of the Heart* (1986). Lange said, "I had just had my second child and wasn't as concentrated as I should have been. But I just love being around Diane and Sissy." Even without her best effort it's a fine movie. This is the only film Jessica keeps in her house for the children to see.

In *Everybody's All-American* (1988) she co-stars with Dennis Quaid as the unhappy wife of an aging college football hero.

Sam Shepard made his directorial debut with *Far North* (1988). Lange enjoyed filming in Northern Minnesota, though the film is not one of her best. Similarly, *Men Don't Leave* (1990) is a minor effort, though as usual with Lange's films, it has its moments.

Jessica is a lawyer in *Music Box* (1990) defending her father in a war crimes trial. It was well received in Germany where it won the Golden Bear Award in 1990 but American critics thought less highly of it, though Jessica herself garnered her fifth Academy Award nomination for her performance.

Martin Scorsese's *Cape Fear* (1991) is a brooding thriller in which Lange has a minor role. In *Night and the City* (1992) she is again cast with Robert De Niro in the story of a small-time lawyer and boxing promoter who has an affair with the wife (Jess) of one of his backers. Entertaining, but—so what? That same year Jessica appeared in "*O! Pioneers,*" a made-for-TV movie based on the classic novel by Nebraska author Willa Cather.

Though few viewers ever saw her next major film, it hit pay dirt for Lange critically. In *Blue Sky* (1994), she played a sexually-obsessed army wife and was awarded the coveted Oscar for Best Actress for her performance. *Losing Isaiah* (1995) was poorly received, but with *Rob Roy* Jessica scored another success. "Oh, God, I was so lucky," she said about appearing in that film. "Rarely do you see characters like mine and Liam's who aren't two twenty-year-olds, but who are sensual and sexual and who are in love with each other and honor each other." Also in 1995 she played Blanche DuBois in Tennessee Williams' play, *Streetcar Named Desire* opposite Alec Baldwin in a made-for-TV movie.

In 1997 Jessica Lange co-starred with Michelle Pfeiffer, Jennifer Jason Leigh, and Jason Robards in *A Thousand Acres,* a variation of the King Lear theme. Robards is an aging farmer who wills his land to his three daughters.

Jessica delivers a great hysterical performance as Martha Baring (against a bland one from Gwyneth Paltrow) in *Hush* (1998). She also shines in *Cousin Bette* (1998) as a seamstress who lives for revenge on her wealthier cousins in old Paris. Elizabeth Shue, Bob Hoskins, and Geraldine Chaplin are co-stars in this darkly photographed but entertaining and meticulously-crafted period film.

In *Titus* (1999) Lange appeared in her first major Shakespeare film, co-starring with Anthony Hopkins. It's bloody, dark, gruesome, sadistic, and masochistic piece, and a bit of a departure for director Julie Taymor, who had previously earned high praise for her Broadway production of the musical *The Lion King*. Miss Lange seemed to be running the gamut of dramatic themes and roles almost as a child who wants to sample all the candy in the sweets shop.

Jessica has been with Sam Shepard for twenty years as of this writing. They have two children, Hanna and Walker. The lived in Stillwater, Minnesota, for many years, but once their kids were out of school they departed for New York and other places.

Jessica says that both she and Sam are difficult people to live with, which is why they can live together so well. "My father was such a passionate man—which is what has directed my life. I have always followed the most passionate course," she admits. "There is nothing I feel I've missed. I lived everywhere and, believe me, did everything. I have gone down the road full tilt."

Tom Laughlin

Thomas Robert Laughlin, Jr.
Born 10 August 1931,
Minneapolis, MN.

Tom "Billy Jack" Laughlin was born in Minneapolis to Tom Laughlin, Sr., a Northern Pacific Railroad switchman in 1931. Tom Sr. had been living as a renter at 3843 N. 4th St. but in 1930 he moved to 2626 Queen Avenue North. The family left Minnesota in 1933 and never returned.

Tom, Jr. broke into television in 1955, just a few months before his debut in movies. He appeared in eleven TV episodes in four years before quitting that medium. Some of those shows were *Climax, Navy Log, The Millionaire* (1956), *The Walter Winchell File* (1957), *Wagon Train* (1957), *Lux Playhouse* (1958), and *M Squad* (1959).

In Tom's early movies he was often given juvenile roles because he had a round face and an easy smile which made him look young. His film debut was as a football player in *These Wilder Years* (1956). He next appeared as a "regular guy" in *Tea and Sympathy* (1956). In *South Pacific* (1958) he delivers some funny lines in the role of the cocky navy pilot Lt. Buzz Adams.

Another flying flick, *Lafayette Escadrille* (1958), followed, with William Wellman directing in the twilight of his career. (Wellman had directed the first Oscar-winning movie, *Wings*, in 1927.)

Tom plays "Lover Boy" in *Gidget* (1959) starring Sandra Dee, Cliff Robertson, and James Darren, and appeared again with Robertson in *The Battle of the Coral Sea* (1959). *Tall Story* (1960) closes out the decade for Tom, and also his contributions to the world of regular commercial film.

At this point Laughlin decided to bring together his talents as a writer, director, actor, and producer in an independent film production. His first film in this capacity is *The Proper Time* (1960). It was followed a year later by *Like Father Like Son,* and in 1965 he came out with a third independent work, *Young Sinner.* None of the three attracted the attention of the critics or made much of a splash at the box office.

However, things were different with *Born Losers* (1967) in which Tom for the first time plays the role of vigilante hero Billy Jack. The film was distributed by American International Pictures and it did well. Yet the frustrations of earlier years continued to dog Laughlin while making *Billy Jack* (1971). Half-way through the filming the money ran out and Laughlin's new producer/distributor, Twentieth Century Fox, wanted to re-edit the film. Eventually Tom got Warner Brothers to agree to distribute *Billy Jack*, but they continued to dilly-dally so long that Tom felt it necessary to sue them. The case was settled out of court, the result being that Tom was given the right to supervise the re-release of the film. It cost him some $800,000—a frighteningly large investment at the time—but the gamble paid off handsomely. *Billy Jack* grossed over $65 million.

Billy Jack is a reserved, anti-establishment half-breed who advocates justice and peace but makes use of the violent martial arts discipline of hapkido karate to achieve these ends. The karate master Bong Soo Han trained Tom for the part. The public so loved this film that it became a cult classic, and even *Newsweek*'s Jack Kroll said the film was "affecting and ...geniune."

Tom's next film, *The Trial of Billy Jack* (1974), continued the roll, grossing $22 million in thirty days—very good for those days. But the magic died with *Billy Jack Goes to Washington* (1977), a stale re-working of Jimmy Stewart's *Mr. Smith Goes to Washington* (1939). Although Richard Corliss described it as "a heart grabber of a movie," nobody much cared. Ten years later Laughlin attempted to stage a comeback with *The Return of Billy Jack*, but public interest was so meager that the film was never released.

Among Tom's other film appearance are *Callan* (1974), *The Master Gunfighter* (1975), *Voyage of the Damned* (1976), *The Big Sleep* (1977), and *The Legend of the Lone Ranger* (1981). Tom wrote and directed *The Babysitter* (1969) and *Weekend with the Babysitter* (1970). His last three acting appearances were in made-for-TV movies.

Tom married Delores Taylor in 1956 and they are still together and have a daughter, Teresa, and son, Frank. Delores shared the screenwriting duties with Tom and also appeared in each Billy Jack movie. In 1974, after studying in Italy with educator and reformer Maria Montessori, the couple founded a Montessori School in Santa Monica.

Tom announced his intention of running against Arnold Schwarzenegger for the Governorship of California but never followed through on the plan. In 1992 he ran in the New Hampshire Democratic Presidential Primary and garnered several thousand votes.

His autobiography, *Wild Bill: Hollywood Maverick*, came out in 1996, and Tom later wrote a booklet entitled "How to Invest in Motion Pictures...and Why You Shouldn't" (1972). It's a good thing he was able to raise the cash he needed at a critical point in his career or we wouldn't have Billy Jack today. Glad you were here, Tom.

Gordon "Porky" Lee

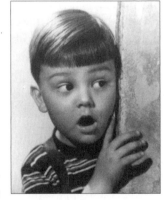

(Eugene "Porky" Lee)
Born 25 October, 1933,
Fort Worth, TX.
Died 22 October, 2005,
Minneapolis, MN.

Porky from the "Our Gang" comedies is a Texa-sotan. He was born in Texas but eventually settled in Minnesota in 1990. Gordon had four very busy years in Hollywood playing Spanky's younger brother, until he grew too tall for the part and had to retire from being a Little Rascal at the age of six.

Gordon was adopted in infancy by a mortician and his wife, who was the head stenographer for the Rock Island Railroad. Mrs. Lee, according to Porky, was the "original liberated woman." She could drive a motorcycle, run a business, do anything and do it well.

The enterprising Mrs. Lee sent of photograph of Porky at eighteen months to Hal Roach, pointing out the resemblance to Spanky. Inspired by a single, positive telegram from Roach, the family moved to Hollywood the very next month and began a happy and prosperous four-year period during which Gordon appeared in forty-two films.

They arrived at the studio gate unannounced and declared, "We came all the way from Texas." They were admitted and registered at the Culver City Hotel. Gordon was cooperative and photogenic, and he did look a lot like Spanky. He was five years old before he realized that most children did not make movies. His very best friend in those days was Bill "Buckwheat" Thomas.

In his movie debut, *Little Sinner* (1935), two-year old Porky couldn't say "okay" but he did say "otay," which the director decided to leave in. After all, producer Hal Roach reasoned, nearly everything kids do or say is cute and this was a new cute twist that would become Porky's signature word.

Porky's usual role was the small kid who's always trailing along behind the gang. In this first feature he tags along behind the older kids who've skipped Sunday school to go fishing down at the river. While at the river they witness some baptisms accompanied by shouts of 'Hallelujah!" and Spanky runs for his life, saying he's learned a great lesson about what might happen to you if you skip Sunday school.

Porky's second film, *Our Gang Follies of 1936* (1935), is loaded with talent from Minnesota, including Jackie Banning from Edina, Therese Bonner from St. Paul, and possibly Mary and Bill McCreary, Jr. from Hibbing. All kids that Roach had available on his lot appeared in this two-reeler. Some perform in the music revue and many of them are audience members either cheering or booing those on stage. The singing and dancing is very natural and unpolished making it very charming to watch. Who wouldn't love these kids?

After making *Auto Antics* (1939), Gordon and family moved back to Texas. Micky Gubitosi (who became Robert Blake) replaced Gordon as the cute toddler and he stayed in the gang until production ended in the spring of 1944. He then became Bobby "Mickey" Blake in film credits, and went on as an adult to star in TV's *Baretta*.

Incidentally, Gordon owned the rights to the name of "Porky" and won a large judgment from a company who used his character without permission in a cartoon.

In Texas Gordon was teased by his fellow high schoolers about his film persona, and for a period he resented the movie-making phase of his life. Over the years identity became a personal issue for him, and he took on the name Gordon, from the director he liked so much as a child, Gordon Douglas. He named his son Douglas Lee. It was because Douglas Lee was stationed in the Twin Cities at the Air Force Reserve Base in 1990 that Gordon came here to live with him. While Douglas subsequently moved away, Gordon opted to stay.

Gordon earned his college degree in education at Texas Tech and the University of Houston. He became a teacher in schools in Texas, Oklahoma, and Colorado. Early on, he developed a specialty of teaching "troubled students." He taught sociology, modern European history, and political science from 1971 to 1990 in an alternative school in Colorado, while devoting his free time to buying, restoring, and selling post-World War II sports cars, especially MGs. He also participated in Democratic Party politics there.

Gordon's "Rascal" days coincided with the best days of the "Our Gang" comedies (1935-1939). In the 1950s a new generation fell in love with these one- and two-reelers when they were shown on the TV show, *Axel and his Dog,* also known as *Axel and His Tree House.* The show ran on WCCO's Channel 4 from 1954 to 1964.

In 1986 Gordon began to attend the Little Rascals' reunions and taking pleasure once again in his Porky identity. He signed autographs at various film festivals around the country and often appeared in the company of Dorothy "Echo" DeBorba and/or Tommy "Butch" Bond.

Speaking of the era when his film-days were over, Gordon once remarked, "The MGM limousine stops coming to your house, and you wonder why the world has ceased loving you so suddenly at age seven."

"My memories are not of the movies, per se," Gordon said. "My memories are of going to get ice cream at the Our Gang Inn, of the lumber yard where everything was made of balsa wood, of wandering around the studio grounds. It was a fair, a circus. It was all play to me, all play. That was the magic of this man, Hal Roach. I didn't know I was making movies; I didn't know that."

Gordon remembered, however, the treadmill ride through the haunted house in **Hide and Shriek** (1938). Halfway through, Buckwheat and he were truly scared to death because no one had prepared them for this scene. Half-kiddingly, Gordon says, "I'm still terrified when I see the film now." He also remembered "tactile and olfactory memories of the men in the bear suits in **Bear Facts** (1938) chasing Alfalfa and the "Gang" members. Buckwheat had to be specially coaxed to do the scene because he was so scared. He also remembered wandering onto the set of **Topper** (1935) because the set involved a smashed-up car. This was a Roach feature with Cary Grant.

Tallness put an end to Gordon's acting career as a six-year-old child, and he eventually reached a height of 6' 4". Even in retirement Gordon had a dark beard and a full head of dark brown hair. He had a company called Otay Products for licensed merchandising. Though he was a trained teacher and had no speech impediment whatsoever, he always said "otay."

Kelly Lynch

Born 31 January, 1959,
Minneapolis, MN.

The theater bug bit Kelly Lynch at a most favorable place—the Guthrie Theater, where she was an apprentice director while in school. After that Guthrie "bite" Kelly studied acting with Sanford Meisner and became a model for the famous Elite Modeling Agency.

Kelly's father Robert is a restaurateur and her mother is a dancer. What other work has Kelly done? Would you believe that she was once an airline hostess? Eventually she got a small part in a film, **Portfolio** (1983), through her employer, Elite Modeling. Her second film was a big step up—the title role in **Osa** (1985).

The next year Kelly gave birth to a daughter, Shane, and for the next two years she devoted herself to giving the baby a proper, healthy beginning in life. In 1988 she returned to films in a big way, appearing in **Bright Lights, Big City** and **Cocktail**. The first stars Michael J. Fox and the second, Tom Cruise. She made three films in 1989: **Warm Summer Rain**, **Road House**, (her first starring role) and **Drugstore Cowboy**. She gained acclaim for his performance in this film, and was nominated for an Independent Spirit Award as best female lead.

Six films and five years later, Kelly was once again nominated for that award for her portrayal of Roberta Bean in **The Beans of Egypt**,

Maine (1994). By this time she had been married to screenwriter Mitch Glazer for two years. Other films of the period include *Curly Sue* (1991), *Three of Hearts* (1993), *Imaginary Crimes* (1994), *Virtuousity* (1995), *White Man's Burden* (1995), *Heaven's Prisoners* (1996), *Cold around the Heart* (1997), *Mr. Magoo* (1997), and *Homegrown* (1998).

Kelly co-starred with Tim Allen in *Joe Somebody* (2001), a film that was shot in Minnesota, featuring Minnesota's Jim Cada and other local actors. She was also in *Charlie's Angels* (2000) and *The Slaughter Rule* (2003). She is busy but selective—sometimes too selective, perhaps. She turned down the Sharon Stone role in *Basic Instinct*.

Kelly has also done four made-for-TV movies: *For Better or for Worse* (1993), *Persons Unknown* (1996), *Brotherhood of Murder* (1999), and *Homeless to Harvard* (2003). She has also made TV appearances on *Miami Vice, Ally McBeal, The Equalizer,* and *Spenser for Hire.*

Kelly is loyal to her Minnesota roots and returns from time to time to important local film events, such as the banquet for Hollywood producer Sarah Pillsbury sponsored by the Minnesota Film Board and several corporate groups.

Mary MacLane

Born 2 May, 1881,
Winnipeg, Manitoba.
Died 6 August, 1929,
Chicago, IL.

Mary became a Minnesotan for a while. Coming down from Winnipeg, the MacLanes (also McLane) lived from 1885 to 1889 in Fergus Falls, Minnesota. As a young woman Mary moved to Chicago and led a wild life there. She later wrote about her libertine activities in an autobiography, *The Story of Mary MacLane—Men Who Have Made Love to Me* (1901). It was an absolute shocker for the times. It was made into a movie in 1917, and Mary herself enjoyed a huge notoriety from this and two other similarly racy books.

For the last four years of her life, however, Mary lived in a dingy room at the Michigan Hotel in Chicago. She died there, alone, at the tender age of forty-eight. She hadn't left her room for several days before her death, but she had arranged all the clippings and photographs of her earlier prosperous days on her bureau as if for a final inspection. She stated in her will that she wished to be buried in Fergus Falls, but the straight-laced dignitaries of the city refused, due to her less-than-wholesome reputation.

(Mary's sister offered a different version of her death, reporting that it came from being tubercular and having an abdominal tumor. The sister-in-law also said that Mary had been employed by a Chicago advertising firm and that on her last days the girls from the office visited her).

Mary was the third of four children of James and Margaret MacLane. Mary had an older brother, John James, a sister, Dorothy Margaret, and a younger brother, James Whitby. Her father was a Highland Scot who had had some success in the California Gold Rush thirty years earlier. In Winnipeg he had a good government job which enabled the family to live in a large house with servants. James had also done piloting of river flatboats and Fergus Falls was on the river route to carry goods to Fort Garry. In 1885 James took the family to Fergus Falls and four years later he died there. At that point his widow took the four children and moved to Butte, Montana.

Mary began primary school in Fergus Falls and finished high school in Butte, where she distinguished herself as the editor-in-chief of the school paper. She read in her spare time and went for long walks with two special friends. Otherwise, she was considered a loner. In her senior year she developed a "crush" on Miss Corbin, her English teacher. Miss Corbin left Butte for further study and later became a professor at the University of Montana at Missoula.

The family had no money for college tuition, so after she graduated from high school Mary immersed herself more than ever in reading. She also began to write. In the course of her reading she came across a lurid journal by the Russian artist Marie Bashkirtseff, which described the woman's amorous adventures from age twelve until her early death at twenty-three. In the preface Bashkirtseff describes her fear of dying in obscurity, and states, "If I should not live long enough to win renown, this journal will interest the psychologists; ...the life of a woman traced day by day, without affectation as if no one in the world should ever read it, and yet at the same time intended to be read; for I am convinced that I shall be found sympathetic—and I tell everything, everything, everything."

Mary was inspired by this tell-all journal and she had similar cravings to live an exciting and amorous life. She took to writing a journal of her own during a three month period in 1901, and she sent the book off to Herbert S. Stone & Co., a Chicago publishing house. Unlike thousands of other writers who must wait for months to learn if their manuscript will be accepted, she heard one week later from her assigned editor, Lucy Monroe, that it would be published in a week.

The Story of Mary MacLane by Herself took the nation by storm and sold 80,000 copies in the first month!! Mary herself earned $17,000 in royalties. Her original title had been *I Await the Devil's Coming*, and she describes herself in the book as without conscience and without virtue. She admitted that there was no vile deed that she would not do to obtain happiness. H. L. Mencken said that he knew no other woman writer who played upon words more magically. Novelist Hamlin Garland was equally enthusiastic. Yet other critics found it a deplorable book and suggested that Mary be soundly spanked. The book made waves from Butte to New York. Butte townspeople were stung by the book's rebuke of them as "dry and warped." Montana libraries would not stock the book and its newspapers denounced it as "inimical to public morality."

With this "storming" success, Mary played the gamut of relationships with other Montanans. She could be as "modest, ladylike, and sensible in manner as any young lady in Butte" while others received the sharp sting of her caustic tongue. She criticized a young lawyer for his loud socks; she told a woman that she looked like a pig and must therefore eat with her feet in a trough. In short, she aroused sensation, controversy, and even some imitation. One Mary MacLane Society consisted of nine sixteen-year-old girls. A young woman from Kalamazoo, Michigan, ate a feast of candy, cakes, and fatal arsenic as she writhed nude on her bed clutching a copy of Mary's book. A few other women died in other bizarre ways all suffering from "MacLaneism." On July 5, 1902, Mary boarded the train for Chicago and left Butte for all time—or so she thought.

In time Mary made peace with Butte, and in the course of her travels she came to the conclusion that the wider world was actually less interesting than Butte had been.

Her second book, *My Friend Annabel Lee*, came out in July of 1903. It had few of the scandalous passages than had made her first so controversial. She merely reflected on Butte and her high school days. There were no profanities, no references to her "kind devil" and no outrageous opinions. Mary had become sane and even conservative in the two years that had elapsed since her first book. This book, too, had several editions but was less of a raging success than the first had been.

Her third and final book appeared in April of 1917. It purported to be a true story of Mary's thoughts and feelings that previously had been "too radical for publication." It exposed the agonized soul-searching of a mature woman who professed a deep desire to bear children yet generally loathed men and admitted to "the subtle guilt of a lesbian tendency."

Mary had resettled in Butte in 1910. After her third book appeared she left for Chicago again. It was there, in the summer of 1917, that she filmed *The Men Who Have Made Love to Me,* both writing the script and playing the heroine.

The story involved six "affairs of the heart." The first is with a callow youth, next a literary man, then a baronet's younger brother, followed by a bank clerk and, finally, the husband of another. Plus one unnamed. These were drawn from Mary's personal experiences.

MacLane wrote an article, "The Movies and Me" for *Photoplay Magazine* in which she explained that movies had for many years provided a pleasurable escape. "I have paid fifteen cents on several thousand afternoons in the far wilds of my native Butte in order to translate me from the somber colors of myself to the passionate prisms of life as presented by various directors." She expressed the belief that there was more sheer beauty to be found in movies than any other form of popular expression. She was confident that she would soon become a movie star. "I had thought that it required a devilish lot of energy and pep and punch and stunningness to become one of those things [a film star]. But not so. It requires languor and clothes and ease and loads of astonishingly yellow make-up. And a kindofa sortofa vampish way with men."

Yet Mary made only one film, and although it generated lots of controversy, it was generally panned. One critic described Mary's performance as "expressionless, unmannerly, and uninteresting," and the subtitles she had provided were widely thought to be laughable. For example: "God has made many things less plausible than me. He has made the sharks in the ocean and people who hire children to work in their mills and mines, and poison ivy and zebras."

Many years after her death, Mary MacLane's body was returned to Minnesota to be reburied next to her father in Fergus Falls.

Grace McDonald

Born 15 June 1918,
Boston, MA.
Died 30 October 1999,
Scottsdale, AZ.

G race and her no-less-talented brother Ray admired Fred and Adele Astaire so much that they developed a brother-sister, song-'n-dance act, too. Their specialty was tap-dancing while singing. They joined the vaudeville circuit when in their late teens. They made it to Broadway in the hit musical, *Babes in Arms,* and they stole part of the show with their version of "I Wish I Were in Love Again." The success of this show gave them their ticket to Hollywood. (Incidentally, **Babes in Arms** was later turned into a popular film starring Mickey Rooney and that great gal from Grand Rapids, Judy Garland.)

The brother-sister act eventually broke up because Ray was picked up by MGM Studios and Grace by Paramount. Grace's first significant film appearance was in *Dancing on a Dime* (1940) but it didn't make a real splash so she did nothing for two years. At that point Universal Studios signed her up and she appeared in twenty-one movies.

Grace had a pert, sweet-faced look and knew how to swing, and what's more, she could convey that magic to the viewing public. She was energetic and led the way in hep and pep through all those morale-boosting "B" movies during World War II. Five of her movies cast her with the Minneapolis-born Andrews Sisters, namely in *What's Cookin'?* (1942), *Give Out, Sisters* (1942), *How's About It* (1943), *Always a Bridesmaid* (1943), and *Follow the Boys* (1944), which had an all-star cast that also included George Raft and W.C. Fields.

Grace also appeared in non-musical shows during those years. For example, she was in Abbott and Costello's comedy *It Ain't Hay* (1943), and the dramas *Murder in the Blue Room* (1944) and *Destiny* (1944). She appeared in *See My Lawyer* (1945) and also in the comedy-mystery *Crazy House* (1943). Both films featured the comic team of Olsen and Johnson. In *Mug Town* (1943) Grace mixes it up with The Bowery Boys. She co-starred with Randolph Scott in *Gung Ho* (1943), a "flag waver" for Marines in the Pacific. One delightful surprise is *Flesh and Fantasy* (1943) a remake of *Tales of Manhattan* starring writer Robert Benchley, Edward G. Robinson, Barbara Stanwyck, Charles Boyer, Thomas Mitchell, and Robert Cummings.

After making the light comedy, *Honeymoon Ahead* (1945), Grace met a Marine from Minnesota, fell in love, retired from movies, and never looked back. The couple moved to Minnesota after his discharge, though in later years they lived in Scottsdale, Arizona in the winters, only returning to Minnesota from May through October. Grace died of pneumonia at the age of eighty-one.

Of local note, Grace became friends with *Minneapolis Star* columnist Barbara Flanagan and film archivist Bob DeFlores, and they dined together occasionally.

June Marlowe

(Gisela Valaria Goetten)
Born 6 November, 1903,
St. Cloud, MN.
Died 10 March, 1984,
Burbank, CA.

This St. Cloud native is especially notable as the beautiful Miss Crabtree in the *Our Gang* comedies that she appeared in from 1930 to 1932. Considered in retrospect, it was her golden era, though she wouldn't have believed it at the time. By that time she had already done a good deal of distinguished work, appearing in Laurel & Hardy's first feature-length film, **Pardon Us** (1931) and in twenty-eight silent movies, the most notable of which was **Don Juan** (1926) which starred John Barrymore, Mary Astor, and Myrna Loy. June also launched the highly successful Rin Tin Tin series in the 1920s.

June was the oldest of five children born to John P. Goetten and Hedwig "Hattie" Himsl. She attended St. Mary's Parochial School with her siblings Louis, Armor, Alona, and Gerald, though only Gisela and Louis graduated before the family moved away about 1919. Gisela also attended St. Cloud Technical High School for one year. Later her brother Louis reminisced, "It seemed everyone skated in those days but none of us were experts. At the time we lived at 503 Seventh Avenue South. We walked down Fifth Avenue to Lake George and in the winter, conditions permitting, we'd skate to St. Mary's…. Dad owned a cottage on Big Spunk Lake near Avon and the family spent every summer there. One day we decided to have a zoo in the garage. We caught snakes, mud turtles, gophers. We had a rabbit and even our Pointer, Trix, became a spotted leopard. He served patiently. After the show, the animals were released in good shape and we had a few pennies to buy candy at Schmidt's store in Avon."

John Goetten ran the family meat market shop on Fifth Avenue near First Street in St. Cloud. His pioneer father, Peter, had started it in 1865. Gisela's mother, Hattie, was born near Vienna, Austria; her brother, J. B. Himsl, became a judge in St. Cloud. Hattie's father, Alois Himsl, born in 1838 in the Upper Alps, came to the United States in 1883. Hattie was one of nine children.

In 1904 John Goetten and his brother Andrew bought their father out of the butcher shop but for health reasons John's family moved to

Minneapolis and he left the business to Andrew and a nephew, Allison (Buster), who continued the market along St. Germain St. While living in St. Cloud, John was a member of the Elks Club and the Knights of Columbus.

Louis continues his recollections of their childhood, "Gisela decided we needed a newspaper, *The Avon Gazette*. She printed it by hand and did a masterful job. The paper gave all the important news such as the birth of Dreher's new calf and Judge J. B. Himsl's visit in a brand new Model T Ford. Gisela and all of us children were fascinated with the old Avon Cemetery. Also, the best strawberries grew there."

In St. Cloud the Goetten children often visited a business on Fifth across from the Goetten Meat Market. A certain Mr. Saunders had a bicycle shop there with a theater upstairs called The Idle Hour. Here, on a hand projector, June saw her first motion picture: a short, all-color, animated cartoon. The children had wonderful memories and June had especially fond ones for the Benedictine Sisters who taught her at St. Mary's.

Shortly after June started Cathedral High School in 1919, the Goettens moved to 2715 Bryant Avenue South in Minneapolis. June went to West High School in her sophomore year, though a year later the family moved to Los Angeles and June graduated from Hollywood High in 1922, intent on a career in art. In L. A. the Goettens moved next to another St. Cloud family, the Henry Puff family, who helped the Goettens find a house.

June's film odyssey began with a successful screen test given by Malcolm St. Clair, a newspaperman-turned-director. He had seen her in the leading role in *My Ideal* at Hollywood High. She appeared in two-reel comedies first with Harry Langdon and Lloyd Hamilton and in a series directed by St. Clair himself called *Fighting Blood* (1923). Screenwriter Harry Carr saw this series and told Sol Lesser, a producer with First National (which was under the umbrella of Warner Brothers), that she would be right for his up-coming movie, *When a Man's a Man*. It was Lesser who gave Gisela Goetten the name June Marlowe.

Carr also convinced Jack Warner sign June to a five-year contract with Warners, and he almost immediately cast her in the Rin Tin Tin series opener *Find Your Man* (1924). She worked with Warners from 1924 to 1927, with Universal from 1927 to 1930, and with the Hal Roach Studios from 1930 to 1932.

The Rin Tin Tin series did much to keep Warner Brothers Studio solvent in the mid-1920s. Darryl Zanuck himself produced and wrote the scripts. June loved animals and being outdoors, so the stories and filming locations suited her perfectly. The titles of the films suggest something of their flavor: *Find Your Man* (1924), *Below the Line* (1925), *Clash of the Wolves* (1925), *Tracked in the Snow Country* (1925), *Night Cry* (1926), and *Fangs of Justice* (1926).

June's first feature-length film with Warners, *When a Man's a Man* (1924), was shot in Prescott, Arizona, and it gave her a chance to show off her fine horsemanship. She played in support of Irene Rich in several melodramas including an adaptation of Willa Cather's novel *A Lost Lady* (1924). Other films for Warners include *The Man without a Conscience* (1925), *The Wife Who Wasn't Wanted* (1926) and *The Pleasure Buyers* (1925), *The Tenth Woman* (1925), and *The Fourth Commandment* (1926).

When it was discovered that Marlowe could write and speak fluent German, she was put to work translating scripts. She was also in several Spanish-dubbed films. In 1929 she traveled to Germany to appear in two German films—*The Glass House* (a highly successful film) and *Through the Brandenburg Gate*. These films were directed by William Dieterle, who later immigrated to Hollywood to direct films. Dieterle worked on two films for Minneapolis producer and movie house owner W. R. Frank, including the highly regarded (and very profitable) *All That Money Can Buy* (1941).

On her trip to Germany June was accompanied by her mother who wanted to see again her 200-room ancestral home, the Castle von Altendorf. June was interviewed on German radio and won over the listening audience with her flawless German. They toured all of Eastern Europe after filming ended and even dined with King Boris of Bulgaria in Prague. On their return to the United Stated, they stopped for a week in St. Cloud where they were the guests of honor at the June Marlowe Film Festival which featured *On the Stroke of Twelve* (1927) at the Sherman (Paramount Theater). *Don Juan* was also screened at the Sherman upon its release in 1926, with audio by the New York Philharmonic. This was the first full-length movie with a synchronized sound track—released a year before *The Jazz Singer* (1927).

On May 2nd, 1929, June appeared on the stage of the Sherman Theater to talk to her many friends and acquaintances from the area. She wore a Le Long costume of the patternneck chiffon from Fandel's store. Later in the day she visited the mayor, James H. Murphy, and other officials at City Hall. She also visited the St. Cloud Orphans Home, the St. Cloud Hospital, and other fondly-remembered people and places.

Though June had been in movies since 1923, she gained some extra publicity and a big boost for her career when she was selected as one of thirteen "Wampus Baby Stars of 1925." She was twenty-two and had already done some ten pictures, seven of which were released in 1925, her Wampus year. Other Wampus Stars were Joan Crawford, Mary Astor, Clara Bow, Janet Gaynor, Faye Wray and Jobyna Ralston who married St. Paulite Richard Arlen. All "Wampus Baby Stars" were chosen by the Western Association of Motion Picture Advertizers.

In a national camera club contest to select the most beautifully photographed woman, she was picked from more than 14,000 entries. She was especially known for her dark brown curly hair and very expressive dark brown eyes.

June continued her career with a series of popular Our Gang films, in which she plays the teacher, Miss Crabtree. The first one, *Teacher's Pet* (1930) opens with the Little Rascals waiting glumly for the arrival of the new teacher with a sour name. When the teacher arrives, they find her to be very sweet, however, and after the shock wears off they scramble to get on her good side.

School's Out (1930), *Love Business* (1931), *Little Daddy* (1931), *Shiver My Timbers* (1931), and *Readin' and Writin'* (1932) followed in rapid succession. Radiantly beautiful, sweet, patient, very understanding of kids' pranks, and very forgiving, June educates the Rascals with good morals and everyone lives happily ever after—the way it's supposed to.

June essentially retired from movie-making after her marriage to Rodney Sprigg on July 2, 1932. The couple were happily married for fifty years. They lived on a large ranch near the Lakeside Country Club near San Diego where Rodney golfed or played cards with John Wayne, Bing Crosby, George O'Brien, and Guy Kibbee while also making arrangements to move or store their worldly goods.

June enjoyed gardening, animals, travel and charities. June wrote a couple of children's stories in the 1960s: *Beesy* and *Furry*. Rodney died in 1982. Her younger brother, Louis, also adopted the name Marlowe and he became a director from 1935 to 1969 of television series and industrial films. All her siblings worked at least for a while in movies.

June had a way with children, though she had none of her own. Early Rascal, Jackie Cooper, said of her, "I had a big crush on her and I adored her. She was a lovely lady—lovely, warm, nice lady." Dorothy DeBorba ("Echo") said, "June Marlowe, now there was a lady. She was such a very kind, sincere person. We were never treated like children by her. She was so sweet."

Sixty years later her producer, Hal Roach, said, "No question that part was suited to her. She was not a great actress; you just liked her, and that was enough. Everyone liked her.... We got fan mail addressed to 'Miss Crabtree' as long as the studio was open."

June's high school class prophecy came true. She had announced "I will become a motion picture actress." And, she did. And she just as easily gave it all up and retired after a busy decade of picture-making.

E. G. Marshall

Born 18 June, 1910,
Owatonna, MN.
Died 24 August, 1998,
Bedford, NY.

W oody Allen so admired the quality of Marshall's acting that he just had to have him in his movie, *Interiors* (1978), where Marshall plays a wealthy, restless patriarch who leaves his wife for a younger woman, thus adding a wrinkle to the severe yet fatherly character he had played for many years on the TV series *The Defenders.*

E.G.'s father, Charles L. H. Grunz, and his mother, Hazel Irene Cobb, were both of Norwegian descent. Charles worked for the telephone company in Owatonna. "Eej" was the oldest of four boys. Over the years he stayed close to his next younger brother, Louis Grunz (later Marshall) who was born in 1914. Gerald was born in 1916 and Joseph in 1918. Some records show the name Grenz instead of Grunz but Louis amended the records to show Marshall as the family name.

Eej remained secretive about his first two initials. He was known on occasion as Everett Gillespie Marshall or Eugene Grunz Marshall. Like Judy Garland's real name of Gumm, Grunz didn't have much of a ring to it.

Marshall attended Carleton College in Northfield, Minnesota—"the Harvard of the Upper Midwest"—from 1928 to 1930 but graduated from the University of Minnesota in 1932. During his two years in Minneapolis Marshall worked at a couple radio stations before moving to Chicago to work in a bigger radio market.

He joined The Oxford Players in 1933 and toured with them for three years "playing Guildenstern and all the really terrible parts," as he later put it. He was Roebuck in George Bernard Shaw's *Man and*

Superman at the Center Stage Theatre in Baltimore, Maryland, his true stage debut. For two more years he acted his way to Broadway joining the Federal Theater Project for his debut in *Prologue to Glory* at the Ritz Theatre in 1938 followed by *The Big Blow* also at the Ritz in 1938.

E.G. was a founding member of the Actor's Studio (known for teaching "method" acting), saying in a 1978 interview, "I try to think what the character is thinking. Then, hopefully, I begin to feel it. I act and react not because I'm recalling a dog killed by a fire engine, but because I'm concentrating on what the character is going through." But Marshall denied using any specific acting method, saying, "I use anything that helps me." Marshall is articulate and witty. He has sharp features, intense eyes,, and a firm, confident voice that's fits his image and is easily identifiable in "voice over" narrations.

Marshall was very busy acting on stage in the 1930s and 40s. He appeared in the original cast of *The Skin of Our Teeth* as Mr. Franklin at the Plymouth Theatre in 1942. This play earned Thornton Wilder his third Pulitzer Prize in three decades. He played Gramp Maple in a re-staging of *The Petrified Forest* at the New Amsterdam Theatre in 1943; he played the Brigadier in *Jacobowsky and the Colonel* at the Martin Beck Theatre in 1944; and he played Willie Oban in the re-staging of Eugene O'Neill's *The Iceman Cometh* in 1946 also at the Martin Beck.

E. G. went back to the airwaves when the Theatre Guild on the Air staged *Iceman* in 1946. His old love of radio returned and he also became host of the long-running radio series, *The CBS Radio Mystery Theater*. Yet he began to appear occasionally in films. For example, he has small parts in *13 Rue Madeleine* (1946) and a detective thriller *Call Northside 777* (1948) starring Jimmy Stewart. His actual film debut was as a morgue attendant in *The House on 92nd Street* (1945).

Among other theater appearances a few stand out. He was in the original cast of Arthur Miller's *The Crucible* in 1953 as Reverend John Hale, and he was also in the original cast of *Waiting for Godot* in 1956, as Vladimir. He later remarked that *Godot* was "a real theater piece—not something that has to be molded and hacked to fit in a theater."

Marshall's film career took flight in 1954 with four notable appearances—*The Caine Mutiny, Pushover, Broken Lance,* and *The Silver Chalice,* which starred a young Paul Newman. The next year he was featured as a doctor in *The Left Hand of God* starring Humphrey Bogart.

Eej did two outstanding performances in 1957. He was Juror Number Four in *Twelve Angry Men* starring Henry Fonda with a very strong cast, and *The Bachelor Party*, in which he plays an aging, hypochondriacal bookkeeper at a colleague's wedding send-off who begins to reveal his most personal tribulations as he falls deeper and deeper into drunkenness. One critic described the film as a "brilliantly observed social study of New York life at its least attractive, and the acting matches the incisiveness of the script."

Meanwhile, between 1949 and 1960 Marshall also managed to appear in over one hundred live television productions.

Marshall is best known, however, for his portrayal of Lawrence Preston on *The Defenders*, which aired from 1961 to 1965. This show is a rare example of social consciousness and mainstream popularity. E. G. took a course in jurisprudence and pressed to add the character of a black judge to the series. A 1962 episode had him defending an abortionist. CBS broadcast that episode despite protests by viewers and cancellations by sponsors. Another still hot topic the show dealt with was blacklisting. He earned Emmy Awards for outstanding continued performance by a lead actor in a series in 1962 and 1963 for *The Defenders*.

Marshall, a liberal Democrat, liked the show so much that he tried for the rest of his life to re-mount it, and age 87 he finally succeeded with the show *Payback* and a new series, *Defenders: Choices of Evils* (1998). In this show he sits at the head of three generations of family lawyers. Beau Bridges plays his son.

A second series he had great success with was *The New Doctors* (1969-1973). This show featured medical issues such as the use of narcotics the way *The Defenders* tackled social justice issues. The umbrella title for four series is *The Bold Ones*.

E. G. had received his professional training in regional theaters, and he continued to appear in roles too numerous to list. He once remarked, "Away from Broadway you have so much respect for serious theater; on Broadway they want jokes and songs and razzmatazz, and a serious actor can die a terrible death." Marshall also praised early "live" television for taking chances, whereas he deplored to tendency of later TV producers to resort to sitcoms and police shows. Some producers of this later period wanted Marshall to portray "establishment daddies" though he vigorously refused to do so. He defined himself as a "utility actor" who "fit in easily."

As a "utility actor" E. G. could move easily from stoic prosecutors in *Compulsion* (1959) and *Town without Pity* (1961) to very humane authority figures like President Harry Truman in *Collision Course* (1976) and Dwight D. Eisenhower in *Ike* (1986). He was less as John Mitchell in *Nixon* (1995) but Mitchell himself wasn't popular either.

His final films were Clint Eastwood's *Absolute Power* (1997), **Billy Jack Goes to Washington** (1977), and **Superman II** (1980).

Everett G. Marshall married Helen Wolf on April 26, 1939, his second marriage. They divorced in 1953; they had two daughters, Degen (Sayer) and Jill. He married a third time to Judith Coy and they also had two children; she was his surviving widow.

Ralph Meeker

(Ralph Rathgeber)
Born 21 November, 1920,
Minneapolis, MN.
Died 5 August, 1988,
Woodland Hills, CA.

Ralph R. Rathgeber was a humble electrician living at 1311 15th Avenue North when his wife, Magnhild Senovia Haavig Meeker, gave birth to the future Ralph Meeker. The family moved to Chicago in 1923, and Ralph eventually grew to be a rough, tough and handsome fellow. He attended the Leelanau School for Boys in Glen Harbor, Michigan, graduated in 1938, and attended Northwestern University, where he majored in music composition and business administration.

Meeker acted in several school plays from his freshman year onward. "The dean thought it was very impractical to be an actor," Ralph recalled in the 1950s, "and painted the blackest picture of the theatrical profession. He pointed at all the other actors who had gone from Northwestern to Broadway and had been failures. He did exactly the right thing."

Ralph enlisted in the U. S. Navy without graduating from Northwestern, was injured on a training cruise, and was discharged. At that point he joined a touring cast of *Doughgirls* (1943) in a walk-on part. He later said he was hired "because he fit the costume." The show toured for nine months. Meeker then joined the cast of *Ten Little Indians,* which made a USO tour of Italy until the end of the War.

After the war Ralph moved to New York City, and while he hunted for acting jobs he worked as a soda jerk at the Whelan Drugstore across from the Roxy Theatre. (The name, Roxy, by the way, comes from S. L. Rothafel from Stillwater, MN., a theater producer and builder of lavish movie houses.)

He eventually made his Broadway debut in Jose Ferrer's *Cyrano de Bergerac* in 1947, and followed Ferrer into his next play, *Strange Fruit*, before taking a small part in the original cast of *Mister Roberts* in 1948. He dropped out a year later when the opportunity arose to replace Marlon Brando as Stanley Kowalski in *Streetcar Named Desire*. He later went on tour with *Streetcar*.

After the tour Ralph made his movie debut in the film, *Teresa* (1951) starring John Ericson and Pier Angeli. He appeared with Viveca Lindfors in *Four in a Jeep* (1951). The movie bug bit him as he plunged into six movies that were released in 1952 and 1953: *Glory Alley, Shadow in the Sky, Somebody Loves Me, Naked Spur, Jeopardy, Code Two.*

In 1954 Meeker landed the starring role in the Pulitzer Prize-winning play *Picnic*. He plays Hal Carter, a bragging vagrant with a large, lanky body, a loud mouth, and a nasty past who mesmerizes five women in a small Kansas town. For his strong performance Ralph won the New York Critics Circle Award in 1954.

MGM wanted him to do *Picnic* on film but he refused the offer. Instead, he starred with Broderick Crawford and Lon Chaney in *Big House, U.S.A.* (1955) and played detective Mike Hammer in *Kiss Me Deadly* (1955). This classic *film noir* directed by Robert Aldrich still plays well today. Meeker went on to play in support of Kirk Douglas in Stanley Kubrick's *Paths of Glory* (1957).

Meeker appeared on many early TV programs, including *Goodyear Television Playhouse, Alfred Hitchcock Presents, Route 66, The Defenders, Wagon Train,* and many others.

His theater credits are no less diverse. In 1961 he took over the role created by Eli Wallach in Eugene Ionesco's *Rhinoceros* and he joined Elia Kazan and Robert Whitehead in 1963-64 at the Lincoln Center Repertory Theater as they staged Arthur Miller's *After the Fall*. Meeker was in the original cast.

Other notable films are *Something Wild* (1962), *The Dirty Dozen* (1962), *The St. Valentine's Day Massacre* (1967), *Gentle Giant* (1968), *The Detective* (1968), *I Walk the Line* (1970), *The Anderson Tapes* (1971), and *Brannigan* (1975).

Though often cast as a policeman or military officer, near the end of his career Ralph made a few science fiction films such as *The Food of the Gods* (1976), and *Without Warning* (1980). He eventually retired to his ranch in Sun Valley, Idaho, which had formerly been owned by Cecil B. De Mille.

Summing up his career, critic Leonard Maltin remarked: "…this dour, sluggish actor didn't have what it took to be a movie star. He was a solid supporting player whose delineation of blustery, cowardly characters revealed a more prodigious talent than was suggested in his infrequent starring turns."

Breckin Meyer

*Born 7 May 1974,
Minneapolis, MN.*

Being born in Minneapolis did little to help Breckin gain a foothold in movieland, but going to Beverly Hills High School with Drew Barrymore, Alicia Silverstone, Johnny Whitworth, Josh Miller, and Brandon Williams did a lot. Maybe what really paid off for him was giving Drew her first kiss when she was ten and he was eleven. (Drew reports this in her teen biography, *Little Girl Lost*.) Drew introduced Breckin to her agent who brought him into commercials and the game show, *Child's Play*. Though he had originally planned to become a kindergarten teacher, Breckin enjoyed the work and turned to the entertainment industry for a career.

Among his half-dozen notable guest appearances on TV are *The Wonder Years, L.A. Law, Clueless, Party of Five, The Tonight Show with Jay Leno* and *Coupling*.

Films where Breckin is featured include *Freddy's Dead: The Final Nightmare* (1991), *The Craft* (1996), *Prefontaine* (1997), *Touch* (1997), *54* (1998), and *Kate and Leopold* (2001). Breckin also appeared in *Clueless* (1995) starring his high school buddy, Alicia Silverstone; *Escape from L. A.* (1996), *The Insider* (1999), and *Road Trip* (2000). He provided the voice for the American version of Roberto Benigni's production *Pinocchio* (2002) and starred in *Garfield* (2004, as Jon Arbuckle).

Breckin was dating Deborah Kaplan until they finally tied the marriage knot on October 14, 2001. She is a writer primarily and wrote and directed "A Very Brady Sequel." She wrote (and met Breckin in) and directed *Can't Hardly Wait* (1998). She also co-wrote *Homeward Bound: Lost in San Francisco* (1996) and the Minnesota-made film *Jingle All the Way* (1996), starring Arnold Schwarzenegger.

Clayton Moore

(Jack Carlton Moore)
Born 14 September 1914,
Chicago, IL.
Died 28 December 1999,
Los Angeles, CA.

The Lone Ranger was an "adopted Minnesotan" and we are grateful for it. Why? During the three years he lived here he once stopped a bank robbery at the Fourth Northwestern National Bank on the West Bank of the University of Minnesota. On another occasion he arrived a moment too late at a supermarket robbery, but was able to untie the store manager, telling him that he had just been rescued by the Lone Ranger.

Moore moved here in 1963 to join his sister and brother-in-law. During his stay he called his business at 4042 Bryant Avenue North Ranger Real Estate. Moore was no stranger to the Twin Cities, however, since General Mills had sponsored both the radio and TV "Lone Ranger" shows.

Jack Carlton Moore grew up on the South Side of Chicago as the son of a real estate broker. On Saturday afternoons he would go to the Devon Theater to watch the serials. Moore, said in his autobiography, *I Was That Masked Man* (1996) that, "I would give anything to be up there on the screen with Ken Maynard, Tom Mix, George O'Brien, William S. Hart, Harry Carey, Sr., so many wonderful cowboy heroes. Whenever anyone asked me what I wanted to be when I grew up, I said either, 'I want to be a policeman,' or 'I want to be a cowboy.'" In playing the Lone Ranger he was both.

Our future hero set out on a career in show business with a trapeze act at the Century of Progress exposition in Chicago (The World's Fair) in 1934. Moore rose through the ranks to aerialist with two different circuses. A few years later he took up a less dangerous profession—working for modeling agencies in Chicago and New York. By this time he was six feet tall, had broad shoulders, had a definite sense of presence, and was handsome besides. In 1937 he went to Hollywood and made his film debut in *Thunder Trail*. Moore also worked as a stuntman. In 1940 he changed his first name at the suggestion of producer Eddie Small to Clayton.

Moore appeared in "B" movies and serials through 1942 and starred in *The Perils of Nyoka* (1942) after which he served in the

164

armed forces. After the war he resumed his cowboy supporting roles at Republic Studios. He was "Ashe" in a very popular serial called *The Crimson Ghost* (1946); then he starred as tough guy, Agent Ted O'Hara, in *G-Men Never Forget* (1948); he starred as Jesse in *Jesse James Rides Again* (1948). Then he co-starred with Minneapolis actress Noel Neill in the serial, *The Adventures of Frank and Jesse James* (1948), again as Jesse.

In 1949 Moore starred in a breakthrough serial, *The Ghost of Zorro*, in which he played the hero while wearing a mask. Detroit businessman-producer, George Washington Trendle, and Fran Stryker, the writer who had created the Ranger show on Detroit station WXYZ in 1933, spotted Moore in the Zorro mask and felt he was perfect for the television version of their hero. The hang-up was Clayton's voice, which was much higher than the sonorous radio voice of Brace Beemer, who had played The Lone Ranger since 1941 and would continue to do so until the show left the airwaves in 1954.

After much vocal training, Clayton was able to match Beemer's resonant voice and the series was off and running. It ran from September 1949 until 1952, when Moore was let go because of a salary dispute. John Hart proved to be less popular in the role, however, and Moore returned to star from 1954 to 1957. There were 169 episodes in all, plus three feature-length Lone Ranger films. In all these episodes Jay Silverheels, a Canadian-born Mohawk, played Tonto, the Lone Ranger's faithful Indian companion. *Kemo sabe*, regardless of the many jokes to the contrary, really does mean "trusty scout."

The filming took place in Utah, Califonia, and Arizona, though the show eventually pitched camp at the Hal Roach Studios. General Mills underwrote the costs, which averaged $12,500 for each of the first fifty-two episodes. Moore himself made only $500 per show, which brought on the salary dispute referred to above.

Clayton made three Ranger features, the two later ones in color: *The Legend of the Lone Ranger* (1952), *The Lone Ranger* (1956), and *The Lone Ranger and the Lost City of Gold* (1958).

Jock Mahoney, a cowboy colleague, said "You couldn't be a successful cowboy star then and not live an exemplary life." Clayton subscribed to the Lone Ranger's credo even after he cornered his last villain. "I will not let my fans down." To the end he reported that, like the Lone Ranger, he never smoked, used profanity, or drank in public. He added, "I think playing the role has made me a better person."

The Lone Ranger was known for his use of precise speech, without slang or dialect. He never shot to kill, and kept out of saloons. Scenes of gambling and drinking were played down.

"Youngsters need heroes today," explained Moore. "Sports figures are not enough. The kind of contact and identification people got from *The Lone Ranger* is missing. I'm for any show that fights for what is right and good. But unfortunately, we don't have very many left."

When the show originally appeared in 1949, the *New York Times* critic Jack Gould called it "just another Western, and not a notably good one at that." Thirty years later it was revered as no other Western show could be. In fact, in later life Moore made a decent living just doing personal appearances at state fairs, rodeos, shopping malls, the Texas Ranger baseball team promotions, and Western Reunions, with a few pizza roll commercials on the side. Moore also did more than 250 radio guest appearances between 1985 and his death in 1999. A court restraining order prohibiting him from wearing the Lone Ranger's mask in public also stirred public interest quite a bit.

Moore identified himself so strongly with the character he was playing that it almost became creepy. Talking about his beloved symbol, the black mask, he once said, "It's my symbol, it's the Lone Ranger, and if I may say, it's Americana. I guess when I go up to the big ranch in the sky, I'll still have it on." Yet he is the only person to have a star on the Hollywood Walk of Fame that includes both his name and the name of the character he was renowned for playing. Moore was inducted into the Stuntman's Hall of Fame in 1982 and the Hall of Great Western Performers of the National Cowboy and Western Heritage Museum in 1990. He also received the Western Heritage Award from the National Cowboy Hall of Fame.

Another Ranger Creed remark often given by Moore as his many personal appearances was, "God put the firewood there, but every man must gather and light it himself."

Noel Neill

Born 25 November, 1920,
Minneapolis, MN.

Yes, Lois Lane is from Minneapolis. Or the real-life actress who plays her is, at any rate. Her name is Noel Neill. Perhaps she plays a *Daily Planet* reporter with such aplomb because her father, David H. Neill, was an editor, a copy desk chief, and staff writer with the *Minneapolis Star* for many years. He had wanted his daughter to become a newspaper woman herself. In being Lois Lane Noel came pretty close. Nor was this just a passing escapade. Ten of Noel's ninety movies are Superman movies, and she was also involved in the TV series from 1953 to 1957.

But let's begin by looking at Noel Neill before she became Lois Lane. The Neill family lived at 4227 12th Avenue South on the edge of the Washburn District. David Neill was working for *Women's Wear Daily* but left that job to become an editor at the *Minneapolis Star*. Her mother had been a singer and dancer and under her influence Noel took tap-dancing lessons and also learned to play the banjo—while dancing. Her role model was Fern Dale who had mastered the same stunt. Noel was four when her lessons began and she performed at the "Kiddie Revues" (recitals) that were staged at the Orpheum Theatre on Hennepin Avenue.

She continued with "Kiddie Revues" through her Bryant Junior High School days. She performed a specialty dance during the presentation of "Purple Towers" at Bryant on April 19, 1934, as noted in the *Minneapolis Star*. By Christmas of 1936 she was performing at the Minneapolis-Moline Girls' Club party at the Minneapolis Armory; she wore a Spanish dress of many folds and pleats and a sombrero on her head. Earlier in 1936 she was part of a trio at Central High that did a vaudeville show with the "Comedy Concert" group. This had been a popular group going back to the days when Eddie Albert and Ann Sothern performed in the group in the mid-1920s. She again wore the Spanish outfit. Noel was the Market Week Queen on February 12, 1937, as she and her three ladies-in-waiting performed at the Curtis Hotel. Her other role models were The Andrews Sisters who became prominent while she was in junior high. All the signs point to her becoming a professional singer and dancer.

At Minneapolis Central Noel became a member of National Honor Society. Next to her class photo in the "Centralian" yearbook is this quote: "A dream of beauty, dazzling bright." She graduated a semester early, in January of 1938, which made it possible for her mother, LaVere, to take Noel to California to get a closer look at the show business world—and to get away from the cold.

LaVere Neill was a true "stage mom." She pushed Noel into accepting an offer to sing at the Turf Club in Del Mar, California, owned by Bing Crosby and his brother. Noel was seventeen at the time and her professional career was already underway. She became a band singer, a World War II pin-up model, and a contract actress with Paramount Pictures. She appeared in a few Henry Aldrich movies, *Here Come the Waves* (1944) with Bing Crosby, and *The Road to Utopia* (1944) with Bing and Bob Hope. She also became known as a "plucky cowgirl," playing in Lash LaRue westerns and opposite Clayton Moore in *The Adventures of Frank and Jesse James* (1948) and other "horse oprys."

Noel also appeared in Sam Katzman's Teenagers series for Monogram Studio. The core group of "teenagers" are Noel, Freddie Stewart, June Preiser, and Warren Mills. As a "teenager" Noel became well known as a sweater girl as well as a sparky 5' 2" redhead.

In 1948 Katzman asked Noel if she wanted to play Lois Lane in his upcoming serial of the Superman comics entitled *The Adventures of Superman*. The success of this serial prompted Sam to ask her to play Lois Lane again in the 1950 film *Atom Man vs. Superman*. Then came the television series in 1952. Noel tried out very confidently but lost out to Phyllis Coates, but Coates dropped out after the first season. Noel played Lois for the next four seasons. Actually, the whole cast was new in that second season, with body-builder actor George Reeves cast now as Superman, Jack Larson as Jimmy Olsen, and John Hamilton, a veteran stage actor, as Perry White, publisher of the *Daily Planet*.

In 1957 everything came to a halt in Gotham City, but the cast was asked to stand by for two years in case funding came through. The comic book writers wrote all the scripts, which saved the producers some money. Noel's naivete was credible and her trademark insouciance made her an appealing foil to Superman's calmness. Either Lois or Jimmy, who were always getting into scrapes, would say in each episode, "Gee, Superman, are we ever glad to see you!"

In the summer of 1957 Reeves formed and financed a musical group which toured state and county fairs. It was both a financial and emotional disappointment—only three people showed up for one performance at a North Carolina fair. One day in 1959 everyone was called and told to "Come back and see if your suit still fits." Reeves was upbeat about the new season and the directing he would do. However, he was found dead of a gunshot wound on June 16, 1959. His death was ruled a suicide though Neill and many of his close friends disagree. (The recent film *Hollywoodville* explores the situation in great detail.)

With Reeves' death the series ended. The next year Neill turned forty, and she thought her career was over. She was married and spent a lot of time playing volleyball on the Santa Monica beach.

After a while she took up public relations work at United Artists. Her residuals for the show, which weren't much to begin with, had run out, and she needed the money. In 1974 some nostalgia-minded college students found her, and she began making appearances at universities around the country talking about her experiences as Lois Lane.

In 1977 Noel was invited to play a cameo role as young Lois's mother in the new *Superman* (1978) series starring Christopher Reeve. It was Noel's eighty-ninth movie. In 2003 a biography of Neill came out, called *Truth, Justice and the American Way.* Jerry Seinfeld read it, and recruited her for an American Express commercial to be filmed in Death Valley.

Aside from her career as Superman's erstwhile girl-friend, Noel did appear in several distinguished movies. In one scene in *American in Paris* (1951), she describes paintings to Gene Kelly in a French accent so delightfully absurd that it's pure camp today. She also appeared in Cecil B. DeMille's *The Greatest Show on Earth* (1952) and *Gentlemen Prefer Blonds* (1953).

Nowadays she travels frequently to Southeast Asia but also appearance regularly at the annual Superman festival in Metropolis, Illinois, and other similar events. Noel has been married twice and divorced twice and she has no children. Her favorite travel destinations are Russia, China, Vietnam, Cambodia, and the Galapagos Islands. She gradually turned from competitive volleyball to golf and has outlasted most of her golfing buddies. She lives in a house she bought forty years ago in Santa Monica Canyon, but after living in California for sixty years, she still has a Minnesota twang.

Noel is proud of the fact that she inspired many working women in the 1950s because of her portrayal of Lois as a journalist in the two-piece suit.

Marian Nixon

(Lillian Maria Nixon)
Born 20 October 1901,
Superior, WI.
Died 13 February 1983,
Los Angeles, CA.

Marion Nixon was born in Superior, Wisconsin—the family lived at 216 Cass Avenue, which was changed later to Thirty-ninth Avenue East. She attended kindergarten in Allouez followed by two years in the Franklin Elementary School, plus a few months in the St. Francis Xavier Parochial School. On April 22, 1912, her family moved to 927 Russell Avenue North in Minneapolis, where Marian spent her later childhood and teen years. She attended Lincoln Elementary and North High School. Her father Fredrick had been a clerk in Superior but got a job as a carpenter at the Soo Line Railroad Shops. Why did they move? Perhaps to be near Marian's grandmother, who lived on Cedar Lake. The entire family often visited Lake Harriet, Lake Calhoun, Lake of the Isles, and Lake Minnetonka together.

By her own account Marion decided at age twelve to become a dancer. While going to North High she worked after school in a department store to earn money for her dance lessons. With the blessing of the dancing teacher, Mrs. Helen S. Noble, she embarked on a vaudeville tour at age fifteen with a troupe of barnstorming acrobats who eventually left her stranded in Los Angeles with $5 in her purse. Being rather short at five feet tall, she had trouble crashing the film studio gates. (A more plausible version, perhaps, has her leaving high school for the first time at seventeen and a half, in the company of her mother, to join an act that was going to the West Coast.)

Marion happened by the Mack Sennett studio one day when a young lady was needed to sit on a beach next to a live (and lively) lion. This was in 1922. Miss Nixon accepted the job and survived the terrors to become a Mack Sennett Bathing Beauty. She was also a Wampus Baby Star in 1924. She became a graduate of the Mack Sennett School where the company churned out two-a-day one-reel comedies.

A third story has Marion dropping out of high school halfway through her senior year at North and going to California in search of work as a dancer. She eventually met a producer at a party, he liked her dancing and her dainty good looks, and gave her a bit part in a film. The bit parts kept on coming until she found herself at Carl Laemmle's Universal Studio, where leading man Reginald Denny took a liking to her. He was considered good box office, and she was given leading roles with him and many other leading men.

Whatever the true story behind her early career may be, her first feature film was *Rosita* (1923) starring America's Sweetheart, Mary Pickford. She appeared in *The Courtship of Miles Standish* (1924) with Charles Ray, and she played opposite Dustin Farnum in *Kentucky Days* (1924), which was a stepping stone to her first meaningful film, *Riders of the Purple Sage* (1925), starring Tom Mix.

All-in-all, Nixon made over thirty feature-length silents through 1928. She made the transition from silent films to talkies fairly easily. Her first important "talkie," *Say It with Songs* (1929), paired her with Al Jolson, the great star from Broadway. Jolson was paid a half million dollars, yet for all his Broadway, radio, and recording success, this movie was a flop. She next appeared with an all-star cast in *The Show of Shows* (1929), a technicolor extravaganza which is of interest today largely because it showcases many of the Warner Brothers silent stars who would not last long in sound films.

In 1932 Marion played the title role in a remake of *Rebecca of Sunnybrook Farm*. (Mary Pickford had played the part in 1921, and Shirley Temple would do again in 1938). She later identified it as her favorite role, although it's Shirley's version that remains stamped in the public consciousness

What isn't well-known is that Marian co-starred with Spencer Tracy in his very first role as a leading man in *The Face in the Sky* (1933). Over the years she was also the leading lady for Will Rogers, James Cagney, Joel McCrea, Warner Baxter, Charles Farrell, Richard Barthemess, Tom Mix, John Barrymore, Dick Powell, Warner Oland, and Al Jolson. A romance had developed between Marion and director William A. Seiter over a period of several movies dating back to 1926, and when the two had completed *We're Rich Again* (1934), Marian and Bill married. Within a year and a half they had a daughter and Marian retired from movie making. (She had also been pretty cozy with a casting director named Ben Lyon during these years, and the ever-patient Ben married Marian in 1971 a few years after Bill Seiter died in 1964.)

Among Marion's notable films of the 1930s are *The Lash* (1930) with Mary Astor; *Courage* (1930) with Belle Bennett; *Too Busy to Work* (1932) starring Will Rogers; and *Winner Take All* (1932) starring Jimmy Cagney. But as the decade progressed her leading men became less distinguished and her parts grew smaller. The handwriting was on the wall, and Marion retired after making *Tango* in 1936. She was thirty-two.

Because her husband Bill Seiter had directed Shirley Temple in two pictures, Marion got to know about her second-hand. She later commented, "She's so clever, and so unaffected. During production on one of her pictures, Bill Seiter had a birthday. Two of the boys on the set presented him with a pen and pencil set. 'Why Mr. Seiter,' Shirley declared, 'I didn't know it was your birthday.' Seiter responded, 'I'm getting so old I don't remember them anymore.' 'But you should have told me,' Shirley insisted. During the rest of that day the usually playful Shirley stayed in her dressing room between shots. At the end of the day she came forth with a little paper ashtray she had woven from little bits of colored paper. She presented it to Director Seiter."

As Marion's success in Hollywood gathered steam, one by one her family members moved to the West Coast to live near her. Her mother arrived first, followed by her father and then her sisters Linda and Florence.

Meanwhile, Marion and Bill Seiter had begun to raise a family of their own. They had a son, Christopher N. Seiter, and a daughter, Jessica Ellen.

In an interview with the *Superior Evening Telegram* in 1939 Marian observed that many changes had taken place in the movie business over the years. In those days casting directors could be approached personally. "We walked around to the casting offices. We'd carry our pictures with us. And those casting directors would take the time to look at them. The picture business has become so big that it is much more difficult to get started."

When asked if she wanted to come back to Minnesota at some future time, she said, "I'd love to go back. I'd like to take a car and drive around and see all the things and places I knew." About Duluth's Minnesota Point, where they spent lots of time as children she said, "We used to go swimming there. Sister and I were talking about it the other day. We'd go down on a picnic taking our lunch with us. We'd build a fire on that beautiful white sand. Then we'd go in the lake…it would be just as cold as ice. Then we'd come out and warm ourselves at the fire. We'd no more do that today. But when you're children, the cold doesn't bother you at all."

Charles Nolte

Born 3 November, 1923, Duluth, MN.

Chuck Nolte was easily the best-liked professor in the Theatre Department at the University of Minnesota during his many years there from the mid-1960s into the 1990s. Students loved Arthur Ballet's introductory course on theater history, but Nolte was very approachable, warm-hearted, a good listener AND he had succeeded on Broadway. Other professors had only visited Broadway but Chuck Nolte was Billy Budd for one year on the Great White Way which he followed with another long run in *The Caine Mutiny Court Martial* (1953-55). George Bernard Shaw once said that, "Those who can, do, and those who can't, teach." Charles Nolte could do both and do them well.

The Nolte family lived at 333 West Victoria Street in Duluth during the 1920s. In 1931 Julius and Mildred M. (Miller) Nolte moved with their four children, Jacqueline, Richard, Mildred and Charles, to 331 Kenilworth. In 1934 they moved to Wayzata.

At Wayzata High School Charles was voted the Most Likely to Succeed by his 1941 graduating classmates. He worked on the school yearbook, the school newspaper, and acted in all the school plays. The summer after he graduated Chuck made his debut in professional theater as Tranio in *The Taming of the Schrew* at the summer stock theater in Excelsior, Minnesota, which later became the Old Log Theater.

Charles spent two years at the University of Minnesota doing lots of dramatics. He won membership to the National Collegiate Players as a freshman. He served in the United States Navy from 1943 to 1945. After the War he resumed his studies at Yale University, the school with the best reputation for dramatic training in the country. At Yale Charles was elected Vice-President of the Yale Dramatic Association. After taking the accelerated program for returning service-men, Charles graduated in 1946 and decided to stay around New York instead of going home.

Nolte debuted on Broadway in 1947 in *Tin Top Valley*. Then he was cast in support of Katharine Cornell in the touring company of *Antony and Cleopatra* (1947). Two years later he received a Theater World Promising Personalities Award for his acting in *Design for a Stained Glass Window* (1948) with Charlton Heston and Martha Scott. When this short-lived production ended, he joined the cast of *Mister Roberts* (1949-51) starring Henry Fonda.

Chuck left the "Roberts" cast to play the title role of *Billy Budd* in 1951. The play was written by University of Minnesota faculty member, Louis O. Coxe, based on the novel by Herman Melville. Nolte's performance was "as honest as the part," said theater critic Brooks Atkinson. Charles had done some weight-lifting so his body fairly rippled when stripped to the waist in this part, and his innocent, roundish face and easy smile radiated youthfulness. Charles won wide acclaim for his performance. Charles and the rest of the cast performed part of the play on the television show *Schlitz Playhouse of Stars*, January 11, 1952.

Nolte next accompanied Fonda in another navy story, *The Caine Mutiny Court Martial*, which ran for nearly two years (1953-55) starting in Los Angeles before being staged on Broadway. He played Lt. Willie Keith to Henry Fonda's leading role as Lt. Barney Greenwald.

While doing Billy Budd, Nolte had spent some of his free mornings doing TV shows, and he now decided to give movies a try. His debut came in **War Paint** (1953). The next film was **The Steel Cage** (1954). This movie was shot during the day while Chuck was still doing "Caine Mutiny" at night. A few years later a big movie came his way—**The Vikings** (1958) starring Kirk Douglas, Ernest Borgnine, Janet Leigh, Orson Welles, and Tony Curtis. Here Charles used his muscles, height, blond hair, and Nordic-blue eyes to great advantage. Then came **Ten Seconds to Hell** (1959) followed by **Under Ten Flags** (1960), starring Charles Laughton and **Armored Command** (1961) starring Howard Keel and the young Burt Reynolds.

After "Caine" closed in 1955 Charles spent much of his time doing theater work in Europe. In Rome he appeared with leading lady Katherine Cornell in *Under Ten Flags*. In Paris he was in *Medea* with Judith Anderson, Christopher Plummer and Mildred Natwick. On the London Stage he appeared in *The Summer People* (1961). The time spent in Europe had changed him, however, and when he returned to the States in 1961 he found the theater scene "hopelessly parochial."

Therefore, Nolte began to write plays, and in 1962 he returned to the University of Minnesota, earning his M.A. in 1963 and his Ph.D. in 1966. At that point the U offered him a sweet contract under which he was required to teach for only six months, leaving the rest of the year free to spend writing, acting and directing.

In 1965 his play, *Do Not Pass Go* was produced on Boradway and was favorably reviewed in the *New York Times*. Charles not only wrote but also acted in the two-person play, and with expenses being quite modest, it actually made money

Over the years Nolte has had a special relationship with the Theatre-in-the-Round Players. He has directed thirteen TRP productions, and they have produced nine of his plays, including *Sister Heeno's Warm Elbow* (1965), *Do Not Pass Go* (1966), *Alexander's Death* (1971), *Roads in Germany* (1978), *The Caine Rehearsals* (1980), and *A Night at the Black Pig* (2002) for TRP's 50th Anniversary Season. His other plays are *The Summer People, Sea Change, End of Ramadan, The Boarding House,* and *A Summer Remembered.*

In its early years TRP staged its productions at the YWCA at 12th and Nicollet, and later at a second-storey space at about 13th and Stevens Avenue, near the present Convention Center site on the fringe of downtown Minneapolis. In 1970 or so the company established a permanent home on Seven Corners in an abandoned pizza restaurant at 245 Cedar Avenue.

Charles has also directed several times on the Minnesota Centennial Showboat, bought for the University of Minnesota's Theater Department by the former head of the Department, Doc Whiting, in 1958.

Charles once directed an old chestnut, *Charlie's Aunt*, which gave his sister an opportunity to host an Opening Night party for the cast and crew. She billed it as "A party for Charlie by Charlie's sister for "Charlie's Aunt."

Among the students who benefited from Nolte's acting and teaching expertise while getting their doctorates at the University are Warren Frost, Peter Michael Goetz, George Muschamp, and Ernie Hudson.

The University of Minnesota honored Charles in 1997 by naming a theater space within the Rarig Center the Charles Nolte Experimental Theatre. Charles taught playwrighting in the Nolte Center, (named after his father, the long-time dean of the Extension Service.) One of his students, Barbara Field, wrote the adaptation of the *Christmas Carol* which is a perennial holiday favorite at the Guthrie Theater. And over the years he has supported a wide variety of student efforts to produce their work in community theaters, on radio, in hospitals, and at public readings.

"Teaching has been a blessing," Nolte once remarked, "a chance to inspire students with a passion about theater. When you're in theater, you are in everything—art, law, psychology, business, religion, design, pathology, history, etymology. I try to inflame young minds to get excited about experiencing something that is rare."

Nolte had been good friends for many years with playwright Tennessee Williams, one of the masters of American drama., so it was not surprising that Williams flew to Minneapolis to see the opening night production of his play, *A Streetcar Named Desire* at Scott Hall on the University campus in early 1972, which Charles was directing. Debra Mooney played Blanche DuBois and throughout his visit Williams just raved about her marvelous, sensitive performance, and comparing it favorably to both Jessica Tandy's initial rendering on Broadway and Vivien Leigh's film version.

Charles, still vigorous, fit, ever-charming, and looking always younger than his years, is finally Professor Emeritus (retired) though he continued to teach at the U of M well into his seventies and still directs at TRP or whenever he's asked.

Nick Nolte

Born 8 February, 1941,
Omaha, NE.

B rash, brawny, and feisty Nick Nolte earned his "adopted Minnesotan" status with three years of trodding the boards at the Old Log Theatre in Excelsior, Minnesota. From August of 1969 to December of 1972 Nick appeared in twenty plays there. At that time the Old Log produced a new play each month so there were frequent rehearsals and little time for goofing off yet he managed his fair share of that. It was not only his looks but also the restless energy of his body language that made his so well suited for the "juvenile" parts in all the plays. Let's touch on those Minnesota connections Nolte made in Excelsior and beyond.

Nick lived in a small house that was originally a cabin, not far from the Excelsior Commons. Though married at the time to a woman in Phoenix, he dated several women, especially an actress at the Old Log named Felicia Soper.

Nick worked hard at the theater—there were no gaffs, pratfalls, pranks, or malapropisms. He loved rehearsing and was generally full of energy and enthusiasm. He was a quick study and learned his lines early. He rewrote each line in his script book to make the words more meaningful for him.

Peter Struder was a good friend and they went around town after the show or in the day in Nick's old beater of a car. Dony Stolz was a good friend, too, but his best friend was Jimmie Wright, who lived in Excelsior until recently. How did he get here? He phoned Old Log owner-director Don Stolz and asked for an audition, which Don granted. Even though he worked well on the stage, he really showed himself in his best light on camera. This was evident even in TV commercials. Everyone urged Nick to go to New York or California. After leaving the Old Log for Los Angeles, he was cast in a new play by William Inge. A studio bigwig saw his performance and invited him to the cast of the TV series, *Rich Man, Poor Man*. This show was a hit for Nolte and won him an Emmy nomination. The rest is history, as they say.

Here is a rundown of his plays at the Old Log. *Cactus Flower, Lovers and Other Strangers, Don't Drink the Water, Catch Me If You Can, Two Dozen Red Roses, The Odd Couple, Love and Kisses, A Thousand Clowns, The Impossible Years, Rumpelstiltskin, Biggest Thief in Town, Harvey, Not Now, Darling, See How They Run, Butterflies Are Free,* and *How the Other Half Loves.*

A local star, Nancy Nelson, who has become Ms Info-Mercial, performed in nine plays with Nolte at the Old Log Theatre. Nancy was the Weather Girl at WCCO TV for a few years in the 1960s. She acted in some two dozen plays at the Old Log and also did commercials, particularly the Embers commercial that played for years on TV. Nancy also had a part in *Airport* (1970, as a counter clerk). Today she is seen every day on TV in cooking-related shows.

Nick was in Los Angeles by early December of 1972. He made a big splash with *Rich Man, Poor Man*, but he was still widely considered to be just a raucous bundle of charm with little depth.

His film debut was *Dirty Little Billy* (1972) made while he was on a sabbatical from the Old Log Theatre. After making several made-for-TV movies, he landed a meaty role in *Return to Macon County* (1975). Other notable films of the period include *The Deep* (1977), *Who'll Stop the Rain* (1978) about a Vietnam Veteran smuggling heroin back to the US, and *North Dallas Forty* (1979). These films are high-energy and action-filled.

He played the very hip Neal Cassady in *Heart Beat* (1980), and starred in *Cannery Row* (1982). Eddie Murphy made his film debut with Nolte in *48 Hrs* (1982). By that time Nolte was a star, and he earned two million for doing the film.

Yet Nolte was also a drinker, and while making *Grace Quigley* (1984) with Katherine Hepburn the actress upbraided him, "Mr. Nolte, you have fallen down drunk into every street gutter in town." His smart reply was, "I've got a few to go yet." In time he curtailed his drinking substantially, though occasional slips were widely publicized in the gossip magazines.

Nick attended Westside High School in Omaha, Nebraska, where Johnny Carson, Marlon Brando, Henry Fonda, and Dick Cavett also went to school. Nolte was given five years probation for selling fake draft cards in 1962. He and Christopher Walken were both considered for the role of Han Solo in *Star Wars* (1977), a part given to Harrison Ford. He was chosen as *People* Magazine's Sexiest Man Alive in 1992. He has been married three times.

Nolte has played quite a few off-beat roles during his long career. He was a bum in *Down and Out in Beverly Hills* (1986), a Texas lawman in *Extreme Prejudice* (1987), a convict playwright in *Weeds* (1987), an army deserter turned South Sea god in *Farewell to the King* (1989), and a beleaguered private eye in *Everybody Wins* (1990).

He received serious attention for his layered performances in Martin Scorsese's *Cape Fear* (1991) and in *Prince of Tides* (1991), for which he won a Golden Globe award and was nominated for an Oscar. Though his choice of films remained uneven, Nolte was now being more widely praised as not only a likeable beefcake, but also a talented actor.

For *Affliction* (1997) Nick was once again nominated for Best Actor by the Academy. Terrence Malick's WWII film *The Thin Red Line* (1998) was also a critical success.

A note on The Old Log Theater of Excelsior is timely here. Don Stolz and family have owned and run this theatre continuously since 1941. It began as summer stock only but in 1960 it became a full-time, year-round, self-supporting theater. It is the longest running theater in America, operating full-time, under one management, and it is the biggest producer of British comedy in the United States. The 655-seat theater is situated on ten acres of well-groomed landscape bounded by the shores of Lake Minnetonka.

Shirley O'Hara

(Shirley Margaret Har)
Born 15 Aug 1924, Rochester, MN.
Died 13 Dec, 2002, Calabasas, CA.

As soon as Shirley Har received her diploma from Rochester High School in June of 1942, she left town for Salt Lake City to visit friends, though she also hoped to squeeze in a side trip to Hollywood. Her stage ambitions were kindled when she studied dancing between ages eight and twelve. Journalism then took the spotlight in her life for a while. She didn't try out for the school plays because she was going to be a journalist, though she rarely missed a movie passing through town.

In the Rochester High School Yearbook for 1942, Shirley Margaret Har had this comment: "'Princess' ought to be able to get plenty of famous peoples' autographs when she becomes a crime reporter." She worked three nights a week at the Chateau Theatre (also the Time and Lawler Theaters) in Rochester for 50 cents a week in her senior year. "The pay wasn't great," she recalled in a 1980 interview, "but I did get to see every movie that came along for free."

Shirley did soon move to Los Angeles, and landed a job as an elevator girl at Saks Fifth Avenue in Beverly Hills. Each girl received a weekly hair-styling and was provided with a smart uniform by the store. Several actresses shopping at the store complimented her on her natural beauty and lovely hair. After a short stint she was promoted to salesgirl in the hosiery department, the youngest salesgirl in the store—and the fastest promoted. She had brown, naturally-curly hair and a face reminiscent of Rita Hayworth. She was just eighteen, weighed 118 lbs, and was 5'4 ½" tall.

The Hollywood elite often shopped at Saks, and one day a producer's wife noticed Shirley and told her husband about her. The producer phoned talent scout Eddie Ruben and agent Marty Martyn, instructing them to go investigate that "freckle-faced dame at the hosiery counter at Saks." They came to see her, liked her looks, rushed her through a screen test and signed her to a contract with RKO Studio.

Her first film was *Around the World* (1943) starring the brilliant comedienne from St. Paul, Joan Davis. Shirley was very pleased that she was given seven wardrobe changes—quite a lot for a newcomer in movieland. She was in several scenes and even had a few lines!

A December, 1943, issue of the *Rochester Post-Bulletin* ran an ad for the film with this caption under Shirley's photo, "Rochester's own movie starlet, Shirley O'Hara, formerly Shirley Har, will make her first screen appearance in Kay Kyser's new production 'Around the World,' starting Friday, February 11, at the Time theatre. Shirley appears in many of the scenes and carries several lines of dialogue." For some of the folks in Rochester seeing Shirley on the screen was a little like seeing her on the Chateau Theatre stage helping people draw for cash prizes on bank nights.

Incidentally, other films showing in Rochester that February were *Presenting Lily Mars* with Judy Garland, *Return of the Vampire* starring Bela Lugosi, and *No Time for Love* with Claudette Colbert and Fred MacMurray. Following Shirley's movie at the Chateau Theater was James Cagney in *Johnny Come Lately*.

Sol Lesser became Shirley's mentor-producer and signed her to a long-term contract. After handling bit parts in seven movies, Lesser put her in *Three Is a Family* (1944) and gave her the second female lead as Athena, the native princess, in *Tarzan and the Amazons* (1945). She had played a lot of native girls, she recalled, "But *Tarzan and the Amazons* was my most important picture." Brenda Joyce was the female lead; this was Johnny Weissmuller's last film performance as Tarzan. Shirley made good friends with "Clark Gable-eared" Cheta, the chimpanzee, during film production.

Shirley found Frank Sinatra to be "a very nice man." She said, "I lived at the Hollywood Studio Club [1215 Lodi Place], which was a home for young girls who worked in the movies. Frank used to stop and pick us up and drive us to work, and drive us home afterwards" during the shooting of his films, *Step Lively* (1943) and *Higher and Higher* (1944) in which Shirley played a Bridesmaid.

Shirley gained a bit of notoriety for her hair style during *Seven Days Ashore* (1944) in which she does her hair "short, brushed up around the head to form an aura, the front being marked by soft bangs." It was called the "O'Hara bob."

She appeared in the "Falcon" series for one film, *The Falcon Out West* (1944) starring Tom Conway. She also appeared in the Andy Hardy film, *Love Laughs at Andy Hardy* (1947). By the time she was 23 Shirley had appeared in sixteen movies. In 1947 she appeared in a new role, as Mrs. Jimmy McHugh, Jr.

Jimmy's father was the songwriter for *Seven Days Ashore* and they met during film production. Jimmy wrote some famous songs: "I Can't Give You Anything But Love, Baby;" "I'm in the Mood for Love;" "It's a Most Unusual Day;" "On the Sunny side of the Street;" and "I Feel a Song Comin' On" among many others. The couple had a son, Jimmy McHugh III. Shirley did no films until 1960 except for a bit part in *Crime Wave* (1954, made in UK). Motherhood and family was the goal for these years. From 1947 to 1959 she, Jimmy and son lived in England.

Upon their return O'Hara jumped back into movie-acting and into TV productions. She appeared in the murder-thriller *The Third Voice* (1960), *Love in a Goldfish Bowl* (1961) and *Sylvia* (1965) co-starring Carroll Baker, Peter Lawford and Minnesota-raised Ann Sothern. A role in *The Ballad of Josie* (1967) gave her the opportunity to work with Doris Day, Andy Devine, George Kennedy, and Minnesota born-Peter Graves. She also did eleven made-for-TV movies in the 1960s and 70s though the best role in her later career was as a secretary in Sylvester Stallone's *Rocky* (1976).

Shirley appeared in fifty TV episodes between 1959 and 1978, running the gamut from *Marcus Welby, M.D.* and *The Mary Tyler Moore Show* to *The Twilight Zone* and *Have Gun Will Travel*.

Her final film was *Getting Wasted* (1980) after which she retired to concentrate on publicity.

What started out as a modest public relations business with her second husband, Milton Krims, eventually became a burgeoning enterprise handling publicity for Warner Bros, Columbia Pictures, First Artists Productions, Orion Pictures, the Ladd Co. and several independent firms engaged in film and TV productions.

Milton Krims was a former Oscar nominee for screenwriting. He was President of the American National Theater Academy and wrote the scripts for several movies. The couple lived in West Hollywood at 2155 North Ridgemont Drive, which is Laurel Canyon until Krims death in 1988.

Among Shirley's duties as a publicist was being a tour guide of the studio. If you had $25 to spare in 1992, and were over the age of ten, she might have escorted you to the studio sets for *Murphy Brown*, *Reasonable Doubt*, *Sisters*, and *Life Goes On*, and also to the sets for the upcoming feature, *Dave* including a replica for the White House. You might have passed some old sets, too, such as the streets used for *Dick Tracy*, *Batman* and even for *Casablanca*.

Shirley might have informed you that the number of tourists to Los Angeles each year is 27.8 million, most of whom want to visit Hollywood, and that there are 60,000 employees in the film industry; that the revenue for *Batman Returns* was $155.5 million and *Lethal Weapon III* brought in $138.2 million. She also personalized each tour with her own experience during Hollywood's golden years. "At that time the studios kept a lot of stock players they were grooming. You would study and hope to become a star. Today actors train in college and work on stage before they're hired for movie roles." Shirley appeared in thirty films or so and was killed in seven or eight of them. "They made a career of killing me."

Shirley's father, William Leo, was a carpenter who worked at Midland Lumber and Coal Company. He expanded his work to become a small builder-contractor though when World War II broke out he took a job as supervisor at a Defense Department facility in Sutton, Nebraska. It is very likely he built homes "on spec" (which builders often do) because they moved nearly every year of their lives in Rochester.

Shirley's parents separated in 1938 and her father lived with his parents at 304 11th Ave. S.E. while her mom lived at 11 2nd Ave. N.E. Shirley is listed as living with her mother in 1940 at 717 3rd Ave. S.E. while her dad is still at his parents' home. William Leo Har has a new residence in 1941 at 418 14th Ave. N.E. while Shirley and her mom stay put. In 1942 her mom remarried, to Otto Neuman of La Crosse, Wisconsin, and Shirley moved into her dad's home at 216 9 ½ S.E.

Perhaps this steady rootlessness and upheaval made it easy for Shirley to leave Rochester as soon as she could in the summer of 1942. Her son, Jimmy, became a freelance photo journalist and did several jobs for *People* Magazine. Her brother, John, grew up to be a contractor like his father. Her father remarried, too, so Shirley had a stepmother named Anne.

Shirley Har remembers Rochester warmly as "a nice place to grow up." It was a great place for Hollywood Cinderella, Shirley O'Hara, to prepare for the ball.

Terry O'Sullivan

Born 7 July, 1915,
Kansas City, MO.
Died Sept 14, 2006,
Mpls, MN.

Growing up on the edge of town, Terry O'Sullivan could have been a modern Daniel Boone because he knew how to ride horses bareback, hunt snakes and game animals, dress out hides, and appreciate the great outdoors. Of course, his father, Timothy Aloysius O'Sullivan, a grain man and President of the Kansas City Board of Trade, expected young Terry to follow him in the grain trade. It was not to be.

One April day on the Kansas City University campus Terry was chatting with a lovely new lassie and she announced that she was going to audition for a play. He went with her and auditioned, too, and was cast in the show with her. The theatrical "acting bug" bit Terry and he was hooked for life. Terry's mother had been a dramatic soprano, and his sister, Barbara, could be seen tap dancing at various local nightclubs, so he knew there was some show business in his blood. Against the wishes of his father he joined a tent show company of actors, the Original McOwen Players. Terry was selected to be the pitchman for the McOwen Company and he pitched candy, "Ladies and gentlemen, I have here in my hand a box of delicious candy...."

Kansas City was the booking center for tent shows in Mid-America so auditions were very convenient for young Terry O'Sullivan. He joined the J. Mickey O'Brien Company of Carthage, Tennessee, and toured the mid-central states playing such small towns as Defeated, Difficult, and Temperance Hall, Tennessee, named such by the victorious Yankee soldiers at the end of the Civil War. At the close of the tour Terry hitch-hiked to New York City. By a huge stroke of luck a farmer heading for New York picked him up. They alternated driving and made it non-stop.

In New York Terry headed for the Irvine School of Drama, where he had won a scholarship. (In the 1930s young women outnumbered the men so that most of the scholarships were given young men to equalize the gender gap in drama school.) Terry found a room on East 52nd Street for $2.50 per week, but drama school had to go on the back burner until Terry could earn some money. He was soon waiting tables in McGowan's Restaurant in Queen's Plaza, Long Island.

Terry's experience as a candy pitchman served him in good stead when a young drama student named Don Stolz asked him if he could perform some plays on radio in Oklahoma City. Terry agreed, and a friendship was started that lasted sixty-plus years. Don has owned and run the Old Log Theatre in Excelsior, Minnesota, since 1941.

Terry's first network job as a radio announcer was on the *Heidt Time for Hire's* hosted by bandleader Horace Heidt. He held several other positions in radio before becoming an announcer for the *Dreft Star Playhouse* in June of 1943. He also worked on *Glamour Manor,* sharing announcing duties in 1944-45 with Jack Bailey, who later hosted the radio and TV shows *Queen for a Day.* This ABC/Blue Network show showcased Cliff Arquette, also known as Charlie Weaver. Terry's future wife, Jan Miner, joined the show for the 1945 run in New York. The show returned to Hollywood in the fall of 1945.

Make Believe Town, Hollywood was Terry's next radio job. It ran from August 1949 to December of 1950. Minneapolis-born Virginia Bruce was the hostess of this light romantic drama of boy-girl tales in Hollywood. On this show Terry had a regular cast job instead of announcing. He also announced on *Today's Children,* a crossover show linking together characters from other soap operas such as *The Guiding Light* and *Ma Perkins* sponsored by General Mills.

After a divorce in 1950 Terry abandoned Los Angeles and lit out for New York. Television was just coming into its own and Terry got in on the ground floor. This was his decade to shine. *Search for Tomorrow* began in 1951 and Terry joined the cast in 1952 playing the male lead, Arthur Tate. Terry was the Favorite Daytime Television Drama Actor in 1953, 1954, and 1955. These awards were given by the *TV-Radio Mirror Magazine.* His co-star was Mary Stuart, who stayed with the show for thirty-five years. Except for a one-year absence in 1956, Terry was in the cast until 1962 when his character died of a heart attack. (During the 1956-57 season he played Elliot Norris on *Valiant Lady).* Terry had rehearsed very hard for his heart attack scene but the writers fooled him and simply announced Tate's death after the fact instead of dramatizing it.

One time Terry was asleep in his car by the side of the road. A New York State policeman investigated and started writing up a ticket until he recognized him as Arthur Tate, the fantasy man of the officer's wife. He tore up the ticket and wished him every success. Terry was given a medal for distinguished service from the National Academy of Television Arts and Sciences.

Terry played Richard Hunter from 1966-68 in *Days of Our Lives* and Judge Sam Stevens from 1968-69 in *The Secret Storm*. Then things were less interesting until 1973, when he moved to Excelsior, Minnesota, and became a regular member of the Old Log Theatre cast, where he performed in some twenty plays over the next thirty years. He also took time out to perform the role of President Franklin Roosevelt in *Annie* for a year's run at the Chanhassen Dinner Theatre. He also played the Cricket Theatre, Theatre 65, the Como Park Pavilion and countless voice-over commercials, print ads, and modeling jobs.

Yes, Terry did it all: tent shows, radio, television, and Broadway theater. He also appeared in eight movies although this is a minor part of his show business life.

His first film, **Men on Her Mind** (1944), starred Mary Beth Hughes, the last girlfriend of John Barrymore. In the movie Terry played (surprise, surprise) a radio announcer.

Not long before leaving Hollywood, Terry also was an on-screen news announcer in Jimmy Cagney's **White Heat** (1949). In 1955 he served the subpoena on Gary Cooper in **The Court Martial of Billy Mitchell**. He fondly remembers the day that he and Coop rode together in a limousine to the shoot site.

In the Twin Cities Terry has spent more time lately on movies as he has eased himself out of doing eight shows a week in the live theater. He played Mr. Crim in the made-for-TV movie, **The Comeback** (1989) starring Robert Urich. He played Mr. Greene in **She Led Two Lives** (1992, TV) starring Connie Sellecca. He was a fan in the stands for **Major League III** (1997). He was Puffy's pharmacist in **The Naked Man** (1998), a Coen-Brothers-esque dark comedy starring Michael Rappaport. He was the old man reading the newspaper aloud to his wife in the opening scenes of **Herman, USA** (1999).

Now in his eighties, Terry still called his agent every day looking for work and he kept busy with independent films such as *Great Lakes* (2002). He is an inspiration for us all.

Terry has been married six times; he has four daughters, eight grandchildren and eight great grandchildren. His last marriage, to Anita Anderson, lasted the longest—over thirty years. Who would have thought a Las Vegas "quickie" chapel wedding would be the best of the lot? Anita is a graduate of the Dudley Riggs' Brave New Workshop and is still active in Twin Cities community theater, especially at the Theatre in the Round Players.

Terry loved to cook, especially old-fashioned roasts. You can read all about him in his autobiography, **Did I Miss Anything (Memoirs of a Soap Opera Star)** (1997).

Emory N. Parnell

Born 29 December, 1890 or 92
St. Paul, MN.
Died 22 June, 1979,
Woodland Hills, CA.

Any movie buff would probably recognize Emory N. Parnell's face, though few would know his name. Emory Parnell made 211 pictures in nearly thirty years, and his image is etched in our collective movie memories. He also appeared in a long-running TV sitcom, *The Life of Riley*, and twenty other television episodes, just to put frosting on the cake of our memories. Emory was a big man, 6' 3" and weighed 220 pounds. We may not remember his name, but seeing his face, we instantly feel that we know *him*.

Emory's father, James Daniel Parnell, worked with the Great Northern Railroad for thirty-six years. In 1900 the family moved to Lakota, North Dakota, and four years later to Sioux City, Iowa, where Emory completed high school and then entered Morningside College, He majored in vocal and instrumental music, and left college in 1912 to earn his living as a concert violinist.

A year later Parnell met and married Effie M. Laird, a Minnesota-born (in 1888) pianist and soloist. They became a singing vaudeville team on the Chautauqua and Lyceum circuits, touring the United States and Canada for thirteen years. In 1926 they settled in Columbus, Ohio, where Emory became head booking agent for the southern Ohio, West Virginia, and Kentucky regions of the bureaus he had previously worked for as an entertainer. He held the job for four years. A typical Chautauqua show included not only theatrical acts but also debates and lectures, and one of the many acts Emory booked was orator William Jennings Bryan, a frequent presidential candidate.

In 1930 he and Effie moved to Detroit where Emory became

a radio actor and narrator in commercial films. His radio resume includes *The Lux Hour* and *The Grouch Club* on station KFI. He appeared in short films advertising for Ford, Chrysler, Standard Oil, etc. and became very well-known and liked. His friends in the Detroit Players Club and the Detroit Yacht Club beseeched him to crash the gates of Hollywood. Yes, he was in the Detroit Yacht Club. Sailing was a major hobby and he owned a 36-ft cutter named the "Effie G." He was also a member of the U. S. Coast Guard Reserve.

In the summer of 1937 Parnell and his wife moved to the West Coast. He picked up radio work right away and after four months he signed his first film contract. Ben Piazza of Major Pictures and head of the RKO Radio casting office put Emory into the Bing Crosby film, *Dr. Rhythm* (1937) but his part was cut from the final edit. His comic abilities were well-known, however, and during the early 1940s he appeared in a number of distinguished films, including *Foreign Correspondent* (1940), *Louisiana Purchase* (1941), *The Maltese Falcon* (1941), *Sullivan's Travels* (1942), *Saboteur* (1942), *Pride of the Yankees* (1942), *King's Row* (1942), and *Mr. Lucky* (1943). After *Government Girl* (1943), he signed a long-term contract with RKO Radio.

Emory could display surprise, shock, sorrow, dismay, frustration, and other emotions easily with his "rubber face." One critic described him as an "American general-purpose character actor [who] could be a villain, prison warden, weakling, or kindly father." He often played a law enforcement officer, moving up in rank as his career progressed from sheriff, policeman, or "beat cop" to sergeant, captain, inspector, and chief. He played judges, mayors, and senators, though he was also adept at salt-of-the-eath characters such as bartenders, used car salesman, ship's captain, and priests.

Emory was often consigned to parts in "B" movies such as three Falcon films starring Tom Conway: *The Falcon in Mexico* (1944), *The Falcon in Hollywood* (1944), and *The Falcon's Alibi* (1946). He joined the Crime Doctor series in *Crime Doctor's Courage* (1945) and *Crime Doctor's Gamble* (1947) as a former gangster who, after an accident, suffered amnesia and becomes a great criminologist and psychiatrist. He appeared in several Blondie films, and five of the Ma and Pa Kettle series.

He was a natural for comedies like *At the Circus* (1939) with the Marx Brothers; *The Dancing Masters* (1943) with Laurel and Hardy; *The Long, Long Trailer* (1954) with Lucille Ball; *Artists and Models* (1955) with Dean Martin, Jerry Lewis and Shirley MacLaine; and *Du Barry Was a Lady* (1943) with Lucille Ball, Gene Kelly, Red Skelton and Zero Mostel.

A few more of Parnell's notable films are *The Miracle of Morgan's Creek* (1943), *Mission to Moscow* (1943), *State Fair* (1945), *Mr. Blandings Builds His Dream House* (1948), *Show Boat* (1951), *The Band Wagon* (1953), and *A Hole in the Head* (1959)

Television came along and he joined that bandwagon, too, finding a juicy, regular role as foreman "Hard-boiled" Hank Hawkins in *The Life of Riley* from 1953-1958 starring Bill Bendix. His notable TV appearances were in *The Lone Ranger, I Love Lucy, Maverick, Perry Mason, Green Acres,* and *The Andy Griffith Show.*

Emory played more than a few Irish characters. At any rate, some of the characters he played were named Kelly, McGuire, McClain, Fitzgibbon, Gallagher, Clancy, Mulloy, Brennan, O'Reilly, Casey, Whalen, O'Leary, McBride, McPherson, Shannon, Haley, Grady, Dolan, O'Casey, Kennedy, Walsh, Higgins, Riley, and McMann It is probably safe to say that he had "the map of Ireland" for a face. We're glad this fellow was a Minnesotan.

Emory and Effie sang on New York stages long before his entry to movies. They lived at 780 W. 71st Street in Manhattan, New York City, according to the 1920 Census. They kept their ties to Minnesota over the years, however, and returned to St. Paul to give birth to their son, James, who was born on October 9th, 1923. James also became an actor, albeit short-lived as he died in Hollywood on December 27th, 1961, after twenty-two movies and thirty-eight TV appearances, nearly all of which were Western or adventure films.

Father and son appeared together in *Pardners* (1956) and *Looters* (1955). His last TV appearance was on 18 December 1961, nine days before he died. James was married and had three children.

Emory and Effie had a second son, Charles Stewart Parnell (Chic) born in 1928. I didn't mention it earlier but, yes, Emory is directly related to the great Irish statesman. Emory honored the relationship by naming his second son Charles.

Strange as it may seem, Effie was granted a divorce from Emory in 1945. He would vanish for weeks at a time, return home, but would offer no explanation for this bizarre behavior. Still, the couple remained together.

Barbara Payton

(Barbara Lee Redfield)
Born 16 November 1927
Cloquet, MN.
Died 8 May 1967
San Diego, CA.

She was described as a "well-built, leggy, moderately talented blonde [who] had a chance for stardom in the early fifties." Early in her career she played opposite James Cagney in *Kiss Tomorrow Goodbye* (1951) and with Gregory Peck in *Only the Valiant* (1951). But her off-screen escapades dominated her life and undercut her career. By age seventeen she had been married twice. At twenty she was a mother. She was romantically linked to a number of men including Howard Hughes, Guy Madison, most of her leading men, and many of the filmmakers she worked with. The wild living took its toll, and Barbara died of heart and liver failure six months shy of her fortieth birthday.

Four years before her death Barbara Payton published her autobiography, *I Am Not Ashamed* (1963). Her scandals and scandalous behavior had long been steak and potatoes for the gossip mongers and tabloid writers, but Barbara substantiates much of it here. Jack Nicholson gave this book to another Cloquet woman, Jessica Lange, to prep her on her role as the wild and lascivious wife in the remake of *The Postman Always Rings Twice.*

Barbara Lee Redfield was born into a blue collar household. Her father, Erwin "Flip" Lee Redfield, was a construction worker. The Redfields were longtime residents of the Redfield Apartments at Avenue C in Cloquet.

Longtime Cloquet resident Mildred Golden said Barbara had such blonde hair as a baby that it was almost snow-white and she had the deepest, most beautiful eyes. She and her younger brother, Frank, seemed like ordinary kids. Barbara's girlfriends remembered her as athletic, bright, and outgoing. She especially loved ice skating, skiing, and sledding. "I loved the winters, the cold, crisp Minnesota winters with a blue-black sky at night and a billion stars you could reach up and grab by the handful. I think I made a wish on every one of those stars," Barbara later wrote to a childhood friend in Cloquet.

As a youngster she was attracted to cooking and by the time she was a teenager she was a really fine cook. As an adult her favorite activity for showing off for boyfriends, husbands, and friends was to prepare them a gourmet meal.

In 1939 the Redfields moved to the Texas oil town of Odessa. Entering high school Barbara was a leggy 5'4". While in Odessa High School she learned how to exploit her sex appeal, developing a tough-talking, brazen personality that attracted both boys and men.

At the very mature age of sixteen Barbara eloped in 1944 with an Odessa boy, William Hodge. His parents had the marriage annulled a few months later. One evening a year later she wore a low-cut dress to a dance at a military base, which impressed Air Force Captain John Payton. The two were married a few weeks later. Barbara enticed her husband to take her to Hollywood for their honeymoon, and she took a screen test at RKO, but nothing came of it. They returned home and eight months later Barbara gave birth to John Lee. Displaying the "What do I care?" attitude that would define her adult life, Barbara gave the baby to her parents, ditched her husband, and returned to Hollywood.

Payton soon landed a job as a carhop at Stan's Drive-In on the corner of Sunset Boulevard and Highland Avenue, and she collected enough there in tips to finance her entry into plush nightclubs like Ciro's, Mocambo, and the Trocadero. With her striking sweet-but-sexy appearance and ribald humor, she was soon dubbed, "Queen of the Nightclubs."

By age twenty-one Barbara had signed a contract with Universal Studios. She appeared in a few B-pictures but was dropped when word got out that she was having an affair with a married man—Bob Hope. She had met Hope in March of 1949 at a hotel party in Houston, and she became a Hope "groupie," following him as he made personal appearances around the country. Upon his return to Hollywood, Hope set Payton up in a little love-nest on Cheremoya Avenue. After six months the relationship ended abruptly as Payton pressed him for more money to cover her living expenses. Hope's advisors paid her off with a handsome sum and the stipulation that she keep quiet and disappear. She went through this cash in a few months and went back to nightclubbing.

As time went on the unsavory aspects of Payton's behavior became more pronounced. She dined with Howard Hughes, mobsters, and wealthy businessmen, and had affairs with numerous actors and directors. Legendary film producer A. C. Lyles remembered Payton fondly, "Barbara never had an itch she didn't scratch."

Her official film debut came in a forgettable film, *Silver Butte* (1949) followed by a starring role opposite Lloyd Bridges in *Trapped*

(1949). In this noirish film she was cast as a cigarette girl in a night-club, but in real life, she had begun to spend time with genuine thugs and drug dealers. One one occasion one of her "friends" beat up her landlady at 3 a.m. in a rent dispute. Barbara seemed to be drawn to seedy, violent people.

Her odd choice of friends had not yet undermined her career, however, and Payton for the first time appeared in a small part in an A-budget film, *Once More, My Darling* (1949) starring Ann Blyth and Robert Montgomery. The studio was pleased with her efforts and signed to her a contract in 1950 at $5,000 a week. Her first assignment was co-starring with Jimmy Cagney in *Kiss Tomorrow Goodbye* (1950), a sequel to Cagney's huge hit, *White Heat* (1949). It is probably Barbara's best film, and it did so well that Warner Brothers doubled her weekly pay.

In her next film, *Dallas* (1950), Payton had a minor part along-side Gary Cooper. She appeared in a similarly small but very decorative role with Gregory Peck in a second Western, *Only the Valiant* (1951). During the filming of both pictures rumors on the set were rampant.

At this time she found a Sugar Daddy, the middle-aged but classy and wealthy Franchot Tone, who took her all over town. He was twice her age but neither seemed to mind a bit. He gave her daily gifts of champagne, flowers, and expensive jewelry, and she made gourmet meals for him. Soon they were engaged and Tone announced he was going to buy a ranch for her in Pomona. Warners was now promoting her as their "white diamond with blue eyes," and Payton was sitting on top of the world.

Yet is seemed nothing could halt the parade of affairs in which Barbara became involved. During her next film, *Drums in the Deep South* (1951, as Kathy Summers), she and Guy Madison became hot and heavy lovers. Tone exposed the liaison and steamy articles soon appeared in the exploitation magazines. Warner Brothers expressed its displeasure with all the bad publicity by casting Payton in the B-budget *Bride of the Gorilla* (1951). Ironically, the film is now considered a cult classic, and it's generally agreed that Payton's performance adds to the appeal, especially the opening scenes during which she does a dance in a sexy sarong.

Tone went to New York City on business in July of 1951 and Payton almost immediately fell in love with Tom Neal, a serious weight lifter and ex-Golden Gloves boxer. " Payton later described their meeting. "It was love at first sight. He looked so wonderful in his trunks, I knew he was the only man in my life."

Though her fidelity was highly suspect, her appeal was great, and Tone and Neal became rivals for her hand. On one occasion Neal pulverized Tone on Payton's balcony, leaving Tone comatose in the hospital for eighteen hours with a concussion and a broken nose. The contest continued throughout the summer, and as late as September 14 Payton announced she was going to marry Neal. Two weeks later she and Tone were married in Cloquet at her Uncle Frank's house at 405 Chestnut. She said, "Hello, husband" and he said, "Hello, darling."

The *Duluth News Tribune* reported the simple wedding ceremony on September 29, 1951. A crowd of between 300 to 400 people, most of them teenagers, gathered outside the white rambler on Chestnut Street. Her maid of honor was a cousin, Miss Marjorie Melby, a student at UM-D. Her uncle, Frank L. (Tim) Redfield gave her away and the Best Man was Captain Robert Redfield, another cousin. The ceremony took five minutes. It was the third marriage for both.

The wedding dinner of eighteen was hosted at The Flame in Duluth, a posh restaurant featuring a piano/string orchestra with the violin players visiting each table.

Barbara's mother called a few minutes after the rites had been concluded and congratulated her daughter who responded, "I'm so happy I could cry." Her divorce from Payton, now a car salesman, had come through on September 13th.

Meanwhile Jack Warner was seething mad with all the bad publicity so he dug into the morals clause of her contract, invoked a dicta found there and broke her contract. Barbara told her buddy, A. C. Lyles, "I know I'm getting bad publicity, A. C., but I couldn't care less. I'm having so much fun!"

The stormy, booze-besotted marriage lasted fifty-three days. She returned to Neal and the couple left for England where Barbara became a star again in B-movies, starting with *Four-Sided Triangle* (1953). In this sci-fi comedy Payton leaves her scientist-husband for another man. He clones her only to find that the clone leaves him, too.

Barbara's other British movies are *Bad Blonde* (1953), (the American title was *The Flanagan Boy*) and *The Woman Is Trouble*, a melodrama where Payton plays a parody of herself as a sex-crazed murderess. This slapstick comedy has Payton dressed up in a cave girl outfit opposite heavy-drinking Sonny Tufts, whose career was also on a downward slide. The underlying element is that a nuclear bomb could send people back to the hills to live as cavemen used to.

Payton starred with Neal for the first time in *The Great Jesse James Raid* (1953). In June of 1953 the two did summer stock theater performing a stage version of *The Postman Always Rings Twice* at the Drury Lane Theater in Chicago. Barbara was so blitzed on opening night that she passed out in Neal's arms; she revived moments later only to collapse again, and he had to carry her off stage.

Their relationship ended in 1955. In the same year Barbara did her last film, **Murder is My Beat** (1955). (In the mid 1960s Neal was convicted of shooting his third wife to death in a jealous rage and spent seven years in prison.)

The rest of the story grows increasingly ugly. Barbara was now referred to in the gossip columns as "Glitterville's Top Tramp." She wore her finest jewelry and furs and seldom went home alone. Barbara had started smoking pot and taking speed, and later heroin.

As she was turning twenty-nine later that year she went to Mexico with a male friend and spent several weeks at the plush Playa de Cortes Hotel in Guaymas. Her companion returned to the States but Barbara lingered behind in the company of her newest lover, (later to become her fourth husband), George Anthony Provas, the twenty-three-year-old manager of a local sport fishing business. They married in Nogales, Arizona, and lived in Kino Bay.

The smitten Provas later said, "We spent the next couple months walking on the beach, fishing for marlin and sailfish, and partying at night. And, of course, making love every chance we got. Without question, Barbara was the most beautiful girl I ever saw....Barbara was happy at first but then we both started drinking way too much and everything went to hell in a hand basket."

Payton eventually returned to Hollywood and attempted to revive her film career, but she met with nothing but derision. She then began a series of low-paying jobs such as waitressing in a strip joint, being a shampoo girl in a West Hollywood beauty shop, and pumping gas on Hollywood Boulevard. Toward the end of her life she was often arrested for drunkenness, passing bad checks, and prostitution.

In 1962 paperback publisher Leo Guild tracked Payton down to audiotape her memories and publish her autobiography, *I Am Not Ashamed*. It is considered by some to be a muddled, untruthful piece of junk but it gave her another brief blast of publicity. She now moved into the Wilcox Hotel, (called a monument to ruined lives), on the corner of Yucca and Wilcox. She was later busted for heroin possession at the Hollywood-Palms Motel, where she was going up and down the hall wearing only a man's pajama top. The policeman who busted her said, "Let me tell you, I was in the 'pool' a long time and I saw a lot of things, but I don't remember ever seeing anyone sink so low as Barbara Payton did." She was thirty-eight and she weighed some 200 pounds at that time.

Following a hospital stay she went to live with her parents, who had moved to San Diego, and she died there a few months later.

A neighbor once said of Barbara Payton, "Nothing wrong with Babs except that she's got a loose-leaf book for a heart." And film producer Herman Cohen once remarked, "Barbara Payton was a gorgeous gal, she was a fun person. She liked to laugh…and she was a little crazy. [You might say] she was a whore who got lucky."

Lucky—but only for a while.

Prince

(Prince Rogers Nelson)
Born 7 June 1958,
Minneapolis, MN.

Jazz musicians John and Mattie Shaw Nelson could not have imagined they were producing a child of musical royalty when their son was born, but the name "Prince" certainly befits this musical genius. On the demo tape Prince made at age sixteen he plays all the instruments himself—drums, bass, piano, and saxophone. Warner Brothers was so impressed that they signed him to a contract immediately. (The name itself comes from the combo Prince's father led, which was called the Prince-Rogers Trio.)

Prince's outstanding soundtrack is for *Purple Rain* (1984) for which he won an Oscar for Best Original Song Score, "When Doves Cry." Prince wrote all the songs in the film and performed them on screen as The Kid. By the time he made *Purple Rain*, however, Prince had long-since invented a new style of music, blending rock, soul, funk, and rhythm-and-blues. In his early albums he also brought a new sexuality to rock lyrics. The album *Purple Rain* sold more than 17,000,000 copies, and "When Doves Cry" rose to number one on the pop, soul, and dance charts. Prince won not only an Oscar, but three Grammy Awards and three American Music Awards for this material, and the film became the most commercially and critically successful rock film since the Beatles' A *Hard Day's Night* (1965).

Growing up had been difficult for Prince. His parents divorced before he finished grade school and he lived with his mother and step-father for a while, then with his father. Finally, he lived with family friends until the family of his good friend Andre Anderson informally adopted him. His stepfather did Prince a big favor, unwittingly, by taking him to a James Brown concert. This music began to percolate in him. By twelve he was teaching himself to play piano. Perhaps the pain of his broken home pushed him to explore music deeply. In any case, by age fourteen he was guitarist for a cover band called "Grand Central" begun by his cousin Charles Smith, a drummer. It featured Andre, who later changed his name from Anderson to Cymone, and Andre's sister, Linda, who played bass and keyboards, joined the group.

In time the band changed its name to "Champagne" and North High School friends Morris Day, James "Jimmy Jam" Harris, and Terry Lewis joined it. Prince became the group leader. At sixteen he made a demo tape, recording the band's instruments on separate tracks, synthesized the tracks through a mixer, and sent the tape to Warner Brothers. They saw the genius in the tape and offered him a contract giving him complete control in music production.

Four years later, in April 1978, Prince released his first album, "For You," which featured the single, "Soft and Wet."

By this time the band was called "Prince and the Revolution," and it was known for funk workouts, soul balladry, metallic wailing guitarwork, and Prince's silky falsetto voice. The albums "Prince" (1979), "Dirty Mind" (1980) and "Controversy" (1981) followed in rapid succession, and all of them went "gold" with sales over 500,000. The single "I Wanna Be Your Lover," went to number one on the soul charts, "1999" was a huge hit, and "Little Red Corvette" stayed on the charts for two years.

However, it was his soundtrack and first film *Purple Rain* (1984) that established Prince as one of pop's megastars. The movie earned ten times what it cost to make notwithstanding the generally poor reviews it got, and the soundtrack was a sensation, reaching sales or more than thirteen million in the USA alone.

Prince went on to write songs for other performers, such as "I Feel for You" which became a huge hit for rhythm-and- blues siren, Chaka Khan. He wrote and recorded "Around the World in a Day" featuring a playful hit, "Raspberry Beret" and "Parade," which served as the soundtrack for his second film, *Under the Cherry Moon* (1986). The critics didn't think much of this film, and fan reaction was also tepid, though "Raspberry Beret" sold four million copies.

Prince's next film was a recorded concert, "The Sign 'o' the Times."

In 1987 Prince opened his own recording studio, Paisley Park, in Chanhassen, Minnesota. It is large enough to hold scale-built film sets and Bill Pohlad's River Road Productions rented it to film *Old Explorers* (1989) starring Jose Ferrer and James Whitmore. It's a multi-purpose sound stage and recording studio but everyone must vacate the premises when Prince comes in to record.

At Paisley Park Prince recorded the soundtrack for Tim Burton's film, *Batman* (1989), and his own third feature film, *Graffiti Bridge* (1990), which the critics found to be mediocre at best.

In 1991 Prince was named Best Songwriter by readers of *Rolling Stone*.

Because of a highly-publicized dispute with Warner's in the early 90s, Prince changed his legal name on June 7, 1993, to an unpronounceable glyph. He dropped the glyph in May of 2000 when the contract with Warner Brothers expired. During these years Prince was known as "The Artist Formerly Known as Prince." It was a odd interlude during which Prince seemed to be adrift creatively.

Prince married Mayte Garcia, a dancer, on February 14, 1996, and they divorced in 2000.

In 2002 Prince released his most eclectic album, "The Rainbow Children," featuring songs inspired by his newly-adopted faith as a Jehovah's Witness. One critic described it as "an ambitious stroll down allegory alley." Prince also took on a succession of protégés including Appolonia, Vanity, Sheena Easton, and Kim Basinger.

Prince was inducted into the Rock and Roll Hall of Fame on March 15, 2004, in his first year of eligibility. He had produced twenty albums in twenty years, had invented a new sound, reinvented it several times, changed his name, then changed it back, made a few films, built a recording studio, and won quite a few awards. At several points in his career it seemed that he had nothing more to say. But each time he has bounced back, making it clear that he is less interested in merely being a pop icon than in producing yet another exciting new sound.

Kane Richmond

(Frederick W. Bowditch)
Born 23 December 1906,
Minneapolis, MN.
Died 22 March 1973,
CA.

Hollywood revolutionized the life of Fred Bowditch as he went from rags to (modest) riches—and acquired a new name in the process. Fred's father Perley was a custodian and it was likely that his poor son would follow in his footsteps, unless he could get a break and become a clerk and then work his way up in some large company.

In 1910 Perley was working at the L. S. Donaldson Company at 3237 37th Avenue. In 1915 he worked at 4200 Hiawatha Avenue and in 1920 Perley lived at the Donaldson Boarding House at 3207 E. 42nd St. In 1923 and 1925 Fred is listed as living with Perley at 2715 E. Minnehaha Parkway and working at the Atlantic Elevator Company. Fred attended Simons Elementary School and Roosevelt High School. Fred should have been in the Class of 1924 but there is no record that he graduated.

In 1928, when Fred was twenty-two, he decided to abandon his clerking job and move to California where the future looked brighter for so many young Americans. He took a new name, Kane Richmond, and with his six-foot height, square-cut jaw, and personable character, he was soon performing as an extra in films.

In fact, Kane's debut as an extra in *Their Own Resort* (1929), caught the attention of the studio bosses who featured him the next year in the serial *The Leather Pushers*. He also distinguished himself in *Cavalier of the West* (1931). Similar roles followed, but it was not until 1935, with the serial *The Adventures of Rex and Rinty*, that he became a genuine star as Frank Bradley. The magic of Rinty had financially saved Warner Brothers Studio from collapse in the mid-1920s and continued to be "gold" for others, too.

Richmond next starred in the serial *The Lost City*, which was such a big hit that he became a challenger for Buster Crabbe's title as "King of the Serials." The first series was based on the adventures of an individual named Colonel William Fawcett, who made some remarkable discoveries in South America while exploring in the late 1920s before he mysteriously disappeared. His intriguing tales fired the public imagination in books, radio shows, and films like those Kane was starring in. The first in the series was subtitled "The Lost City of the Ligurians" and the second was "City of the Lost Men." *Cult Movie Stars* author Robert James Parish lists the second as one of his two Cult Favorites.

Two mainstream films were also big winners for Richmond at this time: *The Silent Code* (1935) and *Thunderbolt* (1935). He appeared in minor roles in *Nancy Steele Is Missing* (1937) and *Boys Town* (1938) one of the best tearjerkers of all time. And he also tried his hand at science fiction movies, including Buster Crabbe's *Flash Gordon's Trip to Mars* (1938) and *Mars Attacks the World* (1938). Leaving few genres unexplored, Kane showed up in *Charlie Chan in Reno* (1939) and *Charlie Chan in Panama* (1940), and in *The Return of the Cisco Kid* (1939) starring Warner Baxter, and the third remake of *Riders of the Purple Sage* (1941).

Aficionados of the era's serials generally agree that *Spy Smasher* (1942) is Kane's finest achievement in movies. He plays Alan Armstrong, an American agent spy smasher, and also Armstrong's twin brother Jack. Secret identities, Nazi spy rings, and stirring romance all play a part in the film's success. (Parts of this film, along with other serial clips, was re-released in 1966 as *The Spy Smasher Returns*.)

Haunted Harbor (1944) was Richmond's next important serial, co-starring Kay Aldrich, the "serial queen." Though the two were good in the love scenes, his stunts were performed by David Sharpe—Kane simply didn't have the athletic ability that his character, Jim Marsden, possessed.

Soon Richmond was doing several serials simultaneously. He was Lt. Larry Farrell in *Brenda Starr, Reporter* (1945) and Bob Moore in *The Jungle Raiders* (1945). In 1946 Kane did the three films for which he is probably most widely remembered, playing Lamont Cranston (aka The Shadow) for Monogram Studios: *Behind the Mask*, *The Missing Lady* and *The Shadow Returns*.

A year later Richmond played his final serial character, Brick Bradford. He retired in 1948 as the last "King of the Serials." He was forty-two years old, and twenty years away from Minneapolis, Minnesota. He had pursued a dream and found fame and a pot of gold at the end of his rainbow in Hollywood.

Marion Ross

Born 25 October 1928,
Watertown, MN.

How many of us have had happy days in our past to recall when times are tough? Marion Ross has had very "Happy Days" indeed, as Marion Cunningham on the ABC-TV sit-com from 1974 to 1984. She received two Emmy nominations for her work on that show, but her varied career also covers the Broadway stage, TV movies, and Hollywood movies.

Marion spent her early years in Waconia, west of Minneapolis. When she was eight her family moved to Albert Lea. Her father, Gordon W. Ross, worked in the management of Interstate Power Company, the local electric utility company. Her mother, Ellen A. Ross, was a homemaker. They lived at 508 High Street on Albert Lea's north side and Marion attended Northside Elementary School and Albert Lea Junior High.

In the spring of 1943, after her sophomore year at Albert Lea High, Marion came to Minneapolis to work as an "au pair" girl so she could take drama lessons at the MacPhail Center for the Arts. She went to Southwest High School for her junior year, then the family moved to San Diego, where she attended San Diego State College. Her older sister, Alicia, stayed in Albert Lea until recently, when she moved to San Diego to be near Marion. Marion also has a younger brother, Gordon A. Ross.

Her Broadway debut came at the Edwin Booth Theatre in 1950s. She also performed at the Globe Theatre in San Diego and at the Summer Theatre in La Jolla, CA.

While TV has been her busiest work arena throughout her career, she has appeared in several fine films, including *Forever Female* (1953), *The Glenn Miller Story* (1954), *Sabrina* (1954), *The Proud and the Profane* (1956), *Lust for Life* (1956), *Some Came Running* (1959), *Operation Petticoat* (1959), *Honky* (1971), *Grand Theft Auto* (1977), *Evening Star* (1996), and *The Last Best Sunday* (1999). She has also made several made-for-TV movies:

Yet TV has been Marion's mainstay as an actress. In fact, she has been a regular on eight different TV series. Her debut series was *Life with Father* (1953, as Nora). Among her other series are *Mr. Novak* (1963-64), and *Paradise Bay* (1965).

Of course Marion Cunningham is her signature role. She played the part on *Happy Days*, week-in-week-out, for eleven years. The show, set in Milwaukee in the late 1950s, was created by comedy writer Garry Marshall who had written for *The Dick Van Dyke Show* and *The Lucy Show*. Ron Howard played "Richie" from 1974-80; he attended Jefferson High and worried about girls all the time. Marion was Richie's mother.

George Lucas was inspired to film *American Graffiti* (1973) after seeing the pilot. The show also led to two successful spin-offs, *Laverne and Shirley* and *Mork and Mindy*.

Marion's next series was ABC's *The Love Boat* (1985-1986), followed by *Brooklyn Bridge* (1991), *The Drew Carey Show* (1997), and *Postcards from Heaven* (1999). Her many guest appearances on TV run from *The Lone Ranger*, *Perry Mason*, and *Rawhide*, to *Seinfeld*, *Hill Street Blues*, and *Dark Shadows*.

In the summer of 2001 Marion had another HAPPY DAY as she was given a star on the Hollywood Walk of Fame, joining the Andrews Sisters, Richard Arlen, Richard Dix, Marguerite De La Motte, Judy Garland, William Demarest, Robert Vaughn, Richard Widmark, and other stars from Minnesota.

She is a spokeswoman for Marion, Illinois, and this duty brings her back to America's heartland a few times each year. On the Lifetime Channel in May of 2002 she was given a movie portrait of her life. In the summer of 2002 she visited Austin, Minnesota, for a SPAM Museum event, and she frequently revives her one-woman show on poet and writer Edna St. Vincent Millay. She has given benefit performances of *Love Letters* by A. R. Gurney in the Twin Cities in recent years. As of this writing she is 78 and still looking for more work.

Marion once told a *Minneapolis Star-Tribune* staff writer that she credits her success in show business to the harsh Minnesota climate and to her immigrant mother's belief in the American Dream (her mother is Canadian). "It's those long winters. If you live in California, there's something swell to do every day. But those long winters, I would sit and think. There's a compression of dreams."

Jane Russell

*(Ernestine Jane Geraldine
Russell)
Born 21 June 1921,
Bemidji, MN.*

Jane was the Hollywood discovery of
Howard Hughes, it's true, but really
Bemidji, Minnesota, was the first to discover her. She was born here during her
parents annual summer vacation to the area.

Jane's father was a lieutenant in the United States Army. Her
father eventually left the service and found work in Van Nuys, California. Jane was nine months old at the time. As a child she took
piano lessons but was something of a tomboy—as the family grew
she found herself with four younger brothers to contend with. Yet
under the influence of her mother, who had once belonged to a traveling troupe of players, Jane also developed an interest in drama and
appeared in several high school plays.

After graduating in 1939 from Van Nuys High School, Russell
worked as receptionist and then a dental assistant. Her father had
died suddenly and she had to work to help support the family. Modelling soon became her chief source of income, and by the end of the
summer she had earned enough money to attend the Max Reinhardt
School of Drama. The regimen bored her, however, and she spent
much of her time at a bowling alley across the street.

Her next stop was Howard Hughes and Hollywood.

Howard Hughes was an aviation pioneer. (His story was admirably told in Martin Scorsese's film *The Aviator*.) He was also a lady's
man and an innovative film-maker. These interests came together in
a project to push the boundaries of what could be shown on film by
making a Western called *The Outlaw*. Jane was chosen for the starring
role largely on the basis of her dramatic and sexy figure. Hughes drew
on his engineering background to personally design clothing that
would highlight her impressive physique, and the results were so provocative that the censors withheld the film from distribution for three
years. *The Outlaw* was finished in 1941, it premiered in 1943 in San
Francisco, but was not given a general release until 1946. Though it
was a box-office success, it did not entirely meet the high level of prurient expectations generated by all the controversy, and there are few
today who would include it among the many classic Westerns being

made at the time. Perhaps if Howard Hawks, the director Hughes originally picked to make the film, had been allowed to pursue his vision, things would have been different. But Hawks walked off the set after a serious disagreement with Hughes about the film's tone, and any magic it might potentially have possessed left with him.

Jane herself, previously an unknown, received a good deal of notoriety as a result of *The Outlaw*, and she became a pin-up girl from coast to coast. Unfortunately, she remained on contract with Hughes from 1941 to 1948 and he was reluctant to loan her out. When she did finally begin appearing in films again, the talent and wit that Hawks had been prohibited from exploiting in *The Outlaw* immediately became plain for all to see. She scored hits with Bob Hope in *Paleface* (1948) and *Son of Paleface* (1952), playing the strong straight-man to his diffident funnyman as he tosses out sexual innuendos in a steady stream. She also had success playing opposite brawny Robert Mitchum in *His Kind of Woman* (1951). Other films of the period include the musical comedy *Double Dynamite* (1951) co-starring Frank Sinatra and Groucho Marx, *The Las Vegas Story (1952)*, *Montana Belle* (1952), and *Macao* (1952).

But Jane's most memorable film is *Gentlemen Prefer Blondes* (1953), a musical in which she teams up with a young Marilyn Monroe under the direction of Howard Hawks. Jane and Marilyn sing a dynamite duet, "Diamonds Are a Girl's Best Friend," while shimmying vigorously in loud, red-sequenced dresses. Fifty years later, that over-the-top song and film are still a treasure. Jane is a great foil for Marilyn who displays a new comic side. Jane's vivacious dancing is great, too. The two became friends on and off the screen.

Jane went on to do *Gentlemen Marry Brunettes* (1955), though neither Marilyn nor director Hawks remained on board, and the results are rather pedestrian. In the drama *The Tall Men* (1956), she appeared with Clark Gable and Robert Ryan. Other films of the period include *The French Line* (1954), *Underwater* (1955), *Foxfire* (1955), *Hot Blood* (1956), and *The Fuzzy Pink Nightgown* (1957) in which she falls in love with her kidnapper, played by Ralph Meeker.

Jane made a few films in the 1960s, but her career was definitely on the wane. In 1970, however, she replaced Elaine Stritch on Broadway in the Steven Sondheim musical *Company*, which gave her the opportunity once again to play a blowsy, boozy broad who can sing, dance, act, laugh, and have a rollicking good time.

Russell made TV commercials in the 1970s for Playtex Bras. These ads—"cross your heart bras for us full-figured gals"—were very successful and ran for several years. In fact, throughout her career

Jane succeeded in exploiting her physique in a good-humored way that her fans found very refreshing. Her co-stars often took the same tack. Bob Hope once famously introduced her as "the two and only Jane Russell," for example.

In the 1980s Jane made some TV guest appearances on *The Yellow Rose,* an hour-long, prime-time serial of a young widow on a sprawling Texas cattle ranch. She also wrote her autobiography, *Jane Russell: My Path and My Detours,* which came out in 1985.

Although Jane's media persona was that of a wise-cracking voluptuous siren, in private life she was noted for her conservatism. She was married for twenty-five years to former football star Bob Waterfield. When they had difficulty conceiving children, they adopted. Wanting to do more for the children, in 1955 Russell founded World Adoption International Fund (WAIF), which was one of the first American agencies to place children from overseas in American families. She and her husband also started the Hollywood Christian Group, a weekly Bible study at her home. She became prominent in Republican politics, and attended the Eisenhower inauguration.

Jane returned to Bemidji in 2002 and was photographed with a "sister," Pat Henry, and a cousin, Judy Jacobi. She signed the guest book, "Back in Bemidji after 81 years." The visit was prompted by a family reunion organized by her cousin, Bud Jacobi, a Bemidji resident. After the reunion she had a scheduled photo-shoot with *Vanity Fair* Magazine.

Winona Ryder

(Winona Laura Horowitz)
Born 29 October, 1971,
Winona, MN.

Note the name of the actress and the town in which she was born. The name means "first-born daughter of the chief" in the Dakota language. Or as we would say, "princess." The Minnesota river town of Winona took the name from the daughter of the Sioux Dakota chief Wapasha III, who lived in the area when the town was settled. And Winona Ryder received that name because she was born in that town.

Ryder, (whose nickname is "Noni" with a long "o" sound) was raised in Minneapolis for parts of a few years of her childhood near the intersection of 19th Street and Fifteenth Avenue South. Born to Michael Horowitz and Cindy Palmer, who were "flower children," Winona grew up in a counter-culture environment that was freer than most, and also, perhaps, more sensitive to political issues and the value of books. Her father was an archivist for Timothy Leary, the LSD guru from Harvard University. When Winona was twelve the family moved to Petaluma, California, where Michael ran the Flashback Bookstore, which was devoted to "hippy" subjects. Later Michael became curator of the Fitzhugh-Ludlow Memorial Library in San Francisco, where the focus was on psychedelic literature. In fact, Timothy Leary was chosen as Winona's Godfather, and frequent visits from "Beat" poet Allen Ginsburg also made Noni feel she that she was in another time zone.

Noni's mother Cindy, along with her former husband, Johnny Palmer, were co-founders of a film society at the firehouse at Minnehaha Avenue and Lake Street. Al Milgrom and a few of his friends later formed the University of Minnesota Film Society from the remnants of this group. Cindy later started a video production company and operated a film society of sorts in Elk, Northern California, where the family lived in a commune environment with seven other families from 1978 to 1981. Movies were so important to Cindy that she allowed Noni to stay home from school if an old classic movie happened to be on TV that day. One of Noni's favorites was *Random Harvest* (1942), and Greer Garson, who played the heroine in that film, became Noni's film idol. "I wanted to be like her. Nothing could compare with Garson's face, her expressions."

The Elk commune was an upscale hippy community, with horses and gardens on a three-hundred-acre plot of land. "You have so much freedom," Ryder later told *Rolling Stone* Magazine, "you can go roaming anywhere. We didn't have electricity, which was weird, but it was great to grow up that way. We didn't have TV, so you'd have to do stuff. My friends' names were Tatonka, Gulliver, and Rio. We'd have hammock contests, sit around and make up stories, make up weird games. I don't know—it was a weird, weird childhood. I mean, it was great."

In 1981 the family moved to Petaluma, just north of San Francisco. Noni wore her hair short and behaved like a tomboy in junior high, and one day she was attacked after school by a group of students who thought she was a very effeminate boy. From that time on her parents taught her at home. She soon became bored with that regimen, however, and at the age of twelve, at her parents' instigation, Noni enrolled in drama classes at the American Conservatory Theatre (ACT) in San Francisco. Her folks wanted her to meet and make friends with other similarly sensitive and creative kids. It never occurred to them that she would actually *become* an actress.

At the age of thirteen Ryder made an audition videotape for the stepdaughter role in Jon Voight's film, *Desert Bloom*. She didn't get the part but she was impressive enough that Triad Artists Agency later agreed to represent her, and she was soon given a role in the teen drama *Lucas*. It was small but it attracted attention.

Ryder is a natural blond but she was told to dye her hair black for the role and it has stayed black ever since. As for her stage name, she told *Rolling Stone* magazine that the inspiration was hers. Her dad was listening to a Mitch Ryder album during a phone interview and she just grabbed the name out of the air.

Her first starring role came in *Square Dance* (1987) in which she played an alienated teenager on the threshold of adulthood. Jason Robards (her stern grandfather) and Jane Alexander (her mother) taught her a lot about the business of acting during the shoot.

"Jane Alexander taught me to be patient, how to hold on to my feelings and then let it all go when it did happen. Jason Robards taught me how to be natural in front of the camera." The film got mixed reviews though Winona herself was singled out for her "touchingly dignified performance."

Winona's career took a giant step forward when she co-starred with Michael Keaton, Geena Davis, and Alec Baldwin in the hit comedy, *Beetlejuice* (1988), playing a death-obsessed teen. She enhanced her reputation further with another dark portrayal in the satire *Heathers* (1989). She was advised by her agents not to appear in this film about teen suicide, which seemed to treat the subject as a joke, but her instincts told her to do it, "[Some people] thought the film was making a joke about teen suicide. But what we were making a joke at was that society makes it so romantic," she later remarked. In playing this role Winona displayed "subtleties beyond her years," according to *Newsweek*'s David Ansen, and the *Village Voice* felt that she played the "conflicted Veronica with deeper-than-Method conviction."

In 1990 Noni plays the long-suffering daughter to Cher's free-spirited mother in *Mermaids*. Her next film, *Edward Scissorhands* (1990), paired her with her long-term love interest, Johnny Depp. (She dated him from the age of seventeen to her mid-twenties, and Depp had a tattoo put on his biceps saying Winona Forever.)

By this time Noni was getting tired of playing teenagers. Yet when asked that year why she played so many teen roles, she answered, "Like, I'm nineteen. What am I supposed to do, play a judge?" Ryder's first adult role came in the Jim Jarmusch film *Night on Earth* (1992), a movie focusing largely on taxi cab conversations.

She had been scheduled to play Mary Corleone, Michael's daughter, in Francis Ford Coppola's *Godfather III* (1990), but she was suffering from respiratory infection, anxiety attacks, depression, and exhaustion, and dropped out of the project.

Ryder later redeemed herself by bringing the Dracula script to Coppola's attention. In that blood-soaked gothic production, *Bram Stoker's Dracula* (1992), she played the British lover of the count-turned-vampire. Though the film did appeal to some tastes, few critics considered it a complete success.

On the other hand, in her next film Ryder teamed up with director Martin Scorsese to make *The Age of Innocence* (1993) for which she was nominated for an Academy Award. The film is based on Edith Wharton's Pulitzer Prize-winning novel about New York aristocracy in the 1870s. Vincent Candy of the *New York Times* found Ryder "wonderful [as a] sweet young thing who's hard as nails, acting as much out of ignorance as of self-interest." Ryder herself later admitted, "It was the first time I ever felt proud of myself as an actress."

Scorsese enjoyed working with the talented actress, saying that it was "like having rampant youth on the set. She'd be jumping up and down, but then when you said, 'Action,' she froze into position. All that energy was put behind her eyes, and I found that really fascinating."

Following convincing performances in *The House of the Spirits* (1993) and *Reality Bites* (1994) Ryder earned another Best Actress Oscar nomination for *Little Women* (1994) playing the central character, Jo March.

Minnesotan Sarah Pillsbury produced Ryder's next film, a charming slice of Americana called *How to Make an American Quilt* (1995). The next year she starred opposite Daniel Day-Lewis in Arthur Miller's *The Crucible* (1996). She was cast as herself in both Woody Allen's *Celebrity* (1998) and *Being John Malkovich* (1999). In *Girl Interrupted* (1999) she returned to teen-roles as a vulnerable young woman in a hospital for the mentally ill.

In October of 1997 *Empire* magazine ranked Ryder as number 42 in their Top 100 Movie Stars of All Time list. The same year she was chosen by *People* magazine as one of the 50 Most Beautiful People in the World. And in 2000 Noni was honored with a star on the Hollywood Walk of Fame.

Premiere magazine once described Winona Ryder as "the witty, wondrous sweetheart of hip America." She has been the idol of Generation X, and although her recent film efforts have not been outstanding, there is little doubt that Ryder has the intelligence, beauty, and depth necessary to move and surprise us all on screen again.

Lili St. Cyr

(Willis Marie van Schaack)
Born 3 June, 1918,
Minneapolis, MN.
Died 29 June, 1999,
Los Angeles, CA.

Willis van Schaack took ballet lessons in her teens, hoping to become a classical dancer someday. As Lili St. Cyr she did become a dancer, and her routines are considered "classic," but not in the way she originally imagined.

Like so many performers of her generation, Lili got her start in vaudeville, as a Florentine Gardens chorus girl. Life in the chorus was less than inspiring, however, and before long Lili began to develop a burlesque routine. She was tall, beautiful, and shapely, she had blue eyes and blond hair, and she found that when she removed her clothing in her skits, she received more than the usual enthusiasm from the men in the audience. Unlike most strippers, however, who were buxom and full-figured, Lili was slender, and the acts she developed, which had names such as "Suicide" "Jungle Goddess," and "Love Moods," became known for their refinement. Her signature act made use of carefully arranged bubbles in a bubble bath.

In time St. Cyr became the most prominent stripper in postwar America, performing in burlesque houses from Montreal and Boston to Seattle and Los Angeles, often making more than $7,500 a week. Not surprisingly, perhaps, she attracted the attention of the authorities and became embroiled in a *cause célèbre*. In spring of 1951 she premiered her bubble bath act at Ciro's, a swanky nightclub on Sunset Boulevard, and on October 15th the police raided the place. Lili was arrested for indecent exposure, lewd and lascivious behavior, and brought quickly to trial. St. Cyr hired the famous lawyer Jerry Geisler (who had earlier won an acquittal for Errol Flynn on a similarly controversial case), and Geisler persuaded the judge to allow Lili to do her bathtub routine in the courtroom, to prove that it was tasteful entertainment. The tub had a glass front and lots of bubbles, though not too many, and after her bath Lili deftly dressed in front of her courtroom audience. The judge demurred on a decision but the jury voted that her act was, indeed, "art." After the verdict, she was photographed holding the flimsy bra and rhinestone studded G-string she wore in her act. They had been introduced at the trial as exhibits A and B. *Look Magazine* did a photo spread of it.

Following her celebrated trial Lili began to appear in "blue movies." These were sexually explicit and provocative films, and the movie houses that showed them ran the risk of police raids and severe fines, not to mention confiscation of their equipment and films. Nevertheless, these films were widely shown, usually along with a bribe to keep the authorities away. Lili's first five films fall into this category. *Love Moods* (1952); *Lili's Wedding Night* (1952, aka as *Her Wedding Night*), which was very loosely based on a movie by the same title made in 1930 with Clara Bow and Charles Ruggles; *Bedroom Fantasy* (1953); *Varietease* (1954); and *Striporama* (1954).

Lili finally cracked the legitimate film world with an appearance as herself in *The Miami Story* (1954) starring Barry Sullivan. This added to her appeal as a mainstream performer and other filmmakers began to take her more seriously as an actress. Howard Hughes was one of them. He cast her in his movie, *Son of Sinbad* (1955) along with Dale Robertson (as Sinbad's son) and Vincent Price (as Omar Khayam). The movie has several extended dance numbers, and is considered good entertainment today, though at the time it was widely thought to be shockingly provocative.

Lili continued to make blue movies, including *Buxom Beautease* (1956), and she had a part in *The Naked and the Dead* (1958), a film based very loosely on Norman Mailer's sensational post-World War II book. Cliff Robertson, Aldo Ray and Raymond Massey starred in this Raoul Walsh-directed film, which Mailer said was, "One of the worst movies ever made." As Sergeant Croft's wife Lili played a cartoon-like woman—selfish, cold, neurotic, and sexually omnivorous. In the book she is merely unfaithful but Walsh turned her into a stripper whose name happened to be Lili. Her striptease is cut short by a MP raid.

That same year Lili made her final legitimate movie, *I, Mobster* (1958), a Roger Corman-directed, bullet-riddled thriller not well received by the few critics who saw it.

At one time or another Lili was linked romantically with Hughes, Orson Welles, and Victor Mature, and she also had six or seven husbands. When she and actor Ted Jordan were married in Las Vegas their cake was in the shape of an atomic bomb explosion.

During an interview for the *New York Times* in 1967, Lili was asked her opinion of the pop fashions of the Sixties. She replied, "1 wouldn't be caught dead wearing net hose, sequined dresses or false eyelashes. Women who wear them in public remind me of strippers."

She used to keep in touch with *Minneapolis Star-Tribune* columnist Barbara Flanagan to say that she was "alive and well and operating a boutique in Los Angeles. I have not been in Minneapolis for many years, but good friends have kept me abreast of the changes there."

In later life she owned a succession of lingerie shops in Los Angeles.

Seann William Scott

Born 3 October, 1976,
Cottage Grove, MN.

Park High School in Cottage Grove can boast of its delegate to Hollywood, Seann William Scott, class of 1994. He worked double shifts at movie houses just so he could see as many of the films that came through town as possible. He also spent some of his teen years at the Eden Prairie Mall, the film location of his favorite movie, *Mallrats* (1995), Kevin Smith's low-budget feature which introduced Ben Affleck to movie audiences. Being so immersed in movies, Seann could not imagine any other kind of career for himself than life as an actor.

He is the youngest of seven children in a "blended family" where each parent brought three children into the new marriage. In 1994, at the age of eighteen, he went to Hollywood with his mother. "My family really thought I was going to come home to Minnesota after two weeks," he later recalled, and added that he really knew nothing about the business of show business at the time. "I was so naïve. I thought when you got an agent they just put you in the movies. I didn't know you had to audition! The first three years were so hard."

His mother left after a month of teaching Seann how to do his laundry and make sandwiches. "She eventually took off and I still couldn't find a job. She was freaking out not knowing how I was going to survive."

He spent a year at Glendale Community College and worked at several odd jobs to pay bills while waiting for "the break." He was a restaurant host and later worked gathering up stray shopping carts at a Home Depot store. His supervisor at the time, Luigi Iezza, remembered Scott as a "cool, laid-back guy," but instead of helping customers he sometimes "would hide out in the plumbing aisle and read movie books."

Scott did occasionally land a bit part on TV which kept his hopes alive. He appeared in episodes of "Unhappily Ever After" and "Sweet Valley High," as well as several commercials. His debut movie came in 1997 in the NBC Movie of the Week, *Born into Exile*.

Then it happened. He went to a talent competition in Los Angeles and he was "discovered." ABC producers loved his looks and flew him immediately to New York to test for "All My Children." Then he won the audition for *American Pie* (1999). Yet, three months before the movie opened, he was still pushing snack carts at the Los Angeles Zoo because he had earned only union scale wages, Hollywood's "minimum wage." "The second day I was there [at the zoo], I had an interview with *Rolling Stone* to promote the movie. I'm thinking, 'What's going on? I have an interview with *Rolling Stone* and I'm selling churros at the zoo!'"

American Pie is a gross comedy about high school kids who are determined to lose their virginity, and it's full of crude jokes and dumbed-down dialog, but young people went in droves to see it, bringing the box office receipts well over a hundred million dollars. Two years later Scott appeared in the sequel, *American Pie II* and was much more amply rewarded for his efforts.

Secure financially for the first time since he left home, Scott spent a few months backpacking in Europe and bought a house overlooking Universal Studios. "I think because of those years of struggling I am really able to appreciate what is happening to me now," he said. "But Home Depot is saving a spot for me, just in case things don't work out."

Parts started to come his way, including *Final Destination* (2000), a film about a psychic student who attempts to save his friends from a fatal plane crash, and **Road Trip** (2000) in which he reprises his character of a clueless but likeable punk. He played the same character again in **Dude, Where's My Car?** (2000).

David Duchovny and Julianne Moore star in Seann's next movie, **Evolution** (2001), which was directed by Ivan Reitman, who had earlier made **Ghostbusters**. The protagonists combat aliens with the help of a well-known dandruff shampoo in this uneven but often quite funny film.

Seann had a chance to work with his teenage idol, director Kevin Smith, in **Jay and Silent Bob Strike Back** (2001). (Seann still has a "one-sheet" of **Mallrats** over his bed, a daily commemoration of the Smith film.) He was excited about doing **Stark Raving Mad** (2002) because it was his first non-comic leading role. "This is the kind of movie I came to L.A. to do."

More recent film appearance include **Bulletproof Monk** (2003), **Old School** (2003), **American Wedding** (2003, also called **American Pie: The Wedding**); and **Rundown** (2003). Like many a restless actor before him, Scott wanted something more of the "pie" (control) and he became a producer of the French film project, **Gregoire Moulin vs Humanity** (2004). He has also become a popular guest on late-night TV shows.

Dick Simmons

Born 19 August, 1913,
St. Paul, MN.
Died 11 January, 2003,
Oceanside, CA.

"On, King! On, you huskies!" "Well, King, this case is closed." These are key phrases in the radio and TV *Sergeant Preston of the Yukon* series, broadcast on CBS-TV from 1955-1958. Dick Simmons was the star, though it had taken him nearly twenty years to find his true calling—sergeant in the Royal Canadian Mounted Police.

Like *The Lone Ranger* and *The Green Hornet* series, *Sergeant Preston* was conceived by George W. Trendle for his Detroit radio station, WXYZ. The TV series was filmed in color, often on location in Ashcroft, Colorado. It was produced by the Wrather Corporation, which also owned the Ranger series.

Simmons did not play Preston on the radio series which ran from 1947 to 1955 on the ABC Radio Network, but he was a perfect fit for the TV show. "Like Clayton Moore was the Lone Ranger, Dick Simmons was Sergeant Preston," wrote Boyd Magers, the editor of *Western Clippings* magazine, who knew Simmons. "...he just looked like what you'd think a typical Mountie would look like." Dick had a deep authoritative voice and a military bearing he'd developed during World War II, where he'd been a pilot in the Air Transport Command. These qualities served him well portraying Sergeant Preston, who relentlessly slogged through snow drifts, alone, looking for fugitives from the law, accompanied only by his horse, Rex, and his faithful lead-dog, Yukon King, a Malamut Husky. He had to ski, drive a dog sled team, snowshoe, swim, horseback ride, wrestle, fist-fight, paddle a canoe, and climb mountains. And Dick did all his own stunts.

Simmons was born to Mr. and Mrs. Parker E. Simons at 348 N. Dale Street in Saint Paul. He attended Hancock Elementary School. The family moved to Minneapolis in 1925 and Dick spent his teen years at 3122 West Lake Street, 3509 West 32nd Street, and 746 Cromwell Avenue near Upton Avenue South and Minnehaha Parkway. His father was a manager-buyer in the purchasing department of St Paul Electric and later at Northland Electric Supply Co. Dick attended Jefferson Junior High, West High School and the University of Minnesota, where he studied drama, fencing, swimming, diving and horseback riding. However, wanderlust took hold of him before he graduated and he took off to see the world.

Between 1934 and 1937 Simmons worked as a deck hand on oil tankers and freighters and a ranch hand and rodeo rider. One of the freighters he signed up on took him to Mexico and South America before reaching its final destination: Los Angeles. Thus acting in movies became another in a long string of odd jobs. Simmons claimed to have done twenty-six pictures in one year, though his officially recorded debut was in Joan Fontaine's *A Million to One* (1937). He was not under contract to anyone so he would just go up to this or that studio's gates and ask if they were hiring that day.

He was eating in a Hollywood restaurant one day in 1938 when MGM producer Hunt Stromberg spotted him and liked his looks. He sent his associate to ask Dick if he had been pictures before and would he like to be in one right away. He was shuttled over to the studio, given a screen test, issued a costume, and assigned to be the Duke de Aiguillon, a minister of state to King Louis XV. Simmons did seem to be in royal company: John Barrymore was playing the king, and Norma Shearer had the title role. The film was *Marie Antoinette*.

Though both Stromberg and director W. S. Van Dyke were satisfied with his performance, nothing ever came of it and Dick went back to doing bit parts, usually uncredited. His third officially recorded movie, *King of the Royal Mounted* (1940), offered a faint foretaste of the fruitful run he would have fifteen years later.

One day in 1942 Howard Strickling of MGM spotted Simmons at a dude ranch rodeo in Palm Springs where Dick was working as a commercial pilot. He had by this time appeared in some thirty-plus movies as an uncredited extra. Strickling was impressed with Simmons' square-jaw and handsome looks and phoned Louis Mayer about him. Without taking the usual screen test, Dick was signed to an MGM contract, and during the next fourteen years he appeared in bit parts in fifty-five films for which he was credited.

After three years of war service, Simmons returned to Hollywood. The best of the post-war films in which he appears are *Love Laughs at Andy Hardy* (1947), *Undercover Maisie* (1947) with Ann Sothern, *Easter Parade* (1948), *A Southern Yankee* (1948) with Red Skelton and Arlene Dahl, *The Three Musketeers* (1948), *Rear Window* (1954), *Brigadoon* (1954), *Love Me or Leave Me* (1955), and *It's Always Fair Weather* (1955).

In 1954 Dick landed the lead role in the serial *The Man with the Steel Whip*, and the next year he was chosen over forty other actors for the role in the *Sergeant Preston* TV series, which ran until 1958.

Dick took a long pause from moviemaking before appearing in the Rat Pack movie, *Sergeants 3* (1963) starring Frank Sinatra, Dean Martin and the gang. He also appeared in the spoof *Robin and the 7 Hoods* (1964) starring Sinatra and newcomer Bing Crosby.

Simmons appeared on other TV shows over the years, including *My Little Margie, Black Saddle, Leave It to Beaver, Rawhide, Perry Mason, The Munsters, It Takes a Thief, The Brady Bunch,* and *ChiPs,* in 1982— his last show business appearance.

Dick was severely injured in a helicopter crash in 1967, and while in the hospital he studied real estate. Once his acting career had come to an end, he took on another odd job—managing a mobile home park in Carlsbad, California.

Eventually health problems forced Simmons to move to Prescott, Arizona. He was survived by his third wife, Billie, his son, Michael, of Thousand Oaks, California, and his daughter, Sue Bryar, of Woodland Hills, California. He also had two grandchildren and two great-grandchildren.

A few bits of trivia:

– Simmons' hair started graying at the age of nineteen.

– Sergeant Preston's first name was Frank though it was never used on the air.

– Brace Beemer played the radio Lone Ranger and also the radio Sgt. Preston whose show was called "The Challenge of the Yukon."

– Though the TV version of the show had only three years of tapings, it ran for decades in syndication around the world.

Ginny Simms

Born 25 May, 1915,
San Antonio, TX.
Died 4 April, 1994,
Palm Springs, CA.

This "adopted Minnesotan" was a true canary. She had intended to be a teacher, but she was pulled toward the hot craze of the time—college dance bands—and when she was an eighteen-year-old student at Fresno State Teachers College in California she put together a trio. Her voice was clearly the best in the group, however, and she did a solo audition with the Guy Lombardo Orchestra. Lombardo didn't give her a job but the positive feed-back she received from the audition encouraged her to seriously consider singing as a career.

After spending time in several obscure bands Ginny landed a job with Tommy Gerun's group, which featured Al Norris as its lead singer. (Norris soon changed his name to Tony Martin and made it into movies.) Her big break came with the Kay Kyser Band in the late 1930s. Kyser's band was hot. He was also popular on radio with his *The Kollege of Musical Knowledge,* a quiz show with music. Ginny sang along with Harry Babbitt and did comic skits with Ish Kabibble. She traveled some 25,000 miles with the band. She was romantically involved with Kyser, and did three movies with him before they parted, amicably, in September of 1941.

Simms made her film debut playing herself in *That's Right, You're Wrong* (1939) which starred Kyser, Adolphe Menjou, Lucille Ball, and Ish Kabibble. Her second film with Kayser, *You'll Find Out* (1940) was also called *Here Come the Boogie Men.* It starred Boris Karloff, Peter

Lorre, and Bela Lugosi, with Kyser and his group playing for a birthday party in a gloomy mansion. Along the way they save the birthday girl from her three tormentors.

Ginny performed alongside The Great Profile, John Barrymore, in *Playmates* (1941) once again with Kyser and his band. Barrymore tries to turn Kyser into a Shakespearean actor in order to get a lucrative radio contract. It's a weird comedy but a good one.

After Ginny and Kay had gone their separate ways, she stayed with RKO Studios for two more pictures: *Seven Days Leave* (1942) and *Here We Go Again* (1942) which starred radio greats Jim (Fibber McGee) Jordan, Molly Jordan, Edgar Bergen, and Charlie McCarthy.

In 1941 NBC Radio Corporation reported that Ginny Simms was one of the top female vocalists in the country. That year she signed on for a new radio series sponsored by Kleenex tissues juggling radio shows with movies. She moved to MGM for *Broadway Rhythm* (1944) where she co-starred with future California Senator George Murphy backed by Tommy Dorsey and his Orchestra. It was based on the Jerome Kern-Oscar Hammerstein operetta, *Very Warm for May*.

She next bounced over to Universal Studios to star in *Shady Lady* (1945) with Charles Coburn. The next year she appeared in *Night and Day* (1946) starring Cary Grant in an entertaining, if inaccurate, biopic of the life of Cole Porter.

In 1945 Simms rather suddenly married an wealthy engineer named Hyatt Dehn, whom she had only known for a month. Many were surprised at this match, but Ginny told Louella Parsons, "He's not a playboy. He's serious-minded…and having a home of my own is something I've lived for all my life." She told Parsons that she wanted marriage and children more than anything, including her Hollywood career, and figured that she could do radio, make records, and also have babies. The couple eventually had two children, David and Conrad.

Hyatt Dehn was a New Yorker from the right social register who was involved in building tract housing for the World War II veterans who were returning to California. The couple settled down on a 65-acre farm near Beverly Hills, Ginny drank quarts of milk and learned to drive a tractor. But the settled-down married life wasn't satisfying in the end, and in 1951 she filed for divorce with, "I wanted to be a housewife. But that didn't work, so I might as well go back to a singing career."

Two months later, in late June, Simms married oilman Bob Calhoun. She refused to move in to the house her husband had just bought, however, and after ten days she broke off the relationship. She filed for divorce that October.

That same year Simms made her final film, *Disc Jockey* (1951). She continued to pursue her singing career, however, doing radio gigs and appearing at the Maisonette at the Hotel St. Regis in New York as late as in 1958.

Now, ladies and gentlemen, you may have begun to wonder where the state of Minnesota figures in any of this. Well, Simms wanted to invest in land development, and she worked with Don Eastvold to develop the Salton Sea area of the California desert. Eastvold was from Minneapolis. He had attended St. Olaf College and the University of Minnesota Law School before moving to Tacoma, Washington in 1950, where he was voted "Young Man of the Year." He served in the Washington State Senate and was elected attorney general. After an unsuccessful run at the governorship, he quit politics and took up land development. It was while working on North Shore Beach Estates on California's Salton Sea that he and Simms met.

The Salton Sea project never really succeeded, but Simms and Eastvold were married in 1961. The next year they moved to Minnesota to develop the Breezy Point resort complex, which at that time was a small resort with tiny rental cabins. Under their ownership the first condominiums in Minnesota were constructed. To make room for the condos, a twenty-seven hole golf course, a shopping center and necessary access roads, the Eastvolds cleared large stands of Jack pine. They also built an airstrip which doubled as a race track on some weekends. They constructed the Marina Dining Room and the Gold View Terrace Motel and lived at the Governor's Home, now a large rental unit with a pool built on a hill overlooking Pelican Lake.

Top-ranked bands like the Tommy Dorsey Band, the Glenn Miller Orchestra, and the Si Zentner Band appeared at the Marina Restaurant, and even Governor Rolvaag was there for the official opening ceremonies.

The Eastvolds did a lot of developing at Breezy Point, but they failed to deliver on many of their wild promises, such a giving a free horse away with each new specified lot. In fact, by 1965 the couple owed money to many small business-owners in the area and they filed for bankruptcy. They blamed their sales people for their financial woes, and others blamed their extravagant management style. Creditors kept Breezy Point open until Hopkins House bought it in 1968. Former bartender Dave Gravdahl, who became director of sales for Hopkins House, said, "It was difficult to get the resort back on its feet. But there were a lot of people who enjoyed coming up here. We just had to start all over. I think the resort wouldn't have been here today if [Eastvold and Simms] hadn't taken it over."

Lawsuits kept on coming through 1969 regarding the Breezy fiasco, however, and the Eastvolds fled to Chevy Chase, Maryland, then back to Hollywood, and finally to Palm Springs, where they lived virtually in hiding for many years to avoid legal entanglements.

Gale Sondergaard

(Edith Holm Sondergaard)
Born 15 February, 1899,
Litchfield, MN.
Died 14 August, 1985,
Woodland Hills, CA.

Little Edith grew up in Litchfield as the star of many neighborhood plays staged in the Sondergaard family barn. In time her star took her to national fame and she was awarded an Oscar for the Best Supporting Actress in 1936, the first year that this category was designated by the Oscar Committee. She was at first the preferred actress to play the Wicked Witch of the West in *The Wizard of Oz* (1940) but it was decided she was too beautiful for the part.

The Sondergaard home was located at 302 Swift Street South at the corner of Swift and Ripley. The house has now been moved to 326 S. Donnelly Avenue. It's a two-storey house with a porch, a roof of several gables, and the narrow, horizontal lap-siding common to many houses of the era. Edith and her sisters, Ragni and Heter, were daughters of Norwegian-Americans, Hans T. and Kristine (Holm) Sondergaard. Hans started as a butter maker in the Litchfield Cream-ery but eventually became a professor of Agriculture at the University of Wisconsin-Madison (1926-1938). He died in 1947.

Edith was photographed in 1910 in one of her many neighbor-hood plays. What was the price of admission to a play in their barn theater? Ten common pins. Gale organized and staged the shows and also played the leading lady. From an early age she was considered "different." Childhood friend Ethel Swanson recalled that Gale had a flair for drama even as a child. "When Gale walked up the stairway of the Sondergaard's lovely old home… she even did that with a certain grace—different from the rest of us ordinary kids."

The family left Litchfield in 1912 when Hans took a job as a federal butter inspector in Minneapolis.

The 1917 *Centralian* yearbook described Gale as having, "the heart to conceive, the understanding to direct and the hand to execute." She also attended the Minneapolis School of Dramatic Art before moving on to the University of Minnesota, where she graduated with a B.A. in 1921.

While at the U Gale was active in the Studio Players, and she also did a short stint in the Chautauqua circuit playing the ingénue, before joining the John Keller Shakespeare Company in 1921. She toured the USA and Canada as Gertrude in *Hamlet*, Jessica in *The Merchant of Venice*, Calpurnia in *Julius Caesar* and a witch in *Macbeth*.

Sondergaard's New York stage debut came in November, 1923, when she took over the role of Edith Somers in *What's Your Wife Doing?* She had come up through the ranks in the hinterlands of Minnesota theater, and now, just two years out of college, she is appearing on Broadway.

Edith spent two seasons with the John Bonstelle Stock Company, 1925-1927, in Detroit, Michigan. Then she joined the prestigious Theater Guild acting in G. B. Shaw's *Major Barbara*. She took over from Judith Anderson (who had replaced Lynn Fontanne) as Nina Leeds (the leading role) in the Broadway production of Eugene O'Neill's *Strange Interlude* in 1929; she was a witch in *Faust* in 1928.

In 1930 Gale married Herbert J. Biberman, the manager (and also sometime writer and stage director) at the Guild. They adopted a son, who became Daniel Hans Biberman. Though domestic responsibilities slowed her down somewhat, Gale continued to appear in plays sporadically until her husband accepted a contract to direct movies in 1935 and the family went West.

Gale herself, like many theater people of the time, had little interest in (or regard for) the movies. But director Mervyn LeRoy was fascinated with her face and asked her to test for his film, *Anthony Adverse* (1936) in the small but important role of Faith Paleologus. Gale was unimpressed with the test results, but LeRoy felt that she would be perfect for the role of Faith. Though the part was small compared to the roles she was used to playing night after night on stage, she took it.

The film itself was an extravaganza. It had 412 scenes and a cast of 2,000. The screenplay ran to five-hundred-thousand words, and sets were built to duplicate scenes in France, Italy, Switzerland, Cuba, Africa, and America. Warner Brothers received 17,437 fan letters requesting that Fredric March be given the title role. Olivia de

Havilland was pre-cast in her part because of her performance in *A Midsummer Night's Dream* (1935). But Gale, a relative unknown to film-goers, won the Oscar.

For the next ten years film offers came in droves, and Sondergaard began a new chapter of life as Queen of the Heavies—the lady you love to hate. Her velvet beauty, high-arched eyebrows, broad-toothed smile, and icy glare could threaten or terrorize even the biggest stars like Bob Hope, Shirley Temple, and Bette Davis. But Gale had not lost her dramatic range, and she was wonderfully sympathetic, for example, as Lucie Dreyfus, the warm, strong wife of Alfred Dreyfus in *The Life of Emile Zola* (1937).

Among Sondergaard's other notable films of the time are *Juarez*, a starring vehicle for Bette Davis and Brian Aherne, and *The Cat and the Canary* (1939) with Bob Hope, Paulette Goddard and George Zucco. It was Gale's job to shock the socks off Bob Hope in this comedy-thriller and she did! She appeared again with Hope in *Never Say Die* (1939).

Gale stars with Tito Guizar in a sleepy Western, *The Llano Kid,* but wakes everyone up again in *The Blue Bird* (1940) in which she outshines the star, Shirley Temple, according to many critics.

She appeared briefly in *The Mark of Zorro* (1940), and in the classic Bette Davis film, *The Letter* (1940). She scares the daylights out of Bette Davis without uttering a word and kills her in the last reel. The film received seven Oscar nominations.

Gale was featured in three Basil Rathbone movies: *Paris Calling* (1941), *The Black Cat* (1941) and *Sherlock Holmes and the Spider Woman* (1944), in which she cultivates an especially evil and charming witch-like persona. Gale was once again a splendid foil for Bob Hope in *My Favorite Blonde* (1942), another comedy-thriller, and she later appeared with Hope and Bing Crosby in *Road to Rio* (1947). She received an Oscar nomination for her role as Lady Thiang in *Anna and the King of Siam* (1946) starring Rex Harrison and Irene Dunne, a film that is hardly less interesting, though far less often screened, than the musical version with Yul Brynner and Deborah Kerr, *The King and I* (1957).

In 1947 Gale's husband, Herbert J. Biberman, appeared before the House Un-American Activities Committee (HUAC) and became part of The Hollywood Ten, who were all sent to prison because they would not give any testimony to the committee. As his wife, Gale, too, was blacklisted. Some three hundred Hollywood persons in all became *personae non gratae*, meaning they could not work in Hollywood (or in any national entertainment media) again.

Just after the blacklisting occurred, Gale's apparently last film opened, *East Side-West Side* (1949) a high-class soap opera about a New York business-man torn between his wife and his lover.

In 1951 Gale was subpoenaed and ordered to testify before HUAC. "Deeply tanned and wearing a black and white checked suit," the New York Times reported, she "agreed that congressional committees should investigate subversive activities but said 'this committee is doing incriminating work.'" Her film (radio and future TV) career ended by her taking the Fifth Amendment with HUAC.

Gale wrote to the Screen Actors Guild asking the union for protection and to consider how to respond to the entire HUAC situation, "I would be naïve if I did not recognize that there is a danger that by the following day I may have arrived at the end of my career as a motion picture actress. Surely it is not necessary for me to say to this Board that I love my profession and that I have tried to bring to it honesty of feeling, clarity of thought and a real devotion. Surely it is also unnecessary for me to state that I consider myself a deeply loyal American with genuine concern for the welfare and peace of my own countrymen and to all humanity... I can find no reason in my conduct as an actress or as a union member why I should have to contemplate a severing of the main artery of my life: my career as a performer."

With the death of Wisconsin Senator Joe McCarthy in 1957, the wind went out of the sails of the communist witch hunts and by the 1960s things were back to normal.

Even though Gale was happy with her family life she was never really wild about the movie business. In talking about the effects of the blacklisting, she said, "Yes, I miss the acting. A part of my life—a part of me, really stopped when my work was taken away from me. I miss it every day. I miss it very much indeed." She added, "I feel no bitterness. If you allow yourself to grow bitter, you only hurt yourself. I'm very proud of having been a part of that period. I am proud to have taken a stand."

The only avenue of artistic freedom and opportunity open to Sondergaard in those days was in stock companies, and from 1948 to 1950 she appeared in several productions. For the next five years she stayed home and read a lot. But an idea was slowly percolating, and Gale began to organize and write a one-woman show which she called *Woman*, gathering materials from Shakespeare, Ibsen, Congreve, Houghton, Corwin, and Sierra. In 1955 she was ready to perform it, and did so intermittently until 1958.

In 1965 the Bibermans sold their home in Hollywood Hills and moved back to New York City, where Gale could return to her first and best love, the stage. In October 1965 she performed *Woman* at the Gramercy Arts Theatre in New York and toured with it to Chicago, Salt Lake City and Los Angeles.

Gale was the guest artist at the Tyrone Guthrie Theater for the 1967 season. She had the leading role of Claire Zachanassian in Dürrenmatt's play, *The Visit* while also appearing in *Tango, Enrico IV* and *Halloween.*

While appearing at the Guthrie Theatre in 1967, she went out to Litchfield to revive her childhood memories of Lake Ripley, the library, the bandstand in the park, and the railroad station. Local resident Phyllis Koenig said, "She was very accepting of the kids when she was here and was quite thrilled, I think, that we had named the Thespian Chapter the Gale Sondergaard Chapter."

In subsequent years Sondergaard appeared in plays in Los Angeles, Seattle, Fort Lauderdale, and New York, among other places. She also continued to appear occasionally in films, including *Slaves* (1969) and *Echoes* (1983), though perhaps the best among her "comeback" roles is as Elk Woman in *The Return of a Man Called Horse* (1976) with Richard Harris.

Ann Sothern

(Harriette Lake)
Born 22 January, 1909,
Valley City, ND.
Died 15 March, 2001,
Ketchum, ID.

Harriette Lake graduated from Minneapolis Central High School in 1926 in the same class with Eddie Albert. Her photo caption on the *Centralian* yearbook that year: "Emotion is the summit of existence; music is the summit of emotion; art is the pathway to God." A year later she began a film career that spanned sixty years.

Ann was red-haired and 5'1½". She was named Minnesota's Outstanding High School Composer in 1925 and she represented Minnesota in the national composition contest in Detroit that year.

Ann's mother, Annette Yde-Lake, a professional singer, was on an opera tour when she delivered baby Harriette in Valley City,

North Dakota. She spent her early years in Waterloo, Iowa, how-ever, before moving north to Minneapolis for junior high school. Ann's father, Walter J. Lake, had deserted the family when Ann was five years old. He was a meat salesman by vocation and a woman-izer by avocation. Ann and her younger sisters, Bonnie and Marion (later-Sally Adams), were raised by their mother and grandmother of Danish heritage.

Upon graduation from Central, Ann studied music at the Uni-versity of Washington for one year before going to Hollywood to join her mother, who was giving voice and diction lessons to actors struggling to make the transition from silent to talking movies. Her mother found her a job with Christie Comedies and soon after with MGM where Ann became an extra in *Broadway Nights* (1927) while still a teenager. Other early films for MGM include *The Show of Shows* (1929), *Doughboys* (1930), and *Hold Everything* (1930).

Somehow in 1930 Florenz Ziegfeld heard Ann sing and hired her right away for a chorus job in *Smiles* starring Marilyn Miller. She next appeared as Geraldine March in *American's Sweetheart* which ran the first six months of 1931 at the Broadhurst Theatre in New York City. She also performed at the Civic Light Opera in 1930-31.

Her next show was *Everyone's Welcome*, which introduced the song "As Time Goes By" by Herman Hupfeld to the world. She played the feminine lead in the road company of *Of Thee I Sing*, by Kaufman, Ryskind and Gershwin, which later won a Pulitzer Prize. She came back to Broadway to replace Lois Moran as the lead of the same show on June 19, 1933. These Broadway musicals were her true aspiration in life, the goal of her talent and her training.

When the show closed, Columbia Pictures invited her to return to Hollywood under contract to play in *Let's Fall in Love* (1934). She was now being credited as Ann Sothern rather than Harriet Lake, and she had also become a platinum blond, which she and others felt more suited to comedy.

She was cast in Eddie Cantor's popular *Kid Millions* (1934), and she starred in *The Blind Date* (1934), *Grand Exit* (1935) and *Eight Bells* (1935). However, after some twenty-five B-features of playing ingénue parts, Columbia dropped her contract in 1936.

On loan-out to Twentieth Century Studio, Ann starred with Maurice Chevalier and Merle Oberon in *Follies Bergère* (1935). She then joined RKO Studios and starred twice with Gene Raymond, in *Hooray for Love* (1935), which also featured tap dancer Bill Robinson and jazz pianist Fats Waller, and in *Walking on Air* (1936). She played the foil off comic Jack Oakie in *Super Sleuth* (1937), and also appeared in *Trade Winds* (1938) and *Hotel for Women* (1939) co-starring with Elsa Maxwell and Linda Darnell.

In their early days at RKO Studio Lucille Ball and Ann Sothern did a lot of crying on each other's shoulders. Miss Sothern complained that she got all the roles that Katharine Hepburn turned down and Miss Ball cried that she got only the parts that Ann Sothern turned down.

Easily Ann's most popular movie was *Maisie* (1939) about a show-girl from Brooklyn who is bold, brassy and energetic but has a heart of gold. Following this totally unexpected success, MGM planned a series to follow up on the little goldmine. Louella Parsons predicted in the *New York Journal American* that Ann Sothern would soon be one of the biggest stars on the MGM lot. In the following decade nine more Maisie movies came out.

Jean Harlow was originally supposed to have been Maisie, but when she died in 1937 the script was shelved until director J. Walter Ruben insisted that Ann Sothern be given the part. The audiences just loved Ann's Maisie role, though none of the follow-up films, with Robert Young as the co-star, measured up to the original MGM also produced a "Maisie" radio series with Ann on CBS from 1945 to 47, and for MGM Radio from 1949 to 1952. At MGM Ann had Greta Garbo's dressing room.

The decade of the 1940s began well for Ann as she was featured in a Warner Bros gangster film, *Brother Orchid* (1940) starring Edward G. Robinson and Humphrey Bogart. She was next in a major MGM musical, *Lady Be Good* (1941), with Ann singing the Oscar-winning song, "The Last Time I Saw Paris." She also played the title role in *Panama Hattie* (1942). In these two movies Ms. Sothern finally got a chance to show off her talent, her timing, and her figure.

As a change of pace (also trying to escape from the Maisie persona), Sothern appeared in war-time drama *Cry Havoc* (1943) which features an all-woman cast of nurses on a Philippine Island treating the beleaguered soldiers. Ann was displeased with playing the second female lead in MGM's *Words and Music* (1948) so she left the studio to join Warner Bros. for *April Showers* (1948).

Sothern's best performance was as Kirk Douglas' spouse in *A Letter to Three Wives* (1949). Joseph Mankiewicz won Oscars for Best Director and Best Screenplay, and the film was nominated for Best Picture.

Joseph Mankiewicz said of Sothern, "Poor Annie. Annie was a damned good musical comedy actress. She had the sexiest mouth any woman ever had. But, at Metro, poor Annie got stuck in the Sam Katz unit. She never got the big break Gene Kelly and others did, of being with the Arthur Freed steamroller of talent."

In 1951 Ann returned to Broadway in *Faithfully Yours* in a brief run. Then, like her good friend Lucille Ball, she plunged into TV with *Private Secretary*. Ann very wisely became her own producer for the show, a half-hour sitcom that lasted four and one-half seasons (1953-1957) before becoming the *Ann Sothern Show* (1958-1961) where Ann is the assistant manager of a plush New York hotel. Though this series starts with a new cast, it gradually brings back all the actors from the earlier series.

Ann was featured in 1964 in two great movies: Gore Vidal's satirical political drama, *The Best Man* with Henry Fonda and Olivia de Havilland's thriller *Lady in a Cage*. She also appeared as the voice of the car in the TV series *My Mother the Car* (1965-66).

Ann did a smattering of movies after her TV series ended, but the big moment came in 1987 with the making of *The Whales of August*, a drama about aging and optimism. Two elderly sisters (Lillian Gish and Bette Davis) live on the coast of Maine and talk about the past. Ann, as Tisha, is their ebullient neighbor. Ann's real-life daughter, Tisha Sterling, is in the cast, too, as is Vincent Price. The director, Lindsay Anderson, commented about Ann, "In a sense she was too good an actress to be a star. Being a star requires elephantiasis of the ego." All the same, Sothern was nominated for an Academy Award for Best Supporting Actress.

Ann Sothern had a high business acumen. She formed Vincent Productions in 1954 to produce her nightclub variety show, Ann Sothern and her Escorts, and she founded Anso Productions in 1958.

In 1953 Ann converted to Catholicism. During the war years she rode a motorcycle back and forth to work at MGM Studios and became an expert in handling it, though she avoided driving cars whenever possible. She loved old rocking chairs for relaxation. Her hobbies included gardening, reading medical books, collecting transoceanic airmail envelopes and small china animals. She had two miniature French poodles named Maisie and Susie.

Though Ann Sothern had been a leading lady, she never attained a high level of stardom so she called herself "a Hollywood princess." She was, however, widely considered "Queen of the Bs" (B-budget features).

Her great-grandfather-in-law, Simon Lake, invented the first submarine, the *Argonaut*.

Ann Sothern was an outstanding athlete until some scenery fell on her back and crushed a vertebra in Jacksonville, Florida. She was told she would never walk again. She had been used to skiing for three months every winter; she was a crack shot in trap shooting, and in 1947 she landed a 259-pound marlin. Ann did indeed walk again, although she had to use a cane; the practice of yoga helped a lot.

Ann was a survivor, living to 92. "I'm exactly like my grandmother. She lived to be 93," she said. "She never gave up. They pulled the sheet over her three times and she pulled it down."

She moved to Ketchum, Idaho, to look at Dollar Mountain every day from her windows—a hill she used to ski frequently. As she summed up her life she said, "I've done everything but play rodeos." She appeared in over seventy films and made 175 TV appearances, but no rodeos.

T-U

Lea Thompson

*Born 3 May, 1961,
Rochester, MN.*

Lea lived at 622 8th SW while attending Edison Elementary School in Rochester. Her parents Barbara and Clifford were both active in the Rochester Civic Theater during the 1960s, when Jim Cavanaugh was at the directing helm. In fact, Barbara had leads in several plays. Says Lea, the youngest of five children, "Everything I know about theater I learned *in utero* while my mom was carrying me through *Macbeth*."

The family moved to the Uptown neighborhood in Minneapolis when Lea was eight. Lea later recalled, "I lived on James (Avenue South) and 32nd (Street), and I mean, we were really poor. That was the greatest place to live. You could walk to school; you just walked to the beach. I stopped and looked at my house. I remember that my mom and dad bought it for $18,000." She made a shocked exhalation-whistle sound when told that the same house in 1995 would sell for at least $88,000. (Nowadays a few hundred thousand might not be unreasonable—for the land alone.) From Uptown Lea traveled to the University area of Dinkytown to attend Marshall-U High, where she graduated at age seventeen in 1978.

Lea was involved in both theater and dance throughout her adolescence, but her dream was to be a prima ballerina. Her first ballet role was as a mouse in the *Nutcracker*. By the time she was twenty, she had performed in forty-five ballet productions with the Minnesota Dance Theatre, the Pennsylvania Ballet Company (who offered her a scholarship when she was seventeen) and The Ballet Repertory. The talented youth also received scholarships to the San Francisco Ballet and the school of the The American Ballet Theatre.

Finally, at age nineteen, she approached a new pinnacle of achievement by auditioning for Mikhail Baryshnikov himself at the

American Ballet Theatre. To her chagrin, Baryshnikov told her she could never be a prima ballerina because her legs were too short, which made her look stocky!

Baryshnikov, the Oracle of the ABT, had spoken—she was a beautiful dancer, but she was too stocky—and Lea abandoned her dream of becoming a great dancer. It was little consolation to observe that she was one of the few ballerinas at ABT without an eating disorder.

At this point Lea directed her energies with equal diligence to a career in acting. After doing twenty-two Burger King commercials as the girl-down-the-street from the Midwest, she made her first feature film as a teenaged water ski "bunny" in *Jaws 3-D* (1983). She could not swim or ski before making the film, and she can't swim or ski to this day. But she could act. And on the set she became acquainted with Dennis Quaid, the movie's star. The two began a three-year engagement, and Quaid gave her some acting tips along the way.

Thompson quickly graduated to being Tom Cruise's level-headed girlfriend in *All the Right Moves* (1983), though Director Michael Chapman wasn't especially happy with her performance and nearly fired her. Several forgettable supporting roles in the cute cheerleader vein followed—*Red Dawn* (1984), and *The Wild Life* (1984). But in her fifth major picture Lea turned a corner, playing a time-warped mother in *Back to the Future*, the biggest hit of 1985. She later told Thomas Schmidt, a Leisure Writer with the *Rochester Post-Bulletin*, "It's very difficult to play a 47-year old woman when you're twenty-three. A lot of people don't believe that I played both parts."

Suddenly the shoe was on the other foot, and every director wanted Lea. She had her pick of parts in several films.

She turned down a role in *The Breakfast Club* (opps!) to appear in *Howard the Duck* (1986) which was a flop, even though it was created by George Lucas. *SpaceCamp* (1986) didn't do too well either. Another teenage-angst role for Lea came in *Some Kind of Wonderful* (1987). The director was her husband-to-be, Howard Deutch. For her work here Lea won the Young Artist Award for Best Young Actress.

Lea's first grown-up role was in *Casual Sex?* (1988). She returned to Minnesota to promote *The Wizard of Loneliness* (1988). D. L. Mabery of the *Rochester Post-Bulletin* interviewed her as they toured her old haunts in South Minneapolis. The next day she went with an old friend to the Minnesota State Fair, telling her, "You know what I really want? Those Tom Thumb doughnuts. They still have those, don't they? I've been dreaming about them."

Lea made sixteen films during the 1980s, including the two sequels to *Back to the Future*. She and Howie Deutch were married in 1989.

After taking a break to be with her newborn daughter Madeline, Lea plunged back into filming in 1993 with *The Beverly Hillbillies,* and *Dennis the Menace*, where she plays the title character's mom.

Though other film roles followed, Lea began to spend more time doing TV shows. Her most recent success has been the star of *Caroline in the City* (1995-1999). She won the People's Choice Award for Best Actress in a new sitcom for her performances. She had her second child, Zoey, in 1994, just before the series commenced.

Besides being a fine actress and dancer, there is also music in Lea's blood. Her mother, also called "Baba," is an accomplished piano player. Lea composed a few songs for *Howard the Duck*. She produced as well as acted in *Electric* (2002), and was the subject of "An Intimate Portrait of Lea Thompson" (TV). Lea appeared with Winona Ryder in *The Vagina Monologues* in Los Angeles and she played Sally Bowles in *Cabaret* both on tour and on Broadway.

In 1988 Lea made a guest appearance on KSTP-TV's "Good Company" with Steve Edelman and Sharon Anderson. And just before a return visit in 1995 she appeared on the *Tonight Show* with Jay Leno, who played a clip from an old Burger King ad which shows her pitching hamburgers in a baseball uniform.

Among a variety of other commitments, in recent years Lea has spent a good deal of time as the star of the Jane Doe mystery series for Hallmark, playing a soccer mom with a secret past as a government spy, who is recalled to service from time to time by the government.

Lenore Ulric

(Lenore Ulrich)
Born 21 July, 1892,
New Ulm, MN.
Died 30 December, 1970,
Orangeburg, NY.

Lenore achieved her real fame on the Broadway stage under Producer David Belasco's guiding hands, where she was known for her smoldering talent, dusky beauty, and intense emotionalism in exotic dramas such as *Tiger Rose, The Son Daughter, Kiki,* and *Lulu Belle*. She did only sixteen films but left her mark nonetheless as a silent film star in *Tiger Rose* (1923) and a few others. This rose was born and partly raised in New Ulm, and was further nurtured in Milwaukee.

Lenore's father, Frank Ulrich, had been a soldier at Fort Snelling before relocating to New Ulm, where he worked as a druggist in the Charles Roos Drug Store. Her mother, Ida (Engenhardt) Ulrich came to New Ulm in 1881 with her sister, Emma, and her father, but a year later their father deserted them, and Ida was adopted by Mr. & Mrs. Mike Ranweiler. After Frank and Ida were married, they lived in the Fred Windland home at 219 North German Street across from Snow's Hatchery on North Minnesota Street. Later they lived at 626 North Broadway in the Alex Ranweiler home. Frank and Ida (sometimes written as Edna) had two daughters, Lenore and Isabel, both of whom entered show business.

Lenore, Isabel and Ida moved to Milwaukee about 1907—possibly earlier. Lenore was soon acting in school plays and she eventually joined a local stock theater company for which she played the role of Carmen in a dramatic version of the opera. By 1910 she was on Broadway and shortly thereafter made her first films. Her debut film was *The First Man* (1911) followed by *A Polished Burglar* (1911). Not being enthralled by movies, she returned to the stage.

By 1914 she was an established star trouper. She appeared in Minneapolis on January 16th at the Metropolitan Theatre in the play, *The Bird of Paradise*, and the following Sunday she opened the same play at the St. Paul Metropolitan. The play deals with the cultural conflicts generated by the arrival of Whites in Hawaii, and its unhappy love story ends with Lenore flinging herself into a volcano.

Under the tutelage of the Bishop of Broadway, David Belasco, a producer-director-manager of immense talent and reputation in New York theater at the time, she appeared in one exotic role after another. On tour at the Metropolitan in St. Paul in 1921 with the Belasco play, *The Son-Daughter*, for example, she plays a Chinese girl forced to marry a rather nasty man: She chokes him right after the ceremony. After watching her performance in *Kiki*, the critic Heywood Broun declared that there were ten powerful dramatic actresses on Broadway and that Miss Ulric was *all* of them.

Lenore made a more extended foray into movies in 1915, appearing as the star in *Kilmeny* (1915), *The Better Woman* (1915), *The Heart of Paula* (1916), *The Intrigue* (1916), *The Road to Love* (1916), and *Her Own People* (1917). But by 1919 she was back on center stage, playing in the hit show, *The Tiger Rose*, at the Davidson Theatre in her adopted native city of Milwaukee. Lenore did these heavy dramatic roles so well, in fact, that during the 1920s and 1930s they were commonly referred to in the New York theater world as "Ulric roles."

After touring the country with *Tiger Rose*, Lenore made a film version in 1923, so as to preserve the fire she had brought to her stage performance. But Ulric found it difficult to express her art in pantomime, and silent films therefore had little appeal for her. However, she did make two more films in 1929, *Frozen Justice* and *South Sea Rose*.

In 1928 Lenore married character actor, Sidney Blackmer, who was seven years older than she. He often played political types or high-class crooks but could play sympathetic roles, too. Their marriage ended in divorce in 1939. Her sister, Isabel, married stuntman/assistant director, Bartlett A. Carre.

When Lenore did turn to talking pictures, it was often in character roles. Her first was as Olympe in Greta Garbo's *Camille* (1936) which also starred Robert Taylor and Lionel Barrymore. In the play *The Doughgirls* (1943), as a Russian sniper named Natasha, she showed she could also do roles on stage other than the heavy, dramatic ones she was often given.

There was a curious connection between Lenore Ulric and Ernest Hemingway. He mentioned her twice in his first novel, *The Torrents of Spring*, and she is also mentioned in his play, *The Fifth Column*, set in Spain in the late 1930s.

Ulric worked for Alfred Hitchcock in *Notorious* (1946) starring Cary Grant, Ingrid Bergman and Claude Rains. The same year she was featured in the Lucille Ball film, *Two Smart People*, and in the Merle Oberon film, *Temptation* (1946). Her final film appearance was as Baroness Kruposny in Nelson Eddy's *Northwest Outpost* (1947).

Lenore frequently walked the from her hotel to the Selwyn Theatre (Chicago), four times on matinee days. Her offstage personality and life were as fascinating as her stage persona. She was always honest and direct and vigorously candid with her opinions.

Lenore's mother, Ida Ulrich, died in Milwaukee in October, 25, 1937, the day before Lenore appeared as a guest artist on WCCO Radio in Minneapolis. She was the guest of Al Pearce and His Gang, on his show, "Watch the Fun Go By," from 8-8:30 PM on WCCO and the CBS network.

Lenore was only 5'2" yet had this powerful stage presence which accords with the old saying, as attributed to some women, that dynamite comes in small packages.

An editorial in the *Minneapolis Journal* of April 24, 1947, summed up her career in the following terms: "In her day Miss Ulric was one of the most effective actresses we ever saw walk the boards. She could make her audience live and feel her parts with her and through them surged the same emotions of love, hate and revenge."

Robert Vaughn

Born 22 November, 1932,
New York City, NY.

Robert Vaughn, better-known to many as The Man from U.N.C.L.E., Napoleon Solo, was raised by his grandparents, Franklin and Marie Gaudel, at 1826 West Broadway in Minneapolis. His father, Walter, was a radio actor who specialized in character roles and had appeared on *Crime Doctor* and *Gangbusters*. Marcella, his mother, was a stage actress who had starred on Broadway with Bela Lugosi in the original production of *Dracula*. (She had graduated from North High in 1926.) The Vaughns could not attend to the needs of a child, however, and Robert was sent west to Minneapolis where grandma and grandpa could. (He is a third generation actor as his grandparents had run a theater company in Glencoe, Minnesota, early in the century.)

Vaughn attended Lowell Grammar School and Jordan Junior High before distinguishing himself at North High, where he was known as Nobby. He was a member of the National Honor Society at North, President and Secretary of Hi-Y, wrote for the weekly school paper and participated in basketball, track, and cross-country.

Nobby used to go with his grandfather to Minnehaha Falls or to the various lakes for walks. The family would picnic together in North Commons Park. On one occasion, when Bobby was five, he recited "Casey at the Bat" and Hamlet's speech, "To Be or Not To Be" to the other picnickers at North Commons. He made his formal debut in theater at age twelve in a summer tent show in Iowa.

One of Vaughn's jobs while a teen was working at Howie's Beer Hall on the corner of West Broadway and Penn Avenue North. Vaughn recalls, "They used the hall above the beer hall for speeches. [Humphrey] came there to make speeches when he was running for mayor in the '40s. He would come in early to practice. My job was setting up chairs. I would always be making a lot of noise. He always tried to talk above the noisemaking. And he would say, 'Can you hear me?' and I would say—because I was 10 or 12 at the time and I thought his name, Hubert, was very funny—'I can hear ya, Hu – bert.'"

Vaughn was in town in 1999 to gather memories for his autobiography but found very few old sites still around. "My grammar school is no longer there – Lowell. My junior high school is no longer there – Jordan. North High School is still there, but it's a different high school in a different place. They tore down the old high school." His childhood home was also torn down so, "I took a piece of wood from the telephone pole that was in the backyard of my house. I don't know how it's going to relate to my writing, but it was kind of a memory." He noted sadly, "It's very strange, because it's like that part of your life didn't exist." He also recounted the parrot that their landlord had trained to squawk, "Gimme the rent! Gimme the rent!"

Robert studied journalism and theater at the University of Minnesota for one year and also worked at the University's KUOM Radio at Eddy Hall. In 1952 he moved to Los Angeles to live with his mother, and two years later he completed his B.A. degree in theater arts at Los Angeles City College. In 1956 he took his M.A. in theater arts at the Los Angeles State College, hanging out with a group of intense young actors that included James Dean and Dennis Hopper.

Robert's film debut was in the Cecil B. De Mille epic, *The Ten Commandments* (1956) playing that classic role, the spear carrier. By the time he made his sixth movie, Good Day for a Hanging (1958), he was being featured with Fred MacMurray. The next year he was nominated for an Oscar as Best Supporting Actor for *The Young Philadelphians* where he played a disabled army veteran accused of murder.

Bob played one of the title characters in *The Magnificent Seven* (1960), a classic Western (though far inferior to its Japanese model, *The Seven Samurai)*, which will certainly give him a measure of immortality.

Vaughn hit the peak of his fame during the sixties in a series of espionage thrillers, starting with *To Trap a Spy* (1964), his first film as Napoleon Solo. The character was taken from Ian Fleming's book, *Goldfinger*. Though he is killed in the book, Fleming allowed producer Norman Felton to use the name of this character for the series

The Man from U.N.C.L.E. (1964-1968), which follows the exploits of a secret agent for the United Network Command for Law and Enforcement, an international crime-fighting organization based in New York. David McCallum was his partner/co-star Illya Kuryakin. Leo G. Carroll was their boss as Alexander Waverly.

Vaughn appeared in several other Napoleon Solo films during the TV show's five-year run, including *The Spy with My Face* (1965), *The Glass Bottom Boat* (1966), *One Spy Too Many* (1966), *One of Our Spies Is Missing* (1966), *The Spy in the Green Hat* (1966), *The Karate Killers* (1967), and *How to Steal the World* (1968). (A reunion film, *The Return of the Man from U.N.C.L.E.* was filmed for TV in 1983.)

"I was very serious about acting," Robert later observed. "I had played Hamlet a couple of times. I never anticipated that my work as an actor would produce 'rock star' reverberations, which indeed it did." Being an international star changed Vaughn's life. "When I arrived at Heathrow Airport in London for the first time the second year of the show, there were thousands of girls screaming and yelling. In those days, you still got off the plane on a stairway. I have pictures. The last one is me getting in a limousine. I've got blood on my face, tie's ripped off, hairs hanging in my face–the result of crazy fans."

But Vaughn has no regrets about this wild and sometimes harmful fan adulation, as it enabled him to go from "working actor" to "negotiating actor." It opened other doors as well. He got to know Bobby and Ethel Kennedy because their kids were crazy about the series, too. About the series Robert said, "It was James Bond on television, and James Bond was the hottest thing in movies. I got the spillover."

Vaughn played the first of many political figures when he appeared as a senator in *Bullitt* (1968) with Steve McQueen and Jacqueline Bisset. But his interest in politics took him well beyond make-believe. When *The Man from U.N.C.L.E.* went off the air in January of 1968 and the filming of *Bullitt* was completed, he became deeply involved in the 1968 presidential campaign. He was "passionately opposed" (to use his own phrase) to the War in Vietnam and a strong supporter of Bobby Kennedy. Vaughn made over a hundred anti-war speeches, the first one as early as January 1966. Even when he was in the midst of "U.N.C.L.E." he debated all comers on the Vietnam War, including William F. Buckley on his PBS-TV show, *Firing Line*.

On one occasion he even debated Hubert Humphrey. Vaughn was in Minneapolis on a promotional tour, "I was on a talk show, and the host brought up my opposition to the war. And Humphrey, who was here in town at his home, called in and started debating with me on the television show." Prior to the war the two famous Minnesotans had once shared a car in the St Paul Winter Carnival parade. Vaughn later recalled, "The Secret Service men who were guarding him were all asking me to give them autographs on U.N.C.L.E. cards. It was before I opposed the war. We had a very pleasant time."

After Bobby Kennedy's assassination and Richard Nixon's presidential victory, Vaughn moved to England in disillusionment and disgust. He did not return for almost five years.

In 1970 Robert completed his Ph.D. in communications, becoming "Dr. Vaughn." But he continued to act regularly in both TV and film. He was featured as Harry Rule in *The Protectors* (1972-74), a show about an elite crew of private eyes which was filmed in Europe and widely syndicated. He joined a huge cast for *The Towering Inferno* (1974) playing a senator. Politics came to the fore again in *The Man from Independence* (1974) in which Bob played former President Harry S. Truman. Dr. Vaughn, now entering middle age, played Charles Desmond in the mini-series based on Taylor Caldwell's hugely popular book, *The Captains and the Kings*, which loosely parallels the origins of the Kennedy family in Boston and their ilk.

Robert won an Emmy for his performance in another mini-series, *Washington: "Behind Closed Doors"* (1977) in which he plays Frank Flaherty, an H. R. Haldeman-like presidential henchman. He performed as Franklin Delano Roosevelt in a one-man stage show, *F.D.R.*, in 1978 and he played former President Woodrow Wilson in the mini-series, *Backstairs at the White House* (1979), earning another Emmy nomination.

More mini-series ensued, sometimes political, sometime science fiction, and occasionally both. *Battle Beyond the Stars* (1980) is a science fiction version of *The Magnificent Seven* in which a small planet hires help to protect itself. The spoof was written by John Sayles and produced by the master modern horror film director, Roger Corman.

His notable productions in the 1980s include *S.O.B.* (1981) written and directed by Blake Edwards, husband of Julie Andrews, who stars along with Robert in the film. He played General Douglas MacArthur in *The Last Bastion* (1984) and F. D. R. again in *Murrow* (1986, TV).

Vaughn continued to work in stage productions as well, including one-man shows on F.D.R. and Truman, and over the years he has racked up over two hundred TV guest appearances.

He was featured in *Delta Force* (1986) and *Black Moon Rising* (1986), co-starring in *Renegade* (1988, made in Italy), and played

Adolf Hitler in *That's Adequate* (1989). With the death of Charles Bronson in August 2003 Vaughn became the sole survivor of the original Magnificent Seven.

Bob Vaughn has been working on his autobiography entitled *Christ, Shakespeare, Ho Chi Min: As I Knew Them*. No publication date has been set.

Vince Vaughn

Born 28 March, 1970,
Minneapolis, MN.

Vince Vaughn was dubbed "the Nicholson of his generation, hands down," by *Gentlemen's Quarterly* magazine in 1998. That may be a bit of a stretch, but when director Gus Van Sant cast him in the Anthony Perkins's role in a recreation of Alfred Hitchcock's *Psycho*, he had already worked with Steven Spielberg in the blockbuster hit film, *The Lost World: Jurassic Park* (1997). What was director Spielberg's opinion of Vince? "A new movie star, an American icon-to-be." Vince is tall at 6'5", has a good physique, boyish good looks, natural charm, and a knack for nailing characters. So, what is the next mountain to climb? First, let's go back to his beginnings.

Vince's father Vernon was a salesman for a toy company, and his mother, Sharon, is a real estate agent turned stockbroker. He was born in Minneapolis, but as his parents become more secure financially they moved the family to Buffalo Grove, Illinois, and later to Lake Forest, an upscale suburb of Chicago, where Vince finished high school in 1988. He has two older sisters, Valerie and Victoria. He is Lebanese, Irish, English, Italian and German.

Vince once told Fred Schruers of *Rolling Stone*, "My family was like the Beverly Hillbillies of Lake Forest. My dad is the first generation off the farm from Ohio. He used to work in steel mills in the summertime to make money for college. My dad always liked country music and blue-collar ways."

As a child Vince enjoyed act out the Westerns his father enjoyed, and he was adept at copying John Travolta's hot dancing act in *Saturday Night Fever*. In fact, he was eventually diagnosed as hyperactive and Ritalin was prescribed to curb his excess energy. His parents refused to give it to him, however. Vince did poorly in school, and was in danger of flunking out. He ran for class president in his senior year, speculating that the school would never flunk the class president. He won the election and he did graduate. He was active in sports until a jeep injury sidelined him. Never idle for long, Vince proceeded to win the lead role in the class play.

Acting appealed to him, and after graduation Vince almost inadvertently won a part in an sex-education film, did an industrial film demonstrating a weight-training set, joined a comedy group called Del Close's ImprovOlympic comedy troupe, and appeared in a Chevrolet "Heartbeat of America" TV commercial which aired at the Superbowl. Though still a teenager, Vaughn received residual checks of nearly $60,000 for this ad.

With the full support of his parents, Vaughn moved to Los Angeles in late 1988. He won small roles on TV shows, the first on *Doogie Howser, M.D.* where he was a patient with a broken leg from a car crash. He appeared on *21 Jump Street* with Johnny Depp and on *China Beach.* His early film roles were nothing to write home about, though he did *telephone* home after the completion of the football drama **Rudy** (1993) to tell his folks, "I'm number forty-four [on his helmet]. Trust me."

During the filming of this picture Vince met Jon Favreau, another transplanted Midwesterner, and they started hanging out together. "[Favreau] was depressed, so I took him to places. The Dresden Room and Three of Clubs, where I hung out, not the hard-to-get-into Beverly Hills clubs." Favreau later wrote the somewhat autobiographical screenplay for the film **Swingers** (1996), and the film was eventually shot in all of Jon's spots—his car, his apartment, his favorite hangouts. Vince was cast as a slightly slick but manic ladies man with sharp suits and hip slang. Favreau shot Swingers for $250,000 and sold it to Miramax for $5 million. It was a "sleeper" hit and the critics also liked it. Owen Glieberman of *Entertainment Weekly* said, "If Swingers has a scene-stealer,... It's Vince Vaughn, who, I predict, is going to be a very big star." He added that Vaughn is "Spooky-cool sexy, like the young Christopher Walken."

On the strength of this performance, Vince was asked to audition for Steven Spielberg for **The Lost World: Jurassic Park.** He was given the high-profile role of the wise-cracking photographer. The Hasbro Company even produced an action doll based on his character, to the great delight of his dad.

That same year Vince appeared with Spielberg's wife, Kate Capshaw, in **Locusts** (1997). He co-starred with Joaquin Phoenix and

Ann Heche in *Return to Paradise* (1998), a thinking person's thriller about three friends whose drug-filled holiday romp in Malaysia is cut short by the authorities, who slap one of them with a death sentence. In order to reduce the sentence, the other two must be convinced to return to Malaysia to share the jail time.

Critics liked the film, and they also liked Vince's next movie, *Clay Pigeons* (1998) a black comedy in which he plays a slick, fast-talking newcomer in a small town in Montana.

Vaughn played Norman Bates in the remake of *Psycho* (1998)—a pointless exercise in the eyes of many viewers. But the cool reception for Psycho did not slow Vaughn's growing film credits. He co-starred with Jennifer Lopez in *The Cell* (2000) and also co-starred three times with Ben Stiller in 2004, including the remake of TV's *Starsky and Hutch*.

He had three new films out in 2004 and three in 2005, with *The Wedding Crashers* being the cream of the crop.

Favreau once told Johanna Schneller in *Premiere* magazine, "[Vaughn] loves America. He loves barbecue, apple pie, Little League, Reagan, all of it." Vince echoed Favreau's statements about himself, "I love America, flat-out. I love what it represents: the pursuit of happiness, individualism, the opportunity for people to change their lives."

Jesse Ventura

James George Janos
Born 15 July, 1951,
Minneapolis, MN.

Jesse "the Body" Ventura wrestled professionally for thirteen years until he became Jesse "the Mind" Ventura for four years as mayor of Brooklyn Park, Minnesota, (1991-1995), a suburban city with a population of 56,000. In 1999 he was elected to a four year term as governor of Minnesota. He also served in the U. S. Navy SEALs for four years.

The "Big Guv" was a natural as a wrestler at 6'4" and 250 lbs. He is also a natural for radio talk shows and football color commentary on radio and TV. Some would dispute his qualifications for political life.

Yet he astounded the nation by being freely elected to be Governor of Minnesota in 1998 over two more-seasoned, professional politicians, becoming the first Reform Party candidate to win a statewide or federal office.

Jesse has also had a career in the movies, appearing as a sidekick to Arnold Schwarzenegger in *Predator* (1987) and *The Running Man* (1987). A line he delivered in *Predator*—"I ain't got time to bleed."— later became the title of his autobiography.

Though he appeared in only a few films, Ventura carried his Screen Actors Guild membership card for eleven years, along with its health and pension benefits. Wrestling, movies, politics—it's all show business, as American humorist, Will Rogers might have said.

Jesse was born to George Janos, a steam fitter, and Bernice, a nurse anesthetist, who are both of Slovak and German heritage.

At Roosevelt High School, class of 1969, James Janos was in the Lettermen's "R" Club for playing football, swimming (as Captain) and track. He was a member of the Twin City Football Championship team of 1968. One of his jobs while in high school was washing dishes at Mama Rosa's Italian Restaurant. Upon high school graduation James joined the United States Navy and applied for the SEALs from which he graduated in 1970. It's considered the toughest military training program in the world. James earned a Vietnam Service Medal but cannot disclose the nature of his missions as a member of Demolition Team 12 because it is still classified.

When his service time was over in 1973 with an honorable discharge, James headed for California, where he joined a motorcycle club known as The Mongols. He was also briefly a bodyguard for The Rolling Stones. In 1975 he returned to Minneapolis and attended North Hennepin Community College for one year before dropping out. He accomplished two things while there, however. He discovered the theater, being cast as Hercules in Aristophanes' play *The Birds*. He also met and married his wife, Terry.

At about this time Jesse became interested in the "in your face" wrestling style of "Superstar" Billy Graham, and Graham gave him encouragement, even though he had never wrestled. Returning to Minnesota again, Jesse began an arduous training program and was eventually spotted by Midwest wrestling promoter, Bob Geigel. Jesse had developed his own style of mouthy, abrasive chatter, and had taken to wearing outrageous costumes. To complete his new persona, James George Janos changed his name. He had always liked the name Jesse so that was an easy decision. He took his last name from a city of the California coast north of Los Angeles.

He wrestled in the Midwest and Pacific Northwest venues for a few years, and joined the American Wrestling Association (AWA) in

1979. Jesse became a "bad guy" who often fought "good guy" Terry "Hulk" Hogan, and almost invariably lost. Jesse did not shine as a wrestler per se but he had a gift for riling up an audience. Vince McMahon, Jr. noticed these vocal talents and in 1985 he hired Ventura as a color commentator for the World Wrestling Federation, a rival group to the AWA. It was his charismatic success in front of the cameras, rather than on the mat, that brought Jesse into the 1987 Schwarzenegger movie thrillers.

Following his work with Arnold, Jesse appeared in *Repossessed* (1990), *Ricochet* (1991), *Demolition Man* (1993) starring a new, muscle-man buddy, Sylvester Stallone, and *Major League II* (1994).

In 1990 Jesse became disenchanted with local politics in Brooklyn Park, where he lived, and he voiced his complaints at several meetings. Finally, one of the council members remarked that if he was dissatisfied with things he should run for office and change them himself. Taking the remark seriously, Ventura mounted a campaign and unseated an eighteen-year incumbent mayor. His four years as mayor (a part-time duty) were uneventful, but the experience undoubtedly whetted his appetite for political life.

During the later years of the decade Ventura appeared on several TV shows and held a variety of radio announcing positions. More importantly, perhaps, after appearing briefly as a guard in *Batman & Robin* (1997), Ventura became active in the Ross Perot's Reform Party and began his run for the governorship of Minnesota. The 1998 gubernatorial campaign in Minnesota involved two lackluster candidates, Norm Coleman and Hubert "Skip" Humphrey III. Coleman, a Democrat from the East Coast who had switched parties, was distrusted by many voters, and Humphrey simply lacked the charisma to match his name recognition. Jesse was considered a buffoon by many voters, but he expressed himself forcefully and made complex issues seem simple, especially to young voters. Fiscally conservative but socially liberal, he wanted to abolish some taxes, cut others, and return the state's budget surplus to the voters. He was Pro-Choice, Pro-Gay Rights, Pro-Gun and Pro-Snowmobiles. Supporting Gay Rights he said, "Love is bigger than government." The flamboyant Ventura outshone the two major-party candidates in a series of televised debates, and squeaked into the governorship with a mere 37% of the vote.

Just after his inauguration, (which was a media extravaganza in itself) Ventura's movie *Beyond the Mat* (1999) appeared, and the same year he played himself in a documentary, *Jesse "The Body" Ventura: The Man, the Myth, the Legend* (1999).

When Ventura voluntarily left office four years later, many people breathed a sigh of relief, feeling that too much of the term had been about Jesse, and too little about the welfare of the state. Ventura himself, always sensitive to criticism, argued in return that the media was too fascinated by his quirks of personality, and not attentive enough to his progressive initiatives.

Whatever the case may be, in 2003 Jesse appeared on his own cable television show on MSNBC called *Jesse Ventura's America*. Originally scheduled as a daily show, it was cut back to once a week before airing began, and canceled soon thereafter.

The following year Jesse was invited to lead a study group at Harvard University as a visiting fellow at the Kennedy School of Government's Institute of Politics. His seminar focused on things he knew a good deal about such as third party politics and campaign finance, and they were widely attended.

From Harvard Ventura moved on to an appearance at Wrestlemania XX as part of the "WWE Hall of Fame Class of 2004." On the more serious side, he also began to speak out about the use of National Guard troups in Iraq, labelling it as "wrong."

Ventura's name is still news, and in September of 2006 he campaigned with independent Texas gubernatorial candidate Kinky Friedman. But his dissatisfaction with the American press had driven him to relocate his home to Baja California, Mexico.

Richard Widmark

*Born 26 December, 1914,
Sunrise, MN.*

The actor who rose to fame as the laughing killer, Tommy Udo, in *Kiss of Death* (1947) was born in the sleepy little town of Sunrise, Minnesota, in Chisago County, just north and east of the Twin Cities. The family moved frequently, however, and Richard and younger brother, Donald, had no choice but to tag along to Sioux Falls, South Dakota; Henry, Illinois; Chillicothe, Missouri; and Princeton, Illinois. Richard went to high school in Princeton, playing football and writing for the school paper. He was the senior class president and gave the 1932 commencement address for his graduating class. His love for movies was kindled by his grandmother, who took him to see his first film when he was three. As a teen he took a job as a doorman at the local movie house so that he could see all the films for free.

Widmark went through Lake Forest College, just outside Chicago, on a full, four-year scholarship majoring in speech and political science. He won first prize in the McPherson Oratory Contest and third prize in the state oratory contest. He belonged to the honorary society, Iron Key, played football and baseball and was once again senior class president.

After graduating with a B.A. in 1936, he toured France and Germany, returning that fall to teach in the college's drama department. During his undergrad and graduate years at Lake Forest College he appeared in some thirty plays. Strongly influenced by his adviser, Professor R. C. Tomlinson, he eventually chose acting as his profession, "I suppose I wanted to act in order to have a place in the sun. I'd always lived in small towns and acting meant having some kind of identity," he later explained in a *New Yorker* interview.

Richard went to New York in 1938 to see a classmate who was producing radio programs and was given a part in a radio series called Aunt *Jenny's Real Life Stories*. For the next ten years he appeared in a number of series, usually as a neurotic young man.

The United States Army rejected Widmark because of a perforated ear drum, and he spent the war years entertaining servicemen under the auspices of the American Theatre Wing. Meanwhile, his Broadway debut in the comedy *Kiss and Tell* came on March 17, 1943.

In December of the following year Richard appeared in a controversial production in which he played a college student fighting to free the girl he loves from the domineering clutches of an older woman. It opened on December 29, 1944, and ran for sixty-seven shows before being closed by the License Commissioner. The reviewer in the *New York Herald Tribune* on December 30, 1944, said, "Widmark does a remarkable job. His tense underplaying sustains the most faltering moments of the play." He left the play early in 1945 to start rehearsals for *Kiss Them for Me*, which deals with three naval aviators on a wild four-day, stateside leave.

Though stage roles continued to come his way, Widmark's goal had always been to work in Hollywood. "I learned the fundamentals of acting on the stage. Movie acting, however, is the most difficult kind of all to do," he later remarked.

Director Henry Hathaway did not want blue-eyed, blond-haired Richard Widmark in his movie, *Kiss of Death*. He felt the actor seemed too intellectual and well-bred to play the sadistic Tommy Udo. Fortunately, he was overruled. This movie introduced a new type of cold-blooded, steely-eyed, homicidal maniac to a thoroughly scared world audience. The cold, blue eyes went well with the heartless, cold-blooded murder. In one famous scene Widmark laughs like a hyena as he pushes an old woman in a wheel chair down a flight of stairs. Writer James Agee said, "It is clear that murder is one of the kindest things he is capable of."

Widmark was confident that this part would launch his movie career, and it did. However, in order to get the role he had to sign a seven-year contract with Twentieth Century Fox. In many of his subsequent films Widmark was type-cast as a villain or a soldier. A few of his bad guy movies are *Street with No Name* (1948, as a gang leader); *Road House* (1948, as a double-crossing proprietor); and *Yellow Sky* (1948, as one of a group of malcontented Civil War soldiers who become outlaws). In *Down to the Sea in Ships* (1951) Widmark plays appears in a sympathetic role for a change, as a sailor who teaches a crusty old sea captain's grandson about the sea.

In his sixth film, *Panic in the Streets* (1950) Widmark got the opportunity to work with the talented director Elia Kazan. This semi-documentary/suspense film deals with tracking down the source of bubonic plague in the streets and waterfront of New Orleans. Richard turns in a great performance as a tired public health official, and the film won an Academy Award for Best Original Story.

Following a few more bad-guy pictures, Richard appeared in the comedy *My Pal Gus* (1952), playing a bon-bon manufacturer too busy to spend time with his small son. After completing the Westerns *Garden of Evil* (1954) and *Broken Lance* (1954) his contract with Fox expired and Richard became an independent. "I knew I had to get away from Fox," he remarked. "I was being switched around from movie to movie without getting a chance to do much that I liked."

Widmark made his debut as a producer with the highly-praised film, *Time Limit* (1957). He next played the Dauphin in Otto Preminger's much pre-publicized *Saint Joan* (1957). His company, Heath Productions, also produced *The Trap* (1960) and *The Secret Ways* (1961) to a lukewarm critical reception. In *The Judgment at Nuremberg* (1961) Widmark had the plum role of the American prosecutor, Colonel Ted Lawson.

In *How the West Was Won* (1962) Richard was surrounded by co-stars including John Wayne, James Stewart, Gregory Peck, Henry Fonda, and Debbie Reynolds. Like many such extravaganzas, the film itself was disappointing, but a *Variety* reviewer observed that, "Widmark makes a vital impression as the head man of the construction team building the railroad."

Richard was a big hit in the title role of *Madigan* (1968), playing a tough New York cop under Don Siegel's direction. The film was so popular that it spawned a TV series in 1972-73 and four "Madigan" film sequels.

In *Murder on the Orient Express* (1973) Richard appears with another all-star cast as the super bad guy who gets killed—by everyone.

Considered in retrospect Widmark's career is unusual in that he worked with the famous directors of Hollywood's Golden Age—men like Henry Hathaway, John Ford, Ed Dmytryk, Vincent Minnelli, and William Wellman—but was also around to work with the next generation—Stanley Kubrick, Elia Kazan, Robert Wise, Joe Mankiewicz, Sidney Lumet, Otto Preminger, Gene Kelly, Fred Zinnemann, and Stanley Kramer. It's also unusual that during his prime Richard starred in nearly every picture he made.

Widmark married Jean Hazlewood on April 5, 1942, and they have one child, Ann Heath Widmark. His wife or his daughter often helped him learn lines. The family has divided its time between a house in Brentwood and a farm-ranch between Santa Barbara and Los Angeles where they grow barley and raise cattle.

Drama departments in colleges often underscore for would-be actors the extreme dedication needed to survive in show business. Widmark has a different story to tell. "Getting launched was easy for me. Too easy, perhaps. That's probably why I never got that dedicated feeling. I never considered myself a dedicated artist, and I don't now. I've never had the feeling I'd die if I didn't get a certain part. Just the same, I love my work, and I work hard. Acting has always been my work, and it's part of my life."

Warren William

(Warren Krech)
Born 2 December, 1895,
Aitkin, MN.
Died September 24, 1948,
North Hollywood, CA.

Warren was known in some circles as a "poor man's" John Barrymore because he had the facial bone structure that showed a dramatic profile, a rich, resonant baritone voice, and a debonair manner. In the course of his career William played such suave and intelligent protagonists as New York detective Philo Vance, defence attorney Perry Mason, and the Lone Wolf, a reformed jewel thief turned sleuth.

Warren's father was the newspaper publisher in Aitkin, and he began his adult life there as a reporter. During World War I he served in France in the Engineer Corps, and while in the service he formed a theatrical troupe which toured army camps in Europe even after the war was over. By the time he got back to the States William was intent upon making acting his career.

He moved to New York City to attend the American Academy of Dramatic Art, which offered a degree after two years of study. (St. Paulite Walter Abel studied there, too.) He also found work almost immediately in stock companies, and took over the Richard Dix role in a touring production of *I Love You*. By the mid-1920s he had become a leading man on the Broadway.

Warren's film debut was in *The Town That Forgot God* (1922) and the next year he appeared with Pearl White in the movie serial *Plunder* (1923). (Pearl had earlier became famous for her film serials, *The Perils of Pauline* (1914)).

Because of his marvelous voice and stage experience, Warren had little trouble making the jump to talking movies. In fact, he was in great demand during those early years. In his first "talkie" film, *Expensive Women* (1931) he co-starring with Dolores Costello, and he went on to play opposite Bebe Daniels in *Honor of the Family* (1931). He co-starred with Marion Marsh in *Beauty and the Boss* (1931), and also co-starred with Bette Davis in two of her early films, *Three on a Match* (1932) and *The Dark Horse* (1932). Warren was outstanding as New York crime lawyer William Fallon in *The Mouthpiece* (1932). He appeared in *Gold Diggers of 1933* (1933), and with Mae West and Randolph Scott in *Go West Young Man* (1936). He co-starred with Gladys George in *Madame X* (1937), and played D'Artagnan in Louis Hayward's *The Man in the Iron Mask* (1939).

Unfortunately, Warner Bros. often restricted Warren to "B" features and low budget serials like the *Lone Wolf* series, which he did on "loan-out" to Columbia Pictures. Warren played the Lone Wolf, a reformed gentleman jewel thief turned sleuth, eight times in all between 1939 and 1943.

A notable exception to this string of B pictures was the splendid Cecil B. De Mille epic, *Cleopatra* (1934), in which he played Julius Caesar to Claudette Colbert's Cleopatra. (The film is worth seeing today largely for its grand photography, which earned an Oscar.) *Imitation of Life* (1934) paired Warren again with Claudette Colbert in a classic tearjerker. And he also worked with director Frank Capra in *Lady for a Day* (1933) co-starring May Robson.

In the mid 1930s Warren played Perry Mason, attorney for the defense, in *The Case of the Howling Dog* (1934) co-starring Mary Astor, *The Case of the Curious Bride* (1935), which showed Errol Flynn in a pre-Captain Blood role, *The Case of the Lucky Legs* (1935), and *The Case of the Velvet Claws* (1936). In a more effete vein, Warren played Philo Vance, the famous detective created by mystery writer, S. S. Van Dine, in *The Gracie Allen Murder Case* (1939).

He starred opposite Alice Faye in *Lillian Russell* (1940), a bio-pic of the flamboyant 1890s entertainer, and he also appeared in a top notch musical, *The Firefly* (1937), starring Jeanette MacDonald and

Allan Jones. To add to the broad mix of film genres William also did a horror film in 1941, *The Wolf Man*, starring Lon Chaney, Jr. and Claude Raines.

In was perhaps because Warren had been raised in Aitkin, on the fringe of Minnesota's north woods, that he grew to love climbing trees. On his ranch in Encino, California, he always trimmed his own trees, using a waist belt and foot spikes just like the pros.

Despite an early death at fifty-three, Warren had a productive acting career. Aitkin lost a newspaper reporter, but it gained a Broadway and Hollywood celebrity which other journalists could write about.

Gig Young

(Byron Ellsworth Barr)
Born 4 November, 1913,
St. Cloud, MN.
Died 19 October, 1978,
Manhattan, NY.

Gig is a snappy name, very "with it." How did John and Emma Barr come up with such a cool, show biz name? Well, they didn't. Byron Barr, who had changed his name to Byran Fleming, was singled out for praise for his performance in the film *The Gay Sisters* (1942), but the critics tended to use his character name, "Gig Young," in their articles, rather than his stage name. The head of Warner's advertising and publicity noticed this and informed Byron, "We're going to change your name." "Was I that bad?" he asked. "No, you were that good!" Jack Warner approved the change and that was that.

As a child Byron lived with his family in St. Cloud at 1209 10½ Avenue South, in a little green house with a white gingerbread porch. When he was five they moved to 727 8th Avenue South. Byron attended

Riverview Grammar School and St. Cloud Technical High School for three and a half years. His family moved to Washington, D. C. in 1932 where Byron completed his high school education at McKinley High. He had his first male lead there in *Little Women*, but he had his credits transferred back to Tech High so he could get a diploma from his old alma mater.

Gig's father owned the J. E. Barr Pickling and Preserving Plant of St. Cloud, and his older brother Donald Barr, a star athlete and scholastic leader, fit right into the family cannery business. Gig avoided the cannery and spent a lot of time during his youth hiking along the Mississippi River banks and hunting ducks there with his dog Shep. He sometimes brought home stray animals and even traded with other kids for their unwanted pets.

When he was fifteen Byron' took a job at the cannery but he was fired right away. (The foreman didn't know he was the boss's son.) He was reinstated, though he would rather have hung out at the filling station at Ninth Avenue and Seventh Street South, not far from school. He liked playing cards with friends and participating in activities at the First Methodist Church to which his family belonged.

He had an eye for the girls, too. His first love was his football coach's daughter. Byron drove up to her house and honked as his friends had done with their girls. The coach appeared and informed him that it was customary to come to the door and inquire respectfully after the young lady.

Mary Ellen Nichols recalled years later that Byron had a beautiful complexion, "We laughed a lot and about the only things we did were go for joyrides and have sodas. But I was so proud to be out with him. I thought he was the handsomest person in town." Of his first paycheck from the cannery, where he made $8 a week, he bought some candy and brought the heart-shaped box to his girlfriend's house. He went there every night until the candy was gone. He added, "I bought myself a flashy tie, too, so I'd look like Jim Dandy when I took my girl out."

As Byron grew into his teen years he became weary of reminders of his brother's accomplishments, so he went regularly to the Saturday movie matinées at the Paramount Theatre in St. Cloud. He was mesmerized by the movies but did not seriously entertain a notion of acting as a career. In high school he took a job as an usher at the Paramount. In recent decades this movie house has been the center of Gig Young Film Fests.

When the family left Washington for North Carolina, Gig elected to stay behind and attend a night course in dramatics. He then joined the Philip Hayden Players where he swapped teaching ballroom dancing for studying drama and tap dancing classes. He stayed with the Hayden Players 1934 to 1937. Though he was also working as a soda jerk, he walked the four miles each way to classes—he was saving money for a trip to Hollywood. Finally, he was awarded a scholarship to the Pasadena Playhouse, and he was ready for departure.

Young set out for California in 1938 with all of $20 in his pocket, calling his mother in North Carolina to tell her he was determined to "make it on my own." He also told her he had a free ride to California. In fact, it took him two weeks to hitchhike there. He earned money on the way by pumping gas for food, worked odd jobs on farms, and slept in barns. With the one dollar he had left when he arrived in Culver City, he rented a room and headed for the Little Theatre.

Although his scholarship at the Pasadena Playhouse covered his tuition, he built sets and painted scenery in exchange for dramatic coaching and took a job as a night clerk in a small hotel until the lack of sleep drove him to the brink of exhaustion. He also acted in thirty plays at the Playhouse during his three years there, all as an unprofessional apprentice. His first professional acting job in Pasadena came in *Pancho* starring George Reeves (who later played Superman). A Warner Brothers film scout came to the play and signed both Gig and Reeves to movie contracts. While at the Playhouse Byron also fell in love with Sheila Stapler, a good-natured, attractive brunette whose parents were prisoners of war in the Philippines at the time of their wedding in 1939. (They were divorced in 1947.)

During his first few years in the film world Young was busy with bit parts in films featuring Humphrey Bogart, Gary Cooper, Errol Flynn, Jimmy Cagney, and Henry Fonda.

Then fate looked kindly upon him. He was featured in *The Gay Sisters* (1942) starring Barbara Stanwyck and George Brent. His is the best performance in this family melodrama about three sisters who resist selling their New York mansion to make way for a development—a plot borrowed from Chekhov. Suddenly the tall, lean, actor from St. Cloud was hot, and he was rushed into an action film, *Air Force* (1943) where he held his own as John Garfield's co-pilot. On the strength of this performance Bette Davis specifically requested that he act in her film, *Old Acquaintance* (1943), and the two became lifelong friends. Miriam Hopkins co-starred as both women are jealous lady novelists who interfere in each others' love lives.

With the onset of World War II, Gig enlisted in the Coast guard and served three years on a submarine. He left with all goodwill from Warner Brothers Studios which expected him back to resume his contract. During the war Gig posed with Jack Warner, Ronald Reagan,

Wayne Morris, and Harry Lewis in a pitch for buying war bonds. Following the war he made two more films with Warners, ended his contract, and free-lanced successfully from then on.

In his first film for MGM Young was Porthos in *The Three Musketeers* (1948). Gene Kelly is superbly acrobatic as D'Artagnan, while Lana Turner is also wonderful as the evil Milady. Gig then played support to John Wayne in *The Wake of the Red Witch* (1948). Other films of the period include *Tell It to the Judge* (1949), *Only the Valiant* (1951), and the Western *Slaughter Trail* (1951).

For his work in *Come Fill the Cup* (1951) Gig received an Oscar nomination as Best Supporting Actor.

In 1950 Gig married his dramatic/vocal coach, Sophie Rosenstein. The same year his brother, Donald, died. After doing five films in 1951 and two in 1952, Gig set off for Broadway and live theater. Poor Sophie died of cancer that same year.

In 1953 Gig starred in *Oh Men, Oh Women* and it became the hit of the 1953-1954 season. Gig himself won a Tony for the Best Male Stage Performance. This made Hollywood buzz again, and he returned briefly to appear in Frank Sinatra's film, *Young at Heart* (1954). After appearing in *Desperate Hours* (1955) with Fredric March and Humphrey Bogart, he returned to Broadway to star as Captain Fisby in *Teahouse of the August Moon* at the City Centre.

When that play closed Gig married for the third time. His new wife, Elizabeth Montgomery, was the daughter of actor Robert Montgomery. She was cute and vivacious, and went on after their divorce in 1963 to star on TV in *"Bewitched"* (1964-1971).

Young shuttled back to Hollywood for four more movie gems in the next few years. He was in *Desk Set* (1957) with Spencer Tracy and Katherine Hepburn, *Tunnel of Love* (1958) starring Doris Day and Minnesota-born Richard Widmark, and *Teacher's Pet* (1958) with Clark Gable. The drinking and hangover scenes in this film are as good as they get. Another fine romantic comedy is *Ask Any Girl* (1959) in which love-hungry receptionist Shirley MacLaine falls first for playboy Gig and then for David Niven, the stable older brother.

Back to live theater in New York Gig played Hogan in *Under the Yum Yum Tree*, and won the Broadway Aegis Award for his efforts.

In 1960 Gig co-starred with Rita Hayworth in *The Story on Page One*, and in a made-for-TV remake of *Ninotchka* without it's essential ingredient—Greta Garbo.

Gig's own personal favorite among his films is *That Touch of Mink* (1962) with Cary Grant and Doris Day. He plays the financial adviser to filthy rich Cary Grant, complaining incessantly about selling his soul for a big salary when he was once so happy as an underpaid professor of economics at Harvard. During the filming Grant told him, "Gig, you can do anything you want in this part." "You can't realize how generous that is," Gig later told a reporter, "because actors playing in a second lead with big movie idols might get a lot of 'no-no's.' Cary Grant believes as I do, that all good pictures are made up of moments. The more moments you have, the greater picture you have. So don't take great moments away from actors if they are there to be had."

An unusual movie was *Kid Galahad* (1962) starring Elvis Presley as a hotel bellhop-turned-boxer. In *For Love or Money* (1963) Gig plays support to Kirk Douglas and Mitzi Gaynor.

The Rogues was a well-cast TV series (1964-65) starring David Niven, Gladys Cooper, Charles Boyer, Robert Coote, and Gig as an international family of jewel thieves. It was sophisticated comedy at its best. Ivan Goff wrote the witty, literate script. It may have been too high-brow and lasted only one season, sad to say. Goff observed about Gig, "He's a much more serious person, much more concerned about his work and life than he shows on the surface. His façade is happy-go-lucky, light-hearted. But he cares enormously, desperately about what he does and what he is."

Just before shooting for *The Rogues* commenced Gig married Elaine Garber Whitman (or Williams), wife number four, a pixyish ex-real estate agent, and they had a daughter, Jennifer, in 1964—Gig's only child. They lived in plush Bel Air, but were divorced in 1966.

In 1965 Gig went on a national tour as Professor Harold Hill in the Broadway smash hit musical, *The Music Man.* He quickly followed that with another stage musical, *On a Clear Day You Can See Forever* followed by *There's a Girl in My Soup,* which won him another Broadway Aegis Award—he's the only actor to have received two Aegis Awards, to accompany his Tony.

Gig's former agent, Marty Baum, had become a producer for ABC Pictures, which was going to make *They Shoot Horses, Don't They?* and Marty wanted Gig to be Rocky, the barker. None of Marty's executives could believe it. "Gig Young??? No way!" Marty was insistent and he also had a challenge talking Gig into it. As the camera was rolling into place on the first day of shooting, Marty said, "You better deliver, pal, or we'll both be behind some lunch counter."

And deliver he did. Young later recalled, "...when Marty put the *Horses* script in my hands, I settled down and gave it everything I had." He played the cynical marathon dance barker so well that he was voted Best Supporting Actor by a 3-to-1 landslide in a public poll conducted by the television stations in Los Angeles and New York.

Gig's character is bursting with false enthusiasm. Interestingly, Gig's 92-year-old father didn't care. Said Gig, "He won't go to a picture if I play a character with any flaws. To him it means I failed."

Gig won the Golden Globe Award and also the Oscar.

Young then returned to the stage to play Elwood P. Dowd in *Harvey*, and many critics felt that he surpassed Jimmy Stewart's film portrayal of the same character in so easily relating to the six-foot imaginary rabbit.

Gig enjoyed both boating and fishing, and he was the proud owner and skipper of the Unicorn, a 36-foot trawler. He spent weekends and time between pictures working on his boat or fishing along the coastal waters.

Ben Roberts, a writer friend of Ivan Goff's, said of Gig, "On the outside, he's gay, sophisticated; a handsome man with a twinkle. Then, surprisingly, you discover he's intelligent, sensitive and real. The juxtaposition is unexpected."

Young's personality had even greater extremes than Goff could imagine. His fifth marriage was to German actress Kim Schmidt. She was 31 and he nearly 65. After three weeks of marriage he shot and killed her and then turned the gun on himself in their Manhattan apartment.

In an attempt to explain this bizarre and tragic turn of events, author George Eells focuses a psychoanalytic lens on Gig's career in *Final Gig: The Man Behind the Murder*. Eells digs up the lurid side of Gig's life—his dependence on alcohol, his tireless search for a substitute mother, his many failed relationships. Did Gig think of himself as a winner? Though he won six prestigious acting awards, and has a star on the Hollywood Walk of Fame, the answer Eells gives is No.

Though we'll probably never know much about Gig Young's health and frame of mind during the last weeks of his life, we do know that he entertained audiences in more than seventy films and countless TV shows for nearly four decades.

He didn't have to work in the family cannery either. He made it on his own.

Blanche Yurka

Born 18 June, 1887,
St. Paul, MN.
Died 6 June, 1974,
New York, NY.

The Buzz Bainbridge Players at the Minneapolis Shubert Theatre proudly announced that Broadway star Blanche Yurka was returning to her hometown to do the leading roles in three Ibsen plays—*The Wild Duck,* *Hedda Gabler,* and *A Doll's House*—and also star in Shaw's *Candida* for their 1926 season.

Antonin Jurka, her father, emigrated to St. Paul from Czechoslovakia in 1865. He had been educated in Prague and served as an assistant government inspector in Hungary and Croatia before leaving Europe because of ill health. He had wanted to be a journalist in his adopted land but settled for a position teaching German in the old Jefferson School. He is credited with introducing music into the curricula of St. Paul schools. He also directed amateur theatrical plays. The family lived at 16 Douglas Street in St. Paul's West Seventh neighborhood, and Blanche definitely grew up in an artistic atmosphere.

At the age of twelve, Blanche already possessed enough beauty and exaltation to warrant special notice, and her father sent her to New York to continue her singing lessons with the Metropolitan Opera Company, where she appeared as the Grail-bearer in Wagner's *Parsifal.* When Henrich Conried became director of the opera house in 1903 he saw that above and beyond her singing abilities, Blanche also had talent as an actress, and in 1907, when she was twenty, he introduced her to the renowned theater impresario David Belasco, who quickly saw her talents and cast her to understudy Charlotte Walker in the leading role of *The Warrens of Virginia.* She next was given the actual leading role in the comedy, *Is Matrimony a Failure?* (1907).

More often than not Yurka's early roles were in comedies, but over the next decade her talent for interpreting the meatier tragic roles from Shakespeare, Ibsen, Shaw, and the Greeks became evident. She was once cast as Gertrude in John Barrymore's *Hamlet.* This distressed her because she was five years younger than Barrymore, yet here she was playing his mother!

As she herself later described the situation: "When I played Gertrude in Mr. Barrymore's *Hamlet*, we all agreed that something ought to be done to justify the opinion which the other characters have of her and which Mr. Shakespeare neglected to support in the four or five silly speeches which he gives her before the closet scene. We decided that for one thing we would make her physically attractive. I made up to look as much as possible like Mary Pickford. It was the only really insincere thing I've ever done in the theater." (By the way, Tyrone Power, Sr. played King Claudius, Queen Gertrude's husband.)

Virtually every role won her praise and increased stature. For example, *New York Times* Critic Brooks Atkinson wrote of her 1929 portrayal of Hedda Gabler, "Miss Yurka is an actress of great depth of emotion, blessed with a voice of almost eerie timbre."

Blanche, like other theatrical superstars of the time, tended to look askance at the movies. Yet she did dip a toe into the celluloid pool a few times by appearing in the ***National Red Cross Pageant*** (1917) and in ***She's Everywhere*** (1919). Unimpressed with the results, she did not appear again until 1935, when she took the part of a strong-willed woman in revolutionary France, Madame DeFarge, in Charles Dickens' ***A Tale of Two Cities*** (1935).

Blanche was an early organizer and active member in Actor's Equity and she served the union in several elected posts.

Fresh on the heels of her success in the *Hamlet* which ran for 101 shows on Broadway, breaking the record of one hundred shows set by Edwin Booth, Yurka came to Minneapolis to be the guest star in Bainbridge Players stock company, reprising the roles that had given her the reputation as the foremost Ibsen actress in America. She opened *The Wild Duck* on May 2, 1926, at the Shubert Theatre, which then stood on 7th Street, a half block west of South Hennepin Avenue.

About Ibsen Miss Yurka said, "Ibsen's plays were radically different from the sort of thing that a commercial manager is wont to do, and the commercial manager, usually timid in exploring a new field, has fought shy of them for a long time. *The Wild Duck* is not highbrow drama for the select few, but vital, powerful, moving drama for everybody with human emotions. There is nothing so stirring as life itself and that is what *The Wild Duck* gives you. It is life through the prism of a great man's imagination and genius."

Hedda Gabler opened on May 9, 1926, and *Minneapolis Tribune* journalist Bradley L. Morison, said on May 10th, "Blanche Yurka contributes another amazingly efficient performance in the title role: her competent hand again is seen in the details of direction; a supporting cast rises spiritedly and vigorously to the exactions of the difficult

Ibsen characterizations....Miss Yurka's performance fully sustains the splendid impression created by her Gina Ekdal. She moves with feline craftiness, gives each furtive look and gesture a maximum significance, and with a fine reserve makes of Hanna the icily indifferent, soulless and hopelessly bored plotter that Ibsen intended her."

Yurka was equally compelling in *Candida,* which opened the following week, and *A Doll's House,* which opened on May 24th.

The month of May was enthralling for playgoers who saw the top-flight, locally- born, Broadway star actress, Blanche Yurka, take them on an Ibsen-Shaw theatrical journey into the lives of four fascinating, strong women. But on June 16 an odd article appeared in the Minneapolis papers wherein Miss Yurka cited her estranged husband in court for unpaid alimony.

Blanche returned to New York that summer, but she returned to Minneapolis is January on 1930 to see a play being produced in Hinckley, Oakley Stout's *Barrens.* What she saw thrilled her and she stated that she would bring it to the East Coast to show off what kind of work was produced in the hinter lands of the Upper Midwest. She took the play East but never succeeded in getting it produced.

While she was in town Blanche also appeared in Richard Herndon's production of *The Vikings of Helgeland.*

The next spring Yurka returned again to perform the leading role of Dolores Mendez in *The Squall* followed by Molla Hansen as *The Sea Woman* at the Minneapolis Shubert Theatre. Both plays had been hits for Yurka on the New York stage prior to being staged in Minneapolis. Also in the cast were Gladys George, Ruth Lee, and Dorrit Kelton, all of whom were later successful on Broadway and in films. During his visit Blanche complained in an interview that the plays were being too hurriedly rehearsed and staged—that one week was simply not enough time to learn lines, build sets, make costumes, props, etc. After the conclusion of *The Sea Woman,* she whisked herself over to Ann Arbor, to play the title role in *Electra* at the University of Michigan.

In 1936 Yurka returned to address a convocation at the University of Minnesota's Northrop Auditorium. Her speech topic was "The Ever Expanding Theater." On another evening she delivered an address "The Art of the Theater," in which, flush from her success in the film *A Tale of Two Cities* she waxed philosophical about the merits of that medium. "I never cease to thrill at the knowledge that into each scene of a motion picture is packed permanently, the very best of the artist's talent. On the radio and stage, where performers must constantly repeat their roles subject to the vagaries of human nature, the best is not always produced. On the screen, perfection reaches the public."

She concluded that all three mediums—radio, stage, and screen—have worked to each other's benefit. She advocated the continuation of the Federal Theater Project and also expressed the hope that the finest of stage productions would somehow be preserved on film. (Nowadays we worry whether the films themselves will survive!)

After twenty years as a leading lady of the stage, in 1940 Miss Yurka began to devote more time to motion pictures. Her only leading role was in *Queen of the Mob* (1940). The story, based loosely on the Ma Barker Gang, came originally from a book by J. Edgar Hoover called *Persons in Hiding*, about public enemies and how the FBI ran them down. Hoover sold the story to Paramount Studios for $10,000, and the studio went on to net $1,500,000 for the film. The film's original title, soon jettisoned, was "The Woman from Hell."

In her next film outing she worked with Jimmy Cagney and Elia Kazan in *City for Conquest* (1940). Several B-features followed, including *Ellery Queen and the Murder Ring* (1941), *Lady for a Night* (1942) with Joan Blondell and John Wayne, *Pacific Rendezvous* (1942), and *A Night to Remember* (1943).

Seen as a character actress now, she was featured in *Tonight We Raid Calais* (1943), *Hitler's Madman* (1943), *The Song of Bernadette* (1943), *The Bridge of San Luis Rey* (1944), based on Thornton Wilder's Pulitzer Prize-winning book, and *The Southerner* (1945), which was directed by French master Jean Renoir. Her last film appearance was in *Thunder of the Sun* (1959), when she was in her seventies. Yurka also appeared frequently on the live TV drama shows during the early days of that medium.

When little, blond-curled Blanche Yurka sat on a branch in an apple tree in St. Paul and her long legs dangled from the limb, she said she had three dreams. She dreamed first she had become a great actress; second that she would marry a wealthy man and live on Summit Avenue; and third that she became a great novelist. Her first dream came true. Some would say that one out of three ain't bad, especially of the caliber of these dreams. She did write an autobiography, *The Bohemian Girl*. And she also wrote an entertaining book about acting technique called *Dear Audience*, which is still sometimes used in college courses.

In a 1955 valedictory essay given to the *New York Times*, when she was sixty-eight years old, Blanche said, "I've had it, the brouhaha, the name in electric lights, the occasional privilege of earning a living, the one-woman tours." She said her career was one that "has given me brief periods of great joy and exultation, as well as long ones of frustration and frequent defeat. And others of comfortable affluence in utterly unimportant plays." Lamenting the poverty of modern theater themes, she said, "Things have taken on a coloration I dislike. I don't like the passion for ugliness that seems so much a part of our theater. I'd like once again to see plays in which the parents don't think their children are horrible and in which children don't think their parents are horrible."

Yurka never really retired from the theater. She just rested a little longer between plays, re-grouped and did another one. In 1970, at the age of 82, she was doing *The Mad Woman of Chaillot* on the London stage.

Steve Zahn

Born 13 November, 1968,
Marshall, MN.

Steve is a "P. K." (preacher's kid.) This reserved young man was an All-Conference defensive back for Cooper High School in New Hope, Minnesota, a suburb northwest of Minneapolis. Though he loved athletics, theater proved to be the more enduring passion. As a young teen he surprised his teacher at Plymouth Junior High, Ert Jones-Hermerding, by demonstrating a fine comic talent in a classroom presentation one day. Ert put him into an improvisational group that rewrote classic fairy tales and performed them as skits at elementary schools. Steve had found his niche.

Zahn acted in several plays at Cooper under the guiding hand of drama teacher Frank Plut, including *Babes in Arms*, *The Dining Room* (where he had multiple roles), *The Music Man* (as Professor Harold Hill), *Oklahoma* (as Will Parker), *Our Town*, and *The Night Thoreau Spent in Jail*. He liked Will Parker, the spunky cowboy, the best "because he both danced and sang where the others just did one thing or the other."

Plut also coached Steve in an oral interpretation of Tennessee Williams' "Portrait of a Girl in Glass" and Steve won the state championship with this selection. Plut also put together a group of twelve boys and one girl called The Hoofers, who danced scenes from

Oklahoma, West Side Story, South Pacific, Godspell, and *Best Little Whorehouse in Texas* at other high schools and eventually at the opening of the State Legislature.

Zahn attended Gustavus Adolphus College in St. Peter, Minnesota, for a few weeks, intending to play football there, but soon dropped out. His break came when he "crashed" an audition for *Biloxi Blues* at the Old Log Theater in Excelsior, Minnesota, and won the leading role. Life was hectic for a while.. He lived in the basement of his parents' home and worked in a machine shop during the day. *Biloxi Blues* ran for twenty-six weeks, and Old Log Artistic Director Don Stolz called Steve "a splendid actor." From the Old Log Steve joined a traveling road show of *A Few Good Men.*

About acting he said, "There's nothing like it in the world. I've been on football teams where we've won important games, and that's a high, but nothing like acting."

Zahn went east to train at the American Repertory Theatre in Cambridge, Massachusetts, then he moved to New York City, where in 1992 he won a role in the touring company of *Bye Bye Birdie* directed by Tommy Tune. They toured for thirteen months. He intended on having lots of romance on the tour. "Then, two weeks after hitting the road, I fell in love," Zahn said sweetly. In this touring company he met his wife-to-be, Robyn Peterman, a dancer and actress. "We met in romantic Long Beach, California, and our big thing was playing gin rummy together."

After living together for two years in an apartment in Hoboken, New Jersey, (when not touring), they married in 1994. "Robyn immediately struck me as being very smart and very funny. The sense of humor is pretty much *it* for me. Everything else wears out, but if you can keep making each other laugh, well, then you'll be okay as a couple." Steve added, "I can't imagine being married to someone who isn't an actress. There's an unspoken understanding about moods and things. Plus, when one person's working, the other gets to visit cool locations." Incurably in love with Robyn, he adds, "How many people have the luxury of desperately missing their loved one a couple of times a year?"

Returning to New York, he landed a part opposite Ethan Hawke in *Sophistry* at the Playwright's Horizon. Ben Stiller saw his performance, and cast both Zahn and Hawke in *Reality Bites* (1994).

Tom Hanks cast Zahn as a wisecracking popster in *That Thing You Do!* (1996) a fictional rock bio-pic. In *SubUrbia* (1996) he plays a blue-haired punk, Buff, an altered escapee from reality. Two sequels followed: *Safe Men* (1998) and *Out of Sight* (1998). "Just before

[*SubUrbia*] wrapped, I asked the haircut guy to shave my head. If you walk around Austin (where the film was shot) with blue hair, people think you're cool. If I went back home with blue hair though, I'd have ended up in a ditch. But with a shaved head, I looked like a serial killer, and people left me alone."

Steve won honors at the Sundance Festival for his inspired comic performance as an escaped convict mistaken for one half of a gay couple of beauty pageant professionals in *Happy, Texas* (1999). Asked why he played in this movie, Steve answered, "It was the only script I've read that the minute I finished reading it I turned to page one and read it again. It made me laugh so hard! I told my manager I had to be in it."

Other notable films of the era are *You've Got Mail* (1998) with Tom Hanks and Meg Ryan; *Stuart Little* (1999); *Saving Silverman* (2001); *Doctor Doolittle 2* (2001); and *Riding in Cars with Boys* (2001).

Fellow actor and good school friend, Mike Saice, said, "Steve gets the good parts, and he earns them. He doesn't seclude himself from other people who have lesser parts; he helps them. He works for the good of the show, not for personal gratification."

Whenever he is in Hollywood on a film assignment, Zahn goes bowling with buddies and checks out swing bands at the retro-chic Derby Club. He is an avid fly fisherman and gardener. Steve and Robyn have one child, Henry James, and they also own a pumpkin farm in Western New Jersey. Steve had done farm chores in Marshall, Minnesota, as a child, and he had imagined he would eventually earn his living doing something manual, never anticipating the success he now enjoys. He finds that running a farm is just the ticket to let off steam in a nice romantic way—that is, if Robyn is too busy to play gin rummy with him.

ABOUT THE AUTHOR

Rolf Canton was born and raised in Minneapolis and graduated from the University of Minnesota in 1969 in theatre arts and humanities. He has been a film buff since kindergarten and he has met eighty-some film stars at various film-events. He has worked as a lumber salesman, a law clerk, a massage therapist, and a writer. He holds degrees in Herbal Studies and Pastoral Wellness Counseling, and has taught English as a second language (in Greece).

His book, *The Moriarty Principle*, was published by Galde Press in 1997. He wrote and co-produced the video, *Conversations with Ancient History*, and wrote, directed, and produced the video, *The Pipe Dream Continues (An Irregular Look at Sherlock Holmes in Minnesota)*.

After living most of his 55 years in Minneapolis, Rolf in 2002 moved to Bonn, Germany, with his wife, Nahid, and sons, Wahid and Yusuf.

He is currently at work on a companion volume to *Minnesotans in the Movies* devoted to directors, screenwriters, producers, composers, and other artists and technicians from Minnesota who have made behind-the-scenes contributions to film.